Between Intrusions:
Britain and Ireland between
the Romans and the Normans

Papers from the 2003 Melbourne Conference

SYDNEY SERIES IN CELTIC STUDIES

1. Early Irish Contract Law
   Neil McLeod

2. The Celts in Europe
   Aedeen Cremin

3. Origins and Revivals: Proceedings of the First Australian Conference of Celtic Studies
   Geraint Evans, Bernard Martin and Jonathan M Wooding (eds)

4. Literature and Politics in the Celtic World: Papers from the Third Australian Conference of Celtic Studies
   Pamela O'Neill and Jonathan M Wooding (eds)

5. Celtic-Australian Identities: Irish- and Welsh-Australian Studies from the 'Australian Identities' Conference, University College Dublin, July 1996
   Jonathan M Wooding and David Day (eds)

6. Nation and Federation in the Celtic World: papers from the Fourth Australian Conference of Celtic Studies
   Pamela O'Neill (ed)

Series Editors:
Aedeen Cremin
Pamela O'Neill

between intrusions:
britain and ireland between the romans and the normans

Papers from the 2003 Melbourne Conference

Edited by
Pamela O'Neill

Editorial Committee:
Julianna Grigg
Neil McLeod

Sydney Series in Celtic Studies 7
University of Sydney

2004

Published in Australia by
THE CELTIC STUDIES FOUNDATION
UNIVERSITY OF SYDNEY

in the
SYDNEY SERIES IN CELTIC STUDIES

ISBN: 1 86487 619 0

This book is copyright. Apart from any fair dealing for the purpose of private study, research, criticism or review, as permitted under the copyright act, no part may be reproduced by any process without written permission from the authors.

Papers delivered at the conference and submitted for consideration for inclusion in this publication were peer reviewed by the editorial committee and other readers before being included.

Contents

John Martyn:
Augustine's failure as mission leader   7

Denise Doyle RSM:
Brigit: from goddess to saint   14

Martin Grimmer:
Memories of the Celts in Bede's *Historia ecclesiastica gentis Anglorum*   22

Melanie Van Twest:
They were there: the population of Anglo-Saxon Sedgeford, Norfolk   33

Pamela O'Neill:
Dimensions and distribution: aspects of Pictish sculpture   39

Kristen Erskine:
A sense of place: sacred sites and assembly sites in Pictland   50

Julianna Grigg:
Aspects of kingship in Pictland and early Scotland   57

Katharine Burke:
Valkyries in Caithness: an exploration of *Darradarliod*   71

Chris Bishop:
Wésten: the birth of 'The Waste Land'   79

Lyn Olson:
The absorption of Cornwall into Anglo-Saxon England   94

Neil McLeod:
The metalworking tradition in medieval Irish law   103

Neil McLeod:
The blood-feud in medieval Ireland   114

David N Wilson:
Heroic epic as propaganda: the manipulation of honour in
    Táin Bó Cúalnge   134

Constant J Mews:
The ambivalent image of Irish Christianity in Gerald of Wales   141

Val Noone:
Culhane of Brunswick on early medieval Ireland   158

Ann Trindade:
Future directions in early Irish studies   169

Augustine's failure as mission leader

John Martyn

The Venerable Bede has long been the main authority for Pope Gregory's very successful mission to England, and he quoted five of the Pope's letters in full, and all of the *Responsa*, which I am sure was written by the Pope, and about a quarter of another lengthy letter that he sent to Augustine.[1] These all appeared in book 1 of the *Ecclesiastical History*. But in fact, fifteen other similar letters of the Pope have survived, and they were all very relevant to this mission.[2] They show how Bede deliberately distorted the truth in Augustine's favour, to suit his English readers, and since then Bede has received very little real criticism from his own countrymen. And yet, as can be seen with his erroneous account of Augustine's consecration, Bede's evidence is far from reliable.[3]

In book I chapter 23, Bede tells us, in Mynors' translation,[4] that in 596 'Gregory, a man eminent in learning and in affairs ... prompted by divine inspiration, sent a servant of God named Augustine and several more God-fearing monks with him, to preach the word of God to the English race.' In fact, the Pope had planned this mission with very great care, over three or more years, and he fully controlled and supervised it for the next five years. It could be argued that his only mistake was his choice of Augustine as the leader of the first mission, rather than his well-tried Mellitus or his most trustworthy and very capable friend, Abbot Cyriacus. Incidentally, a 'servant of God' was the normal term for a 'monk.' In May 594, more than two years before the departure of Augustine, the Pope had heard welcome news from two of his closest friends, both of them brave and talented administrators, the same Abbot Cyriacus and Bishop Felix.[5] These two had successfully converted the Barbaricini, in Sardinia, a lawless

---

[1] For a textual analysis and discussion of the *Responsa*, see the Introduction to my forthcoming annotated translation of Gregory's letters (appearing in 3 vols, printed by PIMS in Toronto, 2003/4). To me there is no doubt that it is genuine.
[2] Letters 6.10, 51, 52, 55, 56, 57, 59, 60; 8.29; 11.38, 41, 45, 48, 50, 51.
[3] Augustine's consecration almost certainly took place at Lyon, while he was on his way to England, thus equipping him with the ecclesiastical powers needed in Kent. Bede argued that, after settling in Kent, Augustine travelled right down to Arles, with the priest Laurence and monk Peter, to be consecrated by Aetherius. But Aetherius was bishop of Lyon, whereas the bishop of Arles was Virgil. Bede was confused.
[4] In B Colgrave and R A B Mynors, *Bede's Ecclesiastical History of the English People [HE]* (Oxford, 1969). In chs 23-32, Bede made use of letters 6.53 and 54, the *Responsa*, and letters 11.45, 39, 56, 36 and 37, a misleading sequence.
[5] Letters 4.23 and 5.38.

and extremely violent mountain tribe of Moors, who had been expelled from Africa by the Vandals. It was this dangerous mission to Sardinia, backed up by a dozen letters, which served as the Pope's trial run, before his next missions to Gaul and then to England.

Then, in September 595, Gregory wrote to the newly appointed manager of his patrimony in Gaul, the priest Candidus. He stressed how small the Church revenue was, and in almost every letter to Gaul, he encouraged the local Christians to pay their proper dues to the Church, especially the bishop of Arles, who was hoarding a great deal of its money. Bede failed to mention this important letter, 6.10.[6] In it, Gregory asked his agent Candidus to use all the gold coins he collected from the Christians in Gaul to buy (a) clothing for the poor, and (b) English captives, about 17 or 18 years old, to be trained as monks. This precise age is of interest. They were old enough to learn fast, and were more likely to be healthy, keen and responsible. As captives, they would already know some Latin, and a year or so in a monastery would have given them time to learn the psalms and gain a good grasp of the main theology of that time. Gregory then asks Candidus to invest any additional funds, and for the interest to be used for the same two purposes later on, when they would provide another group of English speaking monks.[7] Normally all such income would have been sent to Rome, as had happened two years earlier, when 400 gold coins, collected from the Christians in Gaul by the patrician Dynamius, had been sent over to the Pope, thus giving him the problem of converting their substandard gold.[8] But in this case, the Pope made far better use of it. He then asked for the first group of English captives to be sent over to him, together with a priest, who was to baptise any who might seem close to death en route, suggesting a long journey, and he stresses the need for speed. The

---

[6] Dated September 595. This allowed the British monks nearly ten months of monastic life and religious education.

[7] The Pope did his very best to increase the income from the Church's patrimony in Gaul, adding a paragraph to each of the eight letters he sent to the bishops and noblemen about the monks travelling through Gaul to England, in which he described the inadequate contribution so far with a rare and derogatory diminutive, *patrimoniolum* ('pathetic little patrimony', perhaps from Jerome *Ep* 45). By contrast, in the letter below to Candidus, as in his letter to the aristocratic Arigius (6.59), he used the normal noun *patrimonium*.

[8] See letter 3.33, dated April, 593. The aristocratic Dynamius was acting as the Pope's defender, looking after his patrimony in Gaul, especially around Marseilles. The gold coins were worth more in Gaul than if converted to Roman *solidi*, but H Chadwick in 'Gregory the Great and the mission to the Anglo-Saxons' in *Gregorio Magno e il suo Tempo* Vol 1 (Roma, 1991) p 205, note 26, was wrong to concede 'that Gregory's priorities might have been different if there were no difficulty about the currency'. The coins were ancillary to his determination to bring the Roman Church to Gaul and England; he saw them as far more valuable and useful in Gaul, and hence they were not sent to his coffers in Rome in the usual way.

monastery of Saint Andrew would have been the ideal place to train the English captives.[9] This mansion had once housed Gregory's family, and then Gregory himself as a monk, and later on, Augustine.

In his account, Bede goes on to say that the monks
> had already gone a little way on their journey, when they were paralysed with terror. They began to contemplate returning home rather than going on to a barbarous, fierce, and unbelieving nation whose language they didn't understand. They all agreed that this was the safest course, so forthwith they sent home Augustine, whom Gregory had intended to have consecrated as their bishop if they were received by the English. Augustine was to humbly beg Saint Gregory for permission to give up so dangerous, wearisome, and uncertain a journey. Gregory, however, sent them an encouraging letter, in which he persuaded them to persevere with the task of preaching the Word and to trust in the help of God.

So wrote Bede, but almost every word of his account is misleading.

In fact, Gregory had requested support for his first party of monks from no fewer than seven local bishops and potentates before it had even left Rome, and all seven of them were carefully chosen to suit the monks' itinerary. They ultimately proved to be extremely hospitable, from Marseilles, Arles and up through Vienne, Lyon, Autun, Aix, Paris and Rouen, and finally over the Channel to Kent. But when they had reached Arles, it seems that the monks halted, and Gregory says that they were put off through '*maledicorum hominum linguas*' ('the tongues of evil speakers'), some critical Gallic locals, it seems, but they suffered from nothing else. In fact, it was Augustine who got cold feet, and hurried back to Rome, to find someone else as their leader, it seems. The Pope's letter was to tell the monks that the Pope had managed to persuade their leader to rejoin them, using the carrot of his promotion to abbot. Of course, Augustine was always in charge anyway, so the other monks could not order him to return to Rome. The language problem would have been solved by the first batch of newly trained English monks, sent over by Candidus from Gaul to Rome nearly a year earlier. The consecration of Augustine was still some way off, but it was almost certainly carried out when he reached Lyon, rather than during a trip to southern Gaul several months later. Irish and Gallic priests had been active recently in England, Wales had a well-established tribal church, and King Ethelbert's wife, Bertha, was a practising Christian, like her chaplain, Liuthard, and Kent was

---

[9] Most modern scholars have ignored this letter, but Henry Mayr-Hartung in *The Coming of Christianity to Anglo-Saxon England* (London, 1991) pp 58-9, suggested that these British captives were trained in Rome.

far from uncivilized, as any bishop in Gaul could have told Augustine. In south-eastern England, there were no 'barbarous, fierce unbelievers', nor any 'dangerous journeys', unlike in Sardinia's mountains. In fact it was Queen Bertha who played the major role in converting the King and most of his people, and showed great humility over her achievement, which led the Pope to call her a second Helena. This was a great contrast to Augustine's pride.[10]

Bede does quote one letter sent by Gregory to Virgil, the bishop of Arles, asking him to support the monks in their journey to England. But its first part is quite different from Gregory's original, and Bede placed it after the Pope's letter to the monks, although Virgil had already given help to all their party. Most of Gregory's other letters were omitted by Bede, but he does include letter 11.36, dated June 601, a long letter to Augustine, now the 'bishop of the English'. In it, Bede omits the first 22 and last 82 lines of Latin, again to conceal evidence. Gregory starts by praising the bishop's hard work, but then he shows how Christ converted the world 'not through men's wisdom, but through his own virtue, and Jesus chose illiterate fishermen as his preachers.' He went on: 'and Jesus is doing this now also, as he has considered it right to perform courageous works for the English race, by means of 'weak' preachers.' The 'weak', *infirmos*, is picked up later on in the letter, as Gregory warns Augustine against pride, in case 'his weak mind (*infirmus animus*) may be raised up by self-esteem, and may lead through vainglory to its inward fall.' This pride was a problem later on, when Augustine arranged two meetings to bring the Welsh bishops into the fold of the Roman church. His tactless lack of courtesy, combined with his pride, proved too much for them, and when he threatened them, they walked out. As Homes Dudden[11] admitted when commenting on the bishop's *Responsa* to the Pope, Augustine showed 'the scrupulosity and narrowness of a monk, who was unable to divest himself of the ideals of the cloister'. Dudden also accused him of pride.

In his three letters to his metropolitan bishop and vicar in Gaul, Virgil of Arles, the Pope appointed him as the 'minder' of Augustine, his new

---

[10] In letter 11.35, written to Queen Bertha, and sent on 22 June 601, he wrote: 'We praise God, as he has deigned most graciously to reserve the conversion of the English race for your reward', and compares her with 'Helena, the mother of the most pious emperor, Constantine'. In helping to convert her royal husband, she was all-important in the Pope's mission. Bertha was a Frankish princess and a Christian at birth, and with her chaplain soon succeeded in winning over the king. The Pope's letter to the king, 11.37, was also certainly very persuasive. The pride shown by Augustine will appear shortly.

[11] His 946-page study is very dated, but is still the main authority for the life of Pope Gregory. See F Homes Dudden, *Gregory the Great, His Place in History and Thought* Vol 1 (London, 1905; repr New York, 1967) pp 136, 143. He saw the value of letter 6.10.

bishop in England, although he had most probably been consecrated in Lyon, where Virgil could well have been in attendance. But when Augustine, in his *Responsa*, asked the Pope whether he should now 'have control over all the bishops in Gaul' it was clearly a case of foolish arrogance. In the letters, the only two Latin words used to describe Augustine's qualities are *zelus* and *studium*, 'zeal' and 'earnestness'. The two words appear on no fewer than five occasions, and nothing else is added, and they are far from flattering on their own. In ten letters in book 11, Augustine is always greeted as his 'most reverend brother and fellow-bishop,' but this is the impersonal formula of a typical greeting. His real friends had a *dilectissimus* or *carissimus* added to their titles. In just one letter, 11.39, Augustine is 'most holy' also, but it is in a very religious context, where he, or his office, is honoured with a sacred pallium. In his letter to the monks waiting at Arles, Gregory asks them to show lots of *fervor* and *instantia* ('enthusiasm' and 'perseverance'), qualities that were sadly lacking in their leader, as were *fortitudo*, and especially *humilitas*, Gregory's favourite virtue. As the *Responsa* clearly shows, the Pope was very curt in replying to Augustine's arrogant claim of authority over the bishops in Gaul ('We grant you no authority' and 'you will not be able to judge them'), and the Pope tells him curtly that he has already replied over the lengthy sexual questions. One might also add that Augustine showed intellectual pride in dismissing the English as *rudi* ('ignorant').

In a very long letter sent to his friend Eulogius, the archbishop of Alexandria, in July 598, letter 8.29, the Pope told him that he had sent over 'a monk' — note just 'a monk' — who had been elected bishop by the bishops of Germany (which suggests Neustria), to preach to the English. He had heard that this monk was safe and was now hard at work. He went on to mention the 'miracles' that had been done by him, or rather by his fellow monks. Now, this was Augustine's greatest and only real triumph, but in the letter, his name does not appear at all. By contrast, nobody could be more humble than Pope Gregory himself, and he regularly attacked pride as the most insidious sin of all.[12] He ends by appealing to Augustine to be humble, and not suffer as Moses did. In an earlier letter to the same Eulogius, 5.41, he had warned his friend that the 'tempter knows that pride is the beginning of all sin'. Then in letter 9.223, Gregory rewarded Syagrius with the sacred pallium, for all that he had done for Augustine and the first party of monks. He shows that this mission was certainly not a sudden idea: 'After long thought,' he says, 'I was keen to provide the work of preaching for the English race, through Augustine, one-time prior of my monastery, and now our brother and fellow-bishop.' Again he fails to

---

[12] Among Gregory's many biblical quotes, by far the most common is 'whosoever exalts himself' (attacking pride) which appears 11 times (*Mt* 23.12 x 3, *Lk* 14.11 x 4 and *Lk* 18.14 x 4).

praise his choice as leader, with a formulaic title and a pointed reminder of his earlier monastic life, irrelevant in July 599, the date of the letter.

Finally, in letter 11.37 to Ethelbert, king of the English, Gregory provides his one and only character sketch of his arrogant new bishop, and it is a very short one, but with a neat tricolon: *'In monasterii regula edoctus, sacrae scripturae scientia repletus, bonis auctore Deo operibus praeditus'*. In English, 'educated in the monastic rule, replete with knowledge of Holy Writ, and endowed with good works by the grace of God'. Unlike Gregory, it seems that Augustine had spent all of his adult life living according to some monastic rule, learning the Bible off by heart and doing good works as prescribed by God. This unimaginative, bookish monk did well on one occasion during the mission, when he called in to check on an important monastery in Gaul at Lérins, in letter 6.57. He could have become an ideal superintendent of monasteries. Gregory tells the local abbot, Stephen, that he is delighted by Augustine's report to him, which stressed the new concord between monks, priests and officials, and he prays that Stephen can remain vigilant, and thanks him for the cutlery he had sent to Rome to help the poor. Gregory was very much on the side of the poor, and of any women in trouble. It should also be stressed that it was Gregory who decided the long-term organization of the English Church, with the archbishoprics of Canterbury, London and York. And when the Pope died in 604, Augustine was very quick to resign, and the priest Maurice took over in Canterbury. The very capable Abbot Mellitus, who would have been the ideal person to lead the first group of monks to England, had been the bishop of London since late in 601.

But to help the first monks in England to convert the local non-believers, Gregory did three smart things. First, he provided Augustine with some very useful manuscripts, carried there by Mellitus, including a Bible containing the four gospels, with pictures, that still survives, and almost certainly an antiphonary. But the Pope also sent a letter to Mellitus, who took the precious manuscripts and vestments and relics with him, as he set out with the second group of monks to widen the conversion of the English. In the letter, 11.56, dated July 601, he asked the abbot to tell Augustine not to destroy the local shrines and customs, as was the usual practice. In fact, in letter 11.37, sent earlier to Ethelbert, the Pope had urged the King to hunt down idols and pull down their shrines. But now he has changed his mind, as he argues that their temples should be kept intact, once they had been sprinkled with holy water, but the idols in them should be destroyed. This would encourage the people to worship in places familiar to them, but to a new God. And as they were accustomed to slaughtering cattle, while sacrificing to their old devils, they should continue to do so, but while celebrating Saints' days or dedications of new Christian churches.

Thirdly, Gregory kept up a supply of keen young monks, including some who knew the English language, making the task of both groups much easier, and this probably explains the baptism of so many souls. Bede argued that the priests 'had acquired interpreters from the race of Franks, according to the command of the blessed Pope Gregory,' and most modern scholars have agreed. Yet one of these interpreters, Agilbert, was expelled later on by the English king for his 'barbarous speech,' and he even needed an interpreter to present his own case.[13] The numbers converted suggest that a large percentage of monks were able to speak the local language. And as Dudden pointed out,[14] it seems certain that most Franks could not speak intelligible English, despite some trade between the two countries. A few priests may well have come over from Gaul, as interpreters of the Bible, and Bede may well have been aware of some English-speaking interpreters, and this caused his confusion, and he seems to have had no access to the letter explaining their source. But for the mass baptisms, and their sequel, many capable interpreters would have been needed.

This should show that although the Pope's mission to England was successful, thanks mainly to Queen Bertha and the Pope, his choice of his old friend and fellow-monk Augustine as its leader was a serious lapse in his normally shrewd judgement. Besides this monk's incurable pride, I am sure that Augustine was incapable of functioning effectively outside a monastic environment.

---

[13] For the interpreters, see *HE* 1.25: 'They had, by order of the blessed Pope Gregory, taken interpreters of the nation of the Franks.'
[14] Dudden, Vol 3, p 108.

Brigit: from goddess to saint

Denise Doyle RSM

Brigit[1] is of special interest because she seems to have undergone a smooth transition from pagan deity to Christian saint. The historical Brigit is reported as having been born around 450 CE and having died at Kildare in 523 or 525 CE.[2] The earliest biography of the Christian Brigit, *Vita Brigitae*,[3] was written c 650 CE by Cogitosus and is the earliest extant hagiographical work in Hiberno-Latin.[4] In Cogitosus's *Life*, Brigit was represented in such a way that the oral traditions that developed around her had consonance with ancient and local Celtic traditions, with the New Testament, Christian symbolism, Christian apocrypha, and theology as it slowly developed in the early Church.

An incoming religion usually made devils of the gods of preceding religions. Christianity was no exception.[5] The survival of the cult of Brigit in Ireland is an exception. She has remained in the Christian liturgical calendar despite the accretion of mythology, both ancient and medieval, that has accumulated around her. Based on a pattern similar to that used by the early Fathers of the Church to harmonise biblical images of Christ in the Old and New Testaments, Cogitosus's *Life* of Brigit can be seen as a literary basis for a perceived fusion of goddess and Christian saint.

A goddess is the personification of nature, the forces that the male figures struggle to overcome in order to have nature serve them.[6] A goddess of any name in archaic times could be called Brigit, as this was simply an embracing expression or title for 'exalted one'.[7] This title established the divine status of the mythic Irish Brigit, to whom multiple yet separate attributes of healing, craftwork and poetry were linked. In Britain,

---

[1] 'Irish, the exalted one, Brigit, Brighit, Brid, Briid, Brigid': James MacKillop, *Oxford Dictionary of Celtic Mythology* (Oxford, 1998) p 58.

[2] Some traditions consider Brigit to have been a friend and therefore contemporary of Patrick. Patrick arrived as a missionary c 432 and died c 461 or c 493.

[3] Sean Connolly and J M Picard (trans), 'Cogitosus's Life of St Brigit', *Journal of the Royal Society of Antiquaries of Ireland* 117 (1987) 5-27. All quotations given here are from this edition.

[4] Sean Connolly, 'Cogitosus' Life of St Brigit, Content and Value', *Journal of the Royal Antiquaries of Ireland* 117 (1987) 5-27.

[5] Peter Brown, *The Rise of Western Christendom* (London, 1996) pp 34-53; Stephanie Hollis, *Anglo-Saxon Women and the Church* (London, 1992) pp 17-25.

[6] Marie-Louise Sjoestedt, *Celtic Gods and Heroes* (New York, 2000) pp 92ff.

[7] Miranda Green, *Dictionary of Celtic Myth and Legend* (London, 1997) p 50; MacKillop, p 58.

Brigit was known from ancient times as Brigantia, in Gaulish inscriptions as Brigindo, in the formerly Celtic countries of Austria, Switzerland and South Germany she was Bertha or Frau Perchta. Brigida was the deity of the high passes in the Cisalpine region. The names of the cities Bregenz in the Swiss Alps, Brescia in northern Italy, and Brigantium in ancient Portugal all bear testimony to the widespread Celtic cult of Brigit.[8]

Unlike the Greek myths in which the sacred name of Olympus had become a metaphor for a home in the skies where the gods dwelt in palaces of cloud approached by the highroad of the Milky Way,[9] there was no chasm between the supernatural and the natural in ancient Celtic traditions. For the Celts there was continuity in space and time and between worlds. In Brigit, Ireland preserved a legacy of a time when the marvellous was normal.[10]

A titular deity acquired local religious ideals. Some, like Brigit, achieved widespread recognition and devotion. Local rituals and accretion of popular beliefs mean that a titular deity is not identical to, but is equivalent with, other mother goddesses.[11] The mysterious, timeless, many-faceted figure of Brigit was revered as a tripartite goddess of fire, fertility and poetry, attributes which are grounded in the common needs of humanity.[12]

An association of a father-god with a local river-goddess is common in mythology. In Ireland the Dagda is associated with the sacred river Boyne.[13] In the accretion of tradition, the original mythic Brigit, as daughter of the Dagda, was a solar goddess married to a Fomorian, one of the early giant invaders of Ireland. Brian, Iuchar and Iucharba are taken to be Brigit's three sons by Tuireann, son of Ogma, god of eloquence. Ecne, an early Irish personification of knowledge, enlightenment and poetry, is thought to be the grandson of Brigit and thus they are the progenitors of the

---

[8] Claire French, *The Celtic Goddess, Great Queen or Demon Witch?* (Edinburgh, 2001) p 37; T W Rolleston, *Celtic Myths and Legends* (London, 1995) pp 103, 126.
[9] A R Hope Moncrieff, *Classical Mythology* (London, repr 1994) p 22.
[10] Sjoestedt, pp 1-13; Thomas O'Loughlin, *Journeys on the Edges* (London, 2000); James P Mackey, *An Introduction to Celtic Christianity* (Edinburgh, 1995) pp 22-100; Philip Sheldrake, *Living Between Worlds* (London, 1995).
[11] Sjoestedt, pp 24-27.
[12] Kim McCone, *Pagan Past and Christian Present in Early Irish Literature* (Maynooth, 1991) pp 161-77. Fire and cauldrons were potent ancient symbols: fire mediates between nature and society by converting, in the cauldron of plenty and/or wisdom, ore to refine metal, natural products for both culinary and healing activities, and, metaphorically, learning and knowledge in the Cauldron of Poesy.
[13] Green, *Dictionary*, p75. The goddess Brigit was the daughter of the Dagda, the chief of the *Túatha Dé Danann*, associated with abundance and magic. The Dagda, a paradoxical character, mates with the spirit of the River Boyne, Boann, and thus the union of the tribal god and mother goddess is fulfilled. He also mates with the destructive war-goddess the Morrigan: Sjoestedt, p 19.

spiritual lineage to which all poets belong.[14] Myths are often formulated in indirect and religious symbolism which distils human experience.

To call something a myth is not to dismiss it as a legend. Myths in most cases were created to give shape and definition to the otherwise inexplicable wonders of human experience long before scientific proof became the rigid axiom for disciplines of learning. Based on perceptions of truth, myths can be seen as holding the values on which we base our lives, as containing something of fact and something of fiction but as being entirely of neither. Myths provide patterns of understanding which lie outside the normal requirements of justification and progression of time.

In the ancient mythology, Brigit was the territorial deity of Leinster, although venerated all over Ireland and in Celtic Europe. Brigit was both one goddess and three. She was a divinity of healing, crafts and poetry, she was expert in divination and prophecy, she was invoked by women in childbirth and there was a strong fertility aspect to the cult of Brigit associated with the farming year, especially with the lactation of ewes, celebrated at *Imbolc*, 1 and 2 February.[15]

The number three plays a large part in Celtic tradition. The triad which combines three concepts or facts is a genre which dominates the gnomic literature of Wales and Ireland.[16] Tricephalus, the three-faced deity, trios, and triple personages are prominent in both the epic tradition and archaeological excavation of Celtic culture.[17] Amongst the elaborations surrounding the Celtic deity Brigit, we are told that three Brigits guard the entrance to the land of the gods: Brigit the smith-worker, Brigit of medicine and Brigit of poetry.

Each aspect of Brigit the goddess – smithcraft, healing, poetry – dispenses three gifts which promote the livelihood, health and inspiration of the individual. Brigit is chief amongst those who dispense wisdom. She is invoked to keep the hearth-fire and the soul in safety. The flow of inspiration is contained and heated within the cauldron. Brigit and Ceridwen are mistresses of the cauldron of wisdom and inspiration, but the primary function belongs to Brigit, the goddess of inspiration.[18]

The attributes of the Irish goddess Brigit became conflated with, and have been preserved in, the qualities of the Christian Brigit, abbess of

---

[14] MacKillop, pp 58, 173; Rolleston, pp 103, 126.
[15] Green, *Dictionary*, p50; idem, *Celtic Myths* (London, 1993) pp 54f; Peter O'Connor, *Beyond the Mist* (London, 2001) p 64.
[16] Sjoestedt, pp 14-23.
[17] Lancelot Lengyel, *Les Secrets des Celtes* (Tours 1969) pp 68-78, 233-36; Chantal Nerzic, *La Sculpture en Gaul Romaine* (Paris, 1989) p 76; Guy de Bedoyere, *Finds of Roman Britain* (London, 1989) p 150; Sylvia Barnard, 'The Matres of Roman Britain', *Archaeological Journal* 142 (1985) 237-243.
[18] 'Ceridwen, Wales, keeper of the cauldron of wisdom at Bala Lake, Llyn Tegid': MacKillop, p 85.

Kildare. Kildare was undoubtedly once sacred to the druids, as this is a place whose name is linked with an oak grove.[19]

Just as the gospel accounts of Christ's birth, ministry and death were elaborated in apocryphal manuscripts and oral tradition, a similar pattern can be found in the later accounts of the childhood and adult ministry of Brigit. As with Christ, examples of apocryphal anecdotes multiplied with the growth of devotion and the passing of time, many paralleled with the life of Christ. Cogitosus's infancy narrative related quite simply that:

> Brigit ... was born of Christian and noble parents belonging to the good and most wise sept of Echtech. Born of her father Dubhtach and her mother Broiscech, she grew from childhood in the pursuit of good. For, chosen by God, the girl was totally self-restrained and chaste, continually progressing to better things.[20]

This compares to the simple statement Luke recorded of Christ:

> The child grew and became strong, filled with wisdom and the favour of God was upon him ... And Jesus increased with wisdom and in years, and in divine and human favour.[21]

Other traditions elaborate and inform us that Brigit's mother, Broiscech, was a maidservant seduced by her master Dubhtach, prince of Leinster, whose wife was so jealous that she had the girl and her child sold into slavery to a druid, Maithghean, who, impressed by her devoted labour, later freed her and sent her back to her father. This pattern is found in the Old Testament exile of Joseph and Moses and then the New Testament exile of Christ to Egypt.

As a fire goddess, Brigit is said to have been born in a druid's house at sunrise, when the house burst into flames which reached to heaven. The perpetual sacred flame at Kildare, referred to by Gerald of Wales, a twelfth-century cleric, in an account of his travels in Ireland, could have its roots in this tradition.[22] In 1993, under the initiative of the Sisters of St Brigid, a flame was ritually reignited at Kildare, which remains a sacred place of pilgrimage.[23] The theme of light and fire is also a motif in the Old Testament.[24] In the New Testament, the birth of the Christ child is recorded

---

[19] Green, *Dictionary*, p 164: the word druid is sometimes seen as being derived from the root *dru* meaning oak.

[20] Cogitosus 1.

[21] Luke 2:39-52.

[22] Gerald of Wales, *The History and Topography of Ireland* (trans J O'Meara, London, 1982) pp 81f.

[23] Bridget Mary Meehan and Regina Oliver, *Praying with Celtic Holy Women* (Missouri, 2003) p 24: the foundations of a sixth-century fire building where Brigit's nuns are said to have tended the perpetual flame are still in existence.

[24] For example, God appeared to Moses as a flame out of a bush which was not consumed: Exodus 3:2-4.

as being accompanied by the vision of shepherds who witnessed in the night sky the glory of the Lord shining around them.[25]

Brigit is, like Christ, the fruit of an unconventional conception. The genealogy of Christ as presented in Matthew traces the lineage of Christ through the violation of Tamar, the prostitution of Rahab, the adultery of Bathsheba, and the grafting of Ruth's half-Moabite son into the sacred history of the Jewish people. This provocative inclusion by Matthew provides a pattern for his presentation of Mary as a woman pregnant to an unidentified father before marriage.

These four Old Testament women are examples of the achievement of a divine purpose despite violation of morals and cultural expectations.[26] In a similar pattern, the mothers of many Celtic saints are not spoken of as married matrons, but as victims of rape, involved in illicit love or having an absent spouse, which echoes Mary's own conception and pregnancy, of an irregular sexual activity initiated by the Spirit.[27]

It is said that Brigit was born on the threshold, neither within nor without a house, as her mother, bringing milk into a druid's house as sunrise, had one foot outside the threshold. The ancient significance of a threshold is the passing from one state to another. A threshold marked the transition from the profane to the internal sacred state. The ancient Celtic sense of liminality between this world and the next was highly developed. Implied, then, in the theological dramatisation of the threshold birth of Brigit is that she was born between the world of material reality and that of the spirit. The human and divine natures of the Christian saint and the ancient deity had been fused. The existence of the human and divine natures of Christ had been the subject of theological debate in the general councils of the early Christian church since Arius (280-336 CE) had publicly denied the divinity of Christ. The human and divine aspects of Brigit could be accepted by Christians as a theological mystery.

Like Christ at Bethlehem, Brigit was born in no earthly home. In the texts of the Old and New Testaments, the birth of an extraordinary child is related in unconventional and dramatic circumstances, for example Isaac, Ishmael, Moses, John the Baptist and Christ.

Hebridean tradition relates that at the birth of Christ at Bethlehem, Brigit placed three drops of pure spring water on Christ's brow in the reputed ancient Irish tradition of the birth of the Son of Light, at which three drops of wisdom were placed on the brow, the blessing of triple purity.

---

[25] Luke 2:8-15.
[26] Raymond Brown, *The Birth of the Messiah* (London, 1977).
[27] Non, mother of St David of Wales, and Thanea, mother of St Kentigern/Mungo, are examples of irregular/illegitimate conception of sixth-century saints: their *Lives* were written in the eleventh-twelfth centuries: David Farmer, *Oxford Dictionary of Saints* (Oxford, 1997) pp 206, 369.

Ancient Christian litanies and martyrologies speak of Brigit as Mary of the Gael.[28] Continual interweaving of timelessness, of familiar symbols and rites, was an important contribution to the lasting fusion of the goddess and the Christian saint.

As a Christian saint, Brigit is celebrated on the ancient feast of Imbolc, at the beginning of February, which marked the beginning of spring and brought her into close association with fertility, with agriculture and especially with corn and cows. Cogitosus recorded that Brigit's reapers remained dry while the surrounding province experienced a wet day.[29] The synchronised feasts of saint Brigit and Imbolc are interpreted as the Christianisation of the ancient Celtic festival of Imbolc.[30]

Brigit is said to have spent her youth in exile and in agricultural labour for the druid, churning butter, tending the harvest, shepherding flocks. As abbess, Brigit was able to provide food without the supply dwindling.[31] She is portrayed as having the power to multiply such things as butter, bacon and milk, to bestow cattle and sheep, to tame wild animals and to control the weather. The cows were able to be milked three times a day, and one measure of her malt brewed enough beer for her 17 churches at Easter.[32]

The emphasis given by Cogitosus in his life of Brigit to the two theological virtues of faith and charity gives cohesion to his rather random list of folklore. Twenty-three of the 32 chapters present her concern for the poor, the oppressed, the embarrassed and her guests, while 16 involve healing.[33] Cogitosus emphasises that God's power is fruitful through Brigit's faith: 'Hence the faith of our Brigit is similar and comparable to a grain of mustard seed ...'[34] The phrase 'to a grain of mustard seed' recalls for the reader the gospel narrative where the faith of the supplicant was the essential basis for the efficacy of Christ's miracles. Faith was shown to be required for divine intervention. Crowds flocked to Christ as he constantly travelled around his home territories, accessible to everyone who sought him out.[35] Brigit, according to Cogitosus, drew countless people of both sexes from every province in the whole of Ireland, attracted by the fame of her good deeds:

> As a result of these and countless other miracles, the great renown of this handmaiden of God was on the lips of all and,

---

[28] Sean O'Duinn, *Where Three Streams Meet* (Dublin, 2000) p 283; MacKillop, p 58.
[29] Cogitosus 4:1-2.
[30] O'Duinn, pp 284ff.
[31] cf 2 Kings 4:42-44; Matthew 16:9-11; Mark 8:29.
[32] Cogitosus 13-16, 1, 3, 5, 8; cf John 2:1-11.
[33] O'Duinn, pp 284ff.
[34] Cogitosus 11:3.
[35] Matthew 7:28, 8:18, 9:20-23, 28-30, 32-34, 35-36; Luke 8:4, 19, 9:12-17.

not undeservedly but rather with due merit, she was regarded as the most eminent of all.[36] The miracles of Christ, 'who went about doing good',[37] and those enumerated by Cogitosus of Brigit occur among the ordinary misfortunes and material events common in daily life. Matthew's parables of the wise and foolish virgins and the landowner who distributed talents to his slaves[38] provide a foil for Brigit's compassion and tolerance towards, for example, the deceptive and mischievous boy,[39] the exploitation by the ungrateful leper[40] and the beggar whom she clothed in the Bishop's vestments.[41]

The attributes of the pre-Christian deity and the saint Brigit coalesce in the changing energies of the year, in natural, cultural and ritual functions. Seasonal agricultural landmarks symbolise the natural cycle of birth and death, of beginnings, coming to fruition, fading away and regeneration.

The blessing of fire and water is traditional to Brigit. Water images are balanced by those of heat and fire. Fertility of cattle and corn was also linked with fertilising fire. In Celtic traditions it was considered unlucky to cut down the last sheaf of corn as this sheaf represented the corn god. The harvesters would hurl their sickles simultaneously so that no one would know who had killed the corn god. This last sheaf was made into a symbol of the earth mother, a corn dolly decorated with the scarlet ribbons of Ceridwen, another Celtic mother goddess. The corn dolly, frequently called the Biddy, would be hung over the hearth throughout the winter or the year.[42] Saint Brigit's cross is a sheaf of corn[43] formed into the solar symbol of a swastika cross, symbolically linking the successful harvest with the ancient solar attribute of fire and the feminine lozenge shape, in a Christian emblem.

Both Christian and pre-Christian rituals surrounding the corn dolly in a variety of manifestations appear to be continuous among the Insular Celts.[44] Aubrey recorded in 1688 that 'the Irish doe keepe some of last yeares Wheat or Barley, to hang up in their houses, as a Lar [household

---

[36] Cogitosus 7:5.
[37] Acts of the Apostles 10:38.
[38] Matthew 25.
[39] Cogitosus 7:2.
[40] Cogitosus 15:2-4.
[41] Cogitosus 28.
[42] Cassandra Eason, *The Handbook of Ancient Wisdom* (London, 1997) pp 53-57; Iona Opie and Moira Tatem (eds), *A Dictionary of Superstitions* (Oxford, 1993) p 96.
[43] Sometimes rush or straw. One legend is that Brigit converted a pagan on his deathbed while holding a cross plaited from rushes from the floor. Crosses of St Brigit are made from four stalks extending from a square, and are still commonplace in Ireland: MacKillop, p 58.
[44] Opie and Tatem, pp 96f, 378f.

god] ... Some used to hang these idols in their chimneys'.[45] Coleridge noted in the *Annual Anthology* of 1800 a superstition of the West Country, 'if you meet the devil, you may ... cut him in half with a straw.'

In Celtic tradition in both pre-Christian and Christian times, in cases where illnesses do not respond to physical cures or incantations and charms, pilgrimage to a sacred site with healing properties carries its own special healing grace, along with the spiritual motivation and physical effort involved. The practice of pilgrimage to the sacred flame at Kildare and healing rituals at Brigit's well remain current.[46] Ritual celebrations connected with seasonal changes continue to link Brigit with agriculture and the basic life elements of fire and water, the symbols of restoration to life surrounding the cauldron of rebirth.

The fusion of the goddess and the saint reflects the dual nature of woman that is concerned with the solid and earthy, with the provision and moulding of the tangible needs of her family, while at the same time she is close to the mystery of life. The nurturing aspect of life for each woman naturally evolves from the deep-held faith in the link between the feminine and the essential rhythms of nature. Although Brigit herself remained a virgin, her symbolism of fertility is intense. The mysteries of birth and nurture hold a truth beyond the visible and human. The constant act of creating and harmonising is seen in the Old Testament awareness of the presence of God in feminine form, the Jewish concept of motherhood of God, and in the fusion of the Celtic goddess and saint, Brigit.

---

[45] cited in *ibid*, p 96.
[46] Meehan and Oliver, p 24.

Memories of the Celts in Bede's
Historia ecclesiastica gentis Anglorum

Martin Grimmer

Arguably the most important of medieval scholars whose work has informed modern understanding of Anglo-Celtic interaction in the early Anglo-Saxon period is the Venerable Bede (674-735), monk of the joint monasteries of Monkwearmouth and Jarrow in Northumbria. Amongst his extensive corpus, it is his greatest work – the *Historia ecclesiastica gentis Anglorum*; the 'Ecclesiastical History of the English People', completed in 731 – which holds prime position.[1] Indeed, for seventh-century Britain we are almost totally reliant on what he includes in this work, and so we see much of the period only through the lens that he holds up for us. This text also provides the basis for the way in which the early medieval Celts have traditionally been viewed by historians, especially Anglo-Saxon historians. What I aim to examine in this paper is how Bede presented, or how he memorialised, the Celts of early medieval Britain in his *Historia ecclesiastica*.

It has typically been assumed that Bede's attitude to the various Celtic peoples of Britain was unfavourable; that he regarded them with disdain.[2] While this may have some currency as a broad generalisation, such a presumption actually obscures, and trivialises, a deeper complexity in Bede's thinking about the Britons, Irish and Picts.[3] Bede regarded the

---

[1] All references to Bede's *Historia ecclesiastica [HE]* will be cited by book and chapter from L Sherley-Price and D H Farmer (trans), *Bede: Ecclesiastical History of the English People* (Harmondsworth, 1990), with text from C Plummer (ed), *Venerabilis Baedae: Historiam Ecclesiasticam Gentis Anglorum, Historiam Abbatum, Epistolam ad Ecgberctum, una cum Historia Abbatum Auctore Anonymo* (Oxford, 1896). I have chosen to rely mostly on the Sherley-Price and Farmer translation, as it provides a better literal reading of the text than the more literary translation in B Colgrave and R A B Mynors (eds), *Bede's Ecclesiastical History of the English People* (Oxford, 1969).

[2] For example, L Alcock, *Bede, Eddius, and the Forts of the North Britons* (Jarrow, 1988) p 3; D Banham, 'Anglo-Saxon attitudes: in search of the origins of English racism', *European Review of History* 1 (1994) 143-56, p 148; D P Kirby, 'King Ceolwulf of Northumbria and the *Historia Ecclesiastica*', *Studia Celtica* 14-15 (1979-80) 168-73, pp 172f; C A Snyder, 'Celtic continuity in the middle ages', *Medieval Perspectives* 11 (1996) 164-78, p 170.

[3] Bede made use of Latin designations when naming these peoples: *Britanni* (or *Brittones*), *Scotti* and *Picti*. In the case of Bede's use of *Scotti*, it is necessary to consider the context of the passage within which the term occurs so as to determine whether he is referring to inhabitants of mainland Ireland, or of Dalriada, the Scottic

different Celts differently, best illustrated by his treatment of the Britons versus the Irish. For Bede, the Britons were a cowardly (*ignavus*) and lazy (*segnis*) people,[4] who '... for the most part have a national hatred for the English [*quamius et maxima ex parte domestico sibi odio gentem Anglorum*]'.[5] The Scots, on the other hand, were regarded by Bede quite differently: as a people who showed charity (*caritas*),[6] who were inoffensive (*inoxia, innocens*) and who had '... always been friendly to the English [*nationi Anglorum semper amicissimam*]'.[7]

According to Thomas Charles-Edwards, this contrast 'runs deep through the *Historia ecclesiastica*',[8] and it can be argued that the foundation of the difference in Bede's attitudes to these two groups of Celts lay in the disparity between what he saw as their respective efforts to convert the pagan Anglo-Saxons.[9] Bede clearly states that the Britons played no role in the conversion of the Anglo-Saxons. Quite early in the *Historia ecclesiastica* Bede says that:

> Among the other unspeakable crimes [*inenarrabilium scelerum facta*], recorded with sorrow by their own historian Gildas, they [i.e. the Britons] added this – that they never preached the faith to the Saxons or Angles who dwelt with them in Britain.[10]

Bede made the same point when discussing the meeting of St Augustine and the British bishops in the early 600s;[11] and when describing the capitulation

---

kingdom centred on Argyllshire in western Scotland. In modern scholarship, *Scotti* is most commonly translated as 'Irish', a convention which I follow in this paper. I will also make use of the term 'Columban' to describe the community and Christianity of Iona, so as to make a distinction from the churches and clerics of mainland Ireland.

[4] *HE* I.12, I.15. See also *HE* II.2, in which Bede described the flight of Brocmail at the battle of Chester. Charged with protecting the 1200 monks from Bangor, he and his men '... took to their heels at the first assault, leaving those whom they should have protected unarmed and exposed to the sword-strokes of the enemy'.
[5] *HE* V.23.
[6] *HE* III.4.
[7] *HE* IV.26.
[8] T M Charles-Edwards, 'Bede, the Irish and the Britons', *Celtica* 15 (1983) 42-52. This work is still the best examination of Bede's attitude to these two Celtic peoples.
[9] Charles-Edwards, p 42. See also R Cramp, 'Northumbria and Ireland' in P E Szarmach (ed), *Sources of Anglo-Saxon Culture* (Kalamazoo, 1986) 185-201, p 185; C Stancliffe, 'The British church and the mission of Augustine' in R Gameson (ed), *St Augustine and the Conversion of England* (Stroud, 1999) 107-51, p 108; A Thacker, 'Bede and the Irish' in L A J R Houwen and A A MacDonald (eds), *Beda Venerabilis: Historian, Monk & Northumbrian* (Groningen, 1996) 31-59, pp 33-34; E A Thompson, *Romans and Barbarians* (Wisconsin, 1982) p 14; B Yorke, *Kings and Kingdoms of Early Anglo-Saxon England* (London, 1990) p 19.
[10] *HE* I.22.
[11] *HE* II.2. When discussing this passage, Stancliffe, p 108, notes Bede's equanimity about the slaughter of 1200 British monks.

of the community of Iona to Roman practice in 716.¹² He also complained in his concluding statement of the present state of Britain (c 731) that the Britons still refused to accept the Roman Easter.¹³

By contrast, Bede's account of the Irish role in the conversion of the Anglo-Saxons is quite the reverse. The Columbans of Dalriada – that is, those heralding from St Columba's monastery on Iona – are accorded a primary role by Bede in the evangelisation of Anglo-Saxon England, and it is only through him that we even know the extent of their involvement.¹⁴ Bede explicitly acknowledges the debt owed by the Anglo-Saxons to Iona in his chapter on the capitulation of St Columba's monastery to Roman practice, where he refers to them as '... the nation which had willingly and ungrudgingly laboured to communicate its own knowledge of God to the English nation'.¹⁵ His remarks about the Irish were, therefore, noticeably warmer than those he made about the Britons.¹⁶

The distinction between Bede's regard for the Britons and for the Irish is most starkly drawn in his respective accounts of Cadwallon and Aidan. Cadwallon, who was king of the British kingdom of Gwynedd, is in many respects presented as the archetypal barbarian.¹⁷ Having rebelled (*rebellavit*) against King Edwin of Northumbria's *imperium*, with the support of Penda the pagan king of Mercia, Cadwallon is described as '... a barbarian more savage than any pagan [*barbarus erat pagano saevior*]'; a person who professed to be a Christian but '...was utterly barbarous in temperament and behaviour [*adeo ... erat animo ac moribus barbarus*]', and who was:

> set upon exterminating the entire English race in Britain [*totum genus Anglorum Brittaniae finibus erarurum se esse deliberans*], ... [sparing] neither women nor innocent children, putting them all to horrible deaths with ruthless savagery, and continuously ravaging their whole country [*ne sexui quidem muliebri, vel innocuae parvulorum parceret aetati, quin universos atrocitate ferina morti per tormenta*

---

¹² *HE* V.22.
¹³ *HE* V.23. See also *HE* II.20.
¹⁴ I Bradley, *Celtic Christianity: Making Myths and Chasing Dreams* (Edinburgh, 1999) p 25; D P Kirby, 'Bede and the Pictish church', *The Innes Review* 24 (1973) 6-25, p 14; R Sharpe, *Adomnán of Iona, Life of St Columba* (Harmondsworth, 1995) p 39.
¹⁵ *HE* V.22.
¹⁶ Bradley, p 26; H R Loyn, 'The conversion of the English to Christianity: some comments on the Celtic contribution' in *idem*, *Society and Peoples: Studies in the History of England and Wales, c. 600-1200* (London, 1992) 20-44, p 31.
¹⁷ N J Higham, 'Britons in northern England in the early middle ages: through a thick glass darkly', *Northern History* 38 (2001) 5-25, p 21; Stancliffe, pp 109f.

> *contraderet, multo tempore totas eorum provincias debachando pervagatus*].[18]

In Cadwallon's year-long rulership of the Northumbrian provinces after his and Penda's defeat of Edwin in 633, Bede characterised him '... not as a victorious king but as a savage tyrant [*non ut rex victor ... sed quasi tyrannus saeviens*]', who 'ravaged ... with ghastly slaughter [*ac tragica caede dilaceraret*]'.[19] Thus, Cadwallon was for Bede almost worse than a pagan: whereas the pagan Penda of Mercia could not be expected to know or act any better, Cadwallon, as a Christian king, had sinned deeply not only by allying with a pagan but also by attacking a nation of fellow-Christians. Bede's representation of Cadwallon's actions as rebellion against the so-called 'legitimate' *imperium* of Edwin also has overtones of Gildas, mirroring his presentation of the usurper Maximus's rebellion against Rome.[20]

Aidan, the first Columban bishop of Lindisfarne, by contrast, is described by Bede with great admiration.21 He is accounted '... a man of outstanding gentleness, holiness and moderation [*summae mansuetudinis pietatis, ac moderaminis virum*]',[22] a cleric who was

> rightly loved by all, even by those who differed from his opinion on Easter, and was held in high respect not only by ordinary folk, but by Honorius of Canterbury and Felix of the East Angles [*Unde ab omnibus, etiam his, qui de pascha aliter sentiebant, merito diligebatur; nec solum a mediocribus, verum ab ipsis quoque episcopis, Honorio*

---

[18] *HE* II.20. Bede elsewhere referred to Cadwallon's 'callous impiety [*feralis impietas*]' (*HE* III.9).

[19] *HE* III.1. Further on in the same chapter Bede again refers to the '... savage tyranny of the British king [*vesanam Brettonici regis tyrannidem*]', calling him an 'infamous British leader [*infandus Brettonum dux*]'.

[20] Charles-Edwards, p 45. Banham, p 146, notes with irony that Bede's portrait of Cadwallon the Briton differs little from Gildas's earlier description of the Anglo-Saxons. See Gildas, *De excidio Britanniae* 13.1-2. References to Gildas *[DEB]* will be cited according to chapter and section numbers from M Winterbottom (ed and trans), *Gildas: The Ruin of Britain and Other Documents* (London, 1978).

[21] L Bieler, 'Ireland's contribution to the culture of Northumbria' in G Bonner (ed), *Famulus Christi: Essays in Commemoration of the Thirteenth Centenary of the Birth of the Venerable Bede* (London, 1976) 210-28, p 212; Bradley, p 26; D Bullough, 'The missions to the English and the Picts and their heritage (to c.800)' in H Lowe (ed), *Die Iren und Europa im fruheren Mittelalter* (Stuttgart, 1982) 80-98, p 86; N J Higham, *The Northern Counties to AD 1000* (London, 1986) p 281; Kirby, 'Bede and the Pictish church', pp 10, 14; M Richter, *Ireland and Her Neighbours in the Seventh Century* (Dublin, 1999) pp 104f; Thacker, p 43. Bede's account of the life of Aidan (*HE* III.3, III.5) follows closely after his diatribe against Cadwallon (*HE* II.20, III.1). The contrast between the two Celts is thus made more obvious and immediate.

[22] *HE* III.3.

Cantuariorum, et Felice Orientalium Anglorum, venerationi habitus est].[23]

Bede also painted Aidan as an inspiring example of a cleric who practiced what he preached, stating that:

> the highest recommendation of his teaching to all was that he and his followers lived as they taught [*cuius doctrinam id maxime commendabat omnibus, quod non aliter, quam vivebat cum suis ipse, docebat*].[24]

Aidan was also praised for his lack of interest in worldly possessions, his application to the rules of the apostles, as well as for his humility and generosity.[25] His community at Lindisfarne was held in high regard due to their simple desire for an ascetic life serving God.[26] In some respects Aidan is almost too good to be true, with Bede's description of him having a hagiographical flavour that probably tells us more of what Bede wanted Aidan to be, than of what he necessarily was.[27] However, this does not invalidate Bede's overwhelmingly positive attitude to the Columban cleric. Bede's favour towards the Irish in Britain can also be seen in his descriptions of Columba himself,[28] and other Columban or Irish clerics such as Fursa,[29] Colmán,[30] Dìcuil[31] and most especially Adomnán.[32]

Bede's descriptions of Cadwallon and Aidan can, therefore, be used to exemplify the different manner in which he constructed his representations of the Britons and Irish. Cadwallon the British king was presented by Bede as a barbarian, whereas Aidan the Columban cleric was virtually sanctified.[33] While it could be argued that a comparison between the warlike Cadwallon and the saintly Aidan is not strictly a fair one, both these images cohere well with Bede's general view of the two peoples.[34]

That said, the contrast in Bede's attitudes should not be overplayed, as his inter-ethnic views are not always so easy to categorise. For instance, he held at least one Briton in esteem, namely Ninian, the founder of the

---

[23] *HE* III.25.
[24] *HE* III.5.
[25] *HE* III.5, III.17.
[26] *HE* III.26. Bede says something similar of the community of Iona (*HE* III.4).
[27] Bullough, p 85 note 18. Thacker, p 43, argues that Bede was not here expressing support for 'Celtic' practice, as such, but rather vindicating the antecedents of Northumbrian Christianity.
[28] *HE* III.4, V.9.
[29] *HE* III.19.
[30] *HE* III.26, IV.4.
[31] *HE* IV.13.
[32] *HE* V.15, V.21.
[33] Higham, 'Britons in northern England', p 7.
[34] Charles-Edwards, pp 51f. Indeed, both figures are presented as archetypical of their respective *gentes*, and as implied earlier (see note 21), they are juxtaposed in the *HE* itself.

monastery of Whithorn, whom he regarded as '... a most reverend and holy man of British race [*reverentissimo et santissimo viro de natione Brettonum*]',[35] and whom he praised for bringing Christianity to the southern Picts. He also referred to scholars from the British monastery of Bangor-is-y-Coed as 'most learned [*doctissimi*]', and the monastery as 'most noble [*nobilissimo*]'.[36] Similarly, Bede shows some inconsistency in his views of the Irish.[37] Bede's description of Bishop Finán, who succeeded Aidan at Lindisfarne, is noticeably cool. He called him '... a hot-tempered man [*homo ferocis animi*]', who was 'openly hostile [*apertum adversarium*]' to the Roman Easter.[38] Bede also accounted the first unnamed Columban cleric sent to minister to the Northumbrians before Aidan, a man of 'austere disposition [*austerioris amini*]', who himself regarded the Anglo-Saxons as an '... ungovernable people of an obstinate and barbarous temperament [*indomabiles et durae ac barbarae mentis*]'.[39] Bede was also opposed to non-orthodox practice, and in this regard spoke against the Irish. In his description of the Synod of Whitby, for example, he has Wilfrid declare them '... partners in obstinacy [with] the Picts and Britons [*obstinationis ... conplices, Pictos ... et Brettones*]', for being '... stupid enough to contend with the whole world [*contra totum orbem stulto labore pugnant*]' over Easter.[40]

Yet, returning to the contrast between Bede's view of the Britons and the Irish, instead of condemning the Irish for blind pig-headedness, as he does the Britons, he presents their non-orthodoxy as being a function of ignorance.[41] So, in discussing Bishop Aidan, Bede states that '... he had a zeal in God, but *not according to knowledge* [*habentem zelum Dei, quamuis non plene secundum scientiam*]' (emphasis added).[42] He attributed the Columban clerics' ignorance to the location of Iona, explaining that:

> Being so isolated from the rest of the world, there was no one to acquaint them with the synodical decrees about the keeping of Easter [*utpote quibus longe ultra orbem positis*

---

[35] *HE* III.4.
[36] *HE* II.2. Yet in the same chapter he also called the Britons a 'faithless people [*gens perfida*]'.
[37] Sharpe, p 39.
[38] *HE* III.25. Note also Bede's inclusion of the letter from Archbishop Laurentius of Canterbury and his fellow-bishops Mellitus and Justus to the Irish, in which they complain that the Irish bishop Dagan refused to eat with them (*HE* II.4).
[39] *HE* III.5.
[40] *HE* III.25.
[41] Charles-Edwards, p 51; Thacker, p 41.
[42] *HE* III.3. See also *HE* III.17, in which Bede refers to Aidan's 'inadequate knowledge of the proper observance of Easter', of which he 'strongly disapproves', yet still commends Aidan's 'peace and love, purity and humility'. And see *HE* V.22, in which similar comments are made of the Columbans of Iona in general.

nemo synodalia paschalis observantiae decreta porrexerat].[43] Certainly, the Columbans were said by Bede to be 'barbarous and simple [*ut barbari et rustici*]',[44] but their barbarity was not one rooted in evil and slaughter as was the Britons'. In this light, the Columbans could be pardoned for their error as they did not know any better; but having heard the correct teachings of the Roman church they were now expected to conform, or fall into sin.[45] The fact that Iona had actually capitulated to Roman practice by the time Bede was writing the *Historia ecclesiastica* meant that they were not a lost cause for him, that they were ultimately able to gain salvation in his eyes. Thus, he was able to write more favourably of the Irish than of the Britons, who themselves had not yet abandoned their 'improper' practice and had remained obdurate long after exposure to Roman teaching. Bede may have condescended to the Irish, but he was not hostile.[46]

It could be said, therefore, that Bede reserved his favour for those Celts who conformed to his specific Christian agenda. The Columbans had brought Christianity to the Northumbrians, and had been 'rewarded' by their conversion to Roman practice.[47] Those who were treated less positively – bishop Finán and the unnamed Columban missionary – had either shown a wilful disregard for orthodoxy, or had failed to contribute to the success story of the English Church. Ninian, who was the only British saint apart from St Alban even to be named by Bede, brought Christianity to the southern Picts and, significantly, was said to have been '... *regularly instructed* in the mysteries of the Christian faith in Rome [*qui erat Romae regulariter fidem et mysteria veritatis edoctus*]' (emphasis added).[48] In other words, Ninian could act as a model of Roman orthodoxy, in addition to providing some level of legitimacy to Northumbrian ecclesiastical aspirations in southern Pictland and Galloway.[49] Britons as whole, however, were disdained.

This same principle of positive regard in exchange for service to the greater good of Christianity might also be applied to Bede's view of the Picts. While Bede, undoubtedly following Gildas's precedent, refers to the

---

[43] *HE* III.4.
[44] *HE* III.4.
[45] Stancliffe, p 148 note 143.
[46] Thacker, p 41, even refers to Bede as 'defending' Iona.
[47] Stancliffe, p 108.
[48] *HE* III.4. There may have been other British saints' cults in existence in early Anglo-Saxon England which were not mentioned by Bede, for example to St Sixtus in Kent. See Stancliffe, p 121.
[49] Bradley, p 27.

Picts and the Irish both as 'savage races [*gentibus ... vehementer saevis*]',[50] he is otherwise respectful of them. Bridei mac Máelchon, for example, under whose kingship Bede states that Columba had been allowed to convert the Picts, is described as a 'most powerful king [*rex potentissimus*]'.[51] Nechtan son of Derilei, who was the king who introduced Roman orthodoxy to Pictland c 710, was similarly admired. In a letter to Nechtan from Abbot Ceolfrith of Monkwearmouth and Jarrow, reproduced by Bede, he is addressed as '... the most excellent and illustrious lord [*domino excellentissimo et gloriosissimo*]', and called a 'God-fearing king [*rex Deo devote*]'.[52] The general tone of the letter is respectful, as is Bede's treatment of Nechtan in the remainder of his account. For Bede, both these Pictish rulers played an important role in the promulgation of Christianity within their realms. And more particularly in Nechtan's case, he was a champion of Roman orthodoxy. Bede could not have treated him with anything other than affection. In this regard, it is instructive to note that Bede in no way condemns the Picts for killing the Northumbrian king Ecgfrith in 685:[53] if anything, his sympathy appears to have been with the Picts, not with his own ruler.[54]

This attitude actually stands in contrast to other contemporary scholars' remarks about the Picts. For example, in Stephen of Ripon's *Life of Wilfrid*, reference is made to '... the bestial tribes of the Picts [*populi bestiales Pictorum feroci animo*]',[55] and in the later *Continuatio Bedae*, the Pictish king Oengus son of Fergus was said

> from the beginning of his reign right to the end [to have] behaved with bloody crime as a tyrannical slaughterer [*qui regni sui principium usque ad finem facinore cruento tyrannus perduxit carnifex*].[56]

Stephen and the author of the *Continuatio* entry do not appear to have been impelled by the same concerns as Bede.[57]

---

[50] *HE* II.12. By way of comparison see *DEB* 14.1, in which the Picts and Irish are described as 'exceedingly savage overseas nations [*gentibus transmarinis vehementer saevis*]'.
[51] *HE* III.4.
[52] *HE* V.21.
[53] *HE* IV.26.
[54] C Hughes, 'Early Christianity in Pictland', in *idem, Celtic Britain in the Early Middle Ages* (Suffolk, 1980) p 38.
[55] Stephen of Ripon, *Vita Wilfridi* ch 19. See B Colgrave (ed), *The Life of Bishop Wilfrid by Eddius Stephanus: Text, Translation and Notes* (Cambridge, 1927).
[56] *Continuatio Bedae* s.a. 761. See D Whitelock (ed), *English Historical Documents, Volume I, c.500-1042* (London, 1955) no 5, pp 285f, and text from Plummer, *Bede*, Vol I, pp 361-3.
[57] L Alcock, 'A survey of Pictish settlement archaeology' in J G P Friell and W G Watson (eds), *Pictish Studies: Settlement, Burial and Art in Dark Age Northern Britain* (Oxford, 1984) 7-41, p 7. By the time Bede was writing there also existed a

It is thus possible to see that Bede's presentation of the Britons, the Irish and the Picts conformed to a particular ecclesiastical agenda. The extent to which Bede was also motivated by a broader awareness of Anglo-Celtic secular relations has been a matter of debate within the literature. Thomas Charles-Edwards, for example, was of the opinion that Bede's attitudes to the different Celts were solely religious in provenance.[58] He claimed that Bede's view of the Britons, for instance, was in essence a Gildasian-inspired literary construction – a *topos* – based on their refusal to accept Roman patrimony, and that the *Historia* shows 'no evidence for national antipathy'.[59] Nicholas Higham argued along similar lines, stating that Bede was attempting to barbarise the Britons so as to 'prove', within the context of his providential history, the triumph of the Anglo-Saxons as God's chosen people.[60] Bryan Ward-Perkins, on the other hand, has asserted in regard to Anglo-British relations that the perception of difference between the two peoples 'was no mere literary construct' but was actually felt in society.[61] David Dumville also cautions against assuming that Bede 'overdramatised' Anglo-Celtic sentiment.[62]

To a certain extent, it may be a matter of taste as to which opinion one holds and which interpretation of Bede one favours. Certainly, Roman orthodoxy and divine providence were themes of great importance to Bede; after all, he was writing an ecclesiastical history. However, this does not necessarily mean that he would have been unmindful of matters of ethnicity and of the broader socio-political context. Bede was self-consciously English, and was clearly cognisant of the distinct identities of the various

---

peace-treaty between the Picts and the Northumbrians (*HE* V.23). This too may have influenced his portrayal (Kirby, 'Bede and the Pictish church', pp 7f). It should be noted that Bede in his letter to Bishop Ecgberht later expressed concern over the ability of Northumbria to defend itself against invasion by 'barbarians' (*Epistolam ad Ecgberctum Episcopum* ch 11; see Sherley-Price and Farmer, pp 337-51, and text from Plummer, *Bede* Vol I, pp 405-23). If he was here referring to the Picts, which is not at all certain, then he too may have ultimately subscribed to the more generalised anxiety.

[58] Charles-Edwards, pp 42-52.
[59] *ibid*, p 48.
[60] N J Higham, *An English Empire: Bede and the Early Anglo-Saxon Kings* (Manchester, 1995) esp pp 16-18; idem., 'Britons in northern England in the early middle ages', pp 7, 12. See also S Bassett, 'Church and diocese in the West Midlands: the transition from British to Anglo-Saxon control' in J Blair and R Sharpe (eds), *Pastoral Care Before the Parish* (Leicester, 1992) 13-40, p 39.
[61] B Ward-Perkins, 'Why did the Anglo-Saxons not become more British?', *English Historical Review* 115 (2000) 513-33, pp 516f.
[62] D N Dumville, 'The origins of Northumbria: Some aspects of the British background' in S Bassett (ed), *The Origins of Anglo-Saxon Kingdoms* (Leicester, 1989) 213-22, p 219.

peoples of Britain.[63] While his interpretation of Anglo-Celtic relations was skewed by a particular ecclesiastical agenda, there is no *a priori* reason to suppose that he did not overlay this agenda onto an existing framework of ethnic prejudice.[64] And in any event, disagreement amongst historians as to the provenance of Bede's attitudes to the Celtic-speaking peoples of Britain does not alter the fact that he wrote them into his work. Whatever the reason, Bede nevertheless appeared to dislike Britons, and to favour the Irish and Picts.

The representativeness of Bede's work might also be considered from the viewpoint of textuality. The *Historia ecclesiastica* certainly reached a wide audience, as indicated by the number of early manuscripts which have survived, including four from the eighth-century, one of which was probably produced within five years of his death in 735.[65] The popularity of Bede's work can be taken as an indication of its acceptability to its readers.[66] The audience would have been predominantly clerical; however, it is unlikely that the aristocracy remained ignorant of the contents of the work and the attitudes promulgated therein. It was after all dedicated to King Ceolwulf of Northumbria, who appears to have read it.[67] We might presume too much to state that Bede's text reflected mainstream thought at the time,[68] but it *must* have influenced how people thought about Anglo-Celtic relations.

What I have attempted to show in this paper is that Bede adopted an eclectic attitude to the different Celtic peoples residing in Britain, which was informed by what he perceived as their respective contributions to the success story of the Christian church of the Anglo-Saxons. Bede wrote with due attention to what he saw as the different roles played by the Britons, the Irish and the Picts. He presented the Britons as obdurate barbarians who refused to take any part in the Christianisation of their Anglo-Saxon neighbours and who still, when Bede was compiling the *Historia ecclesiastica*, held out against orthodox Roman practice. He painted the Irish as saintly missionaries who willingly brought the word of God to the kingdoms of the Anglo-Saxons, and who could be forgiven their

---

[63] Banham, p 148; Charles-Edwards, p 43; Ward-Perkins, pp 513f, 516.
[64] Banham, pp 147f; Snyder, pp 170f.
[65] The earliest surviving manuscript is *Cambridge University Library MS Kk.5.16*, which was probably produced in the late 730s. This manuscript also contains the *Moore Memoranda*. See D N Dumville, 'On the northern British section of the *Historia Brittonum*', *Welsh Historical Review* 8 (1977) 345-54, p 350; Plummer, *Bede* Vol I, p lxxxvi; R W Hanning, *The Vision of History in Early Britain* (New York, 1966) p 67.
[66] Banham, p 153; H E J Cowdrey, 'Bede and the "English people"', *Journal of Religious History* 11 (1980-1) 501-23, pp 519f.
[67] *HE* Preface. See also Kirby, 'King Ceolwulf of Northumbria', pp 168-73.
[68] As is suggested by Banham, p 153.

previous non-orthodox practices due to their isolation and simplicity. The Picts, while not in the same league as the Irish, were nonetheless a people also to be respected due to their voluntary pursuit and acceptance of Roman practice. Any treatment of the Celtic peoples of Britain which relies on Bede needs, therefore, to recognise these complexities in his writing.

They were there: the population of Anglo-Saxon Sedgeford, Norfolk

Melanie Van Twest

The village of Sedgeford is located on the east coast of England, in the north-western part of Norfolk, East Anglia, and forms a part of Smithdon Hundred. It is mentioned in Domesday Book, along with the (now deserted) neighbouring villages of Eaton and Gnatingdon. Its inland location means that it is bordered on all sides by other parishes, one of which is Snettisham, the famous site of the Iron Age torc hoards of high status that call to mind the East Anglian Iceni and Boudicca's revolt against the Romans. Because of this long association, archaeological and historical interest – both amateur and professional – in this area has had a long history of its own.

Sedgeford is, even now, a very small village boasting over 500 residents but possessing only one pub, one small general store and part-time post-office, and one daily bus to service them. The population was mainly employed in local agriculture to within the last 25 years: it is now becoming increasingly a dormitory satellite to larger local centres, such as King's Lynn and Cambridge.

The site which is the subject of this paper is located on the southern slope of the Heacham river valley, facing the village. It comprises two fields: the Boneyard and the Reeddam. The Boneyard is so-called for the amounts of bone – apparently recognised as human – that were turned up each time the field was ploughed. The Reeddam, as the name implies, was once used for the commercial production of Norfolk reed, once a valuable crop used in thatching house roofs.

The Boneyard has been archaeologically investigated twice prior to 1996, as far as we have been able to ascertain. Both of these investigations were short: a matter of a few weeks. 35 years later a chance meeting between the landowner and Dr Neil Faulkner[1] led to the establishment of the Sedgeford Historical and Archaeological Research Project, or SHARP.

SHARP aims to reconstruct, as far as possible, a coherent history of human occupation in Sedgeford parish. With this in mind, we have spent six to eight weeks of every British summer since 1996 attempting to research, dig, read, explore, survey, plan, photograph and interview everything and everyone that presents itself to us! Naturally this has led to

---

[1] Dr Faulkner is an academic archaeologist based at the Institute of Archaeology, University College London.

the accumulation of a vast archive, even at this relatively early stage. In this paper, I will briefly discuss the investigations and findings of the human remains research.

The Anglo-Saxon burials at Sedgeford are found in both the Boneyard and the Reeddam. The former, as noted above, has long been known as an ancient cemetery, and is a dry, hillside environment, with quite homogenous, sandy soils (especially in the upper layers), well-dispersed adult burials and few juvenile graves.[2] The Reeddam, by contrast, was found to contain burials only by accident in the second (1997) season: these turned out to be very densely packed — in up to six layers — into thick grey clayey mud, with a high proportion of juvenile burials. It has been concluded, using evidence from a variety of sources, that the Reeddam represents the first phase of usage of this area as a cemetery: only later, once the Reeddam area was full, did burials start to take place up the hillside on what is now the Boneyard. Alternatively, it is possible that the later Reeddam burials may be contemporary with the early Boneyard graves.

Research into the human skeletons excavated from both the Reeddam and the Boneyard commenced in earnest in 1998, at which time the skeletal archive consisted of the remains of 25 individuals in varying degrees of completeness, as well as large amounts of loose, disarticulated bone. We implemented a system of observational and metric recording, based on an international standard,[3] which attempted to retrieve all the information from each individual that could easily be noted on site. A file was compiled on each individual, and all the data collected, including photographs and field records.

By the end of the 2000 excavation season, at which time I formally concluded my active association with SHARP, we had evidence for over 300 burials, approximately 150 of which were in varying states of completeness. The accumulated evidence from these, as well as from other parts of the site, has allowed us to draw some valuable conclusions about the status, health and quality of life enjoyed by the Anglo-Saxon community in this part of England.

Looking first at the method of burial, we can make some educated guesses about the length of use of the cemetery. There are a number of examples of burials intersecting other burials, which suggest that the

---

[2] A small discrete area of mainly juvenile burials was identified during the 2000 excavation season and is slowly being explored as the constraints of time and other archaeology permit. Prior to this, very few juvenile burials had been found.

[3] J E Buikstra and D H Ubelaker (eds), *Standards for Data Collection from Human Skeletal Remains* (Arkansas Archaeological Survey Research Series 44, 1994).

cemetery was in use long enough for some graves to be forgotten, and other graves dug too close for comfort.[4]

The position of the arms of the individuals as buried also gives us a clue as to the method of burial: some are by the sides, some across the pelvis, some varied. Our current belief is that those with arms placed to the side and head turned to one side were coffined burials, while other arm placement variations were shrouded burials that were placed in the grave wrapped in linen or another cloth. The latter theory is based upon the surmise that although the corpse was probably wrapped quite securely, there may have been enough room for the arms to move about as the body was manoeuvred into its grave, and to remain in a variety of positions post-burial. Accepted wisdom is that shroud burials are fairly low-status, the belief being that the amount of expense represented by a length of linen, compared to a wooden coffin with metal brackets and clasps, is minimal.[5]

The evidence for a small number of coffined burials at Sedgeford includes material evidence as well as skeletal burial position. One of the first coffin burials to be noted made itself evident only by one rusted piece of angled ironwork found near the head of the Reeddam skeleton S1041, suggesting that before other parts of the skeleton were disturbed, there had been a series of these brackets at each corner of the burial binding the corners of a wooden box, and good evidence for a wooden structure in which the individual was buried.

The nature of the burials[6] and their dates[7] strongly suggests that this community was Christian by religion. The period is also just prior to the Viking occupation of northern England and the establishment of the Danelaw.

Before I discuss what we have found out about the population, I should note that cultural indicators, such as chance finds of metalwork as well as pottery and coins, indicate that parts of the Middle-Saxon community in Sedgeford may have been both literate and capable of fine craftsmanship. A large number of pins, or parts thereof, have been found. Only one was in direct relationship with a skeleton, but its position balanced upon the pelvis suggests that they may all be shroud pins. A

---

[4] Alternatively, inter-cutting graves may represent a desire to bury within family groups where a desire to preserve discrete graves was not an issue; Patricia Reid, SHARP. *pers comm* (2003).

[5] This belief may in fact be erroneous: the hours of labour represented by a sheet of linen (planting and harvesting flax, making thread, weaving cloth) are probably far more than those required to make a sturdy wooden box for burial, even if the latter is more substantial; Reid, *ibid*.

[6] All the burials appear to be of unclothed persons (no buckles, clasps or other dress ornamentation) and without gravegoods, in an east-west supine orientation.

[7] Dating has been by a variety of methods, including radiocarbon, to the Middle to Late Saxon period, c 750 onwards.

number of styli, writing implements for re-usable wax tablets, have also been found, as well as some jewellery such as the lovely Saxon knotwork brooch now used as the SHARP logo. These all suggest more than a simple rural, pastoral community: there is reason to believe that the structure of the village was more stratified with a greater range of education and skills than we may at first think likely.

In considering the community itself, I will deal first with those quality of life indicators that allow us to assess the population's level of health. We have looked particularly at their stature, teeth, bone density and morphology, evidence for disease and injury, and mortality. Other quality of life indicators are those giving us an idea of their society: evidence of violence and the status of women.

Surprisingly, the Sedgeford population displays statures similar to modern British populations. The height of most males falls between 170 and 180 cm, and that of females between 160 and 170 cm. Association between stature and dental age of juveniles also suggests that growth in children was at optimal rates. All of these figures indicate that the Middle-Saxon population at Sedgeford enjoyed a good level of nutrition and a degree of activity and childhood lifestyle that allowed the achievement of maximum growth potential for most individuals.

The condition of their teeth gives us some very interesting insights. Although heavily worn even by full adulthood, probably due to the grit content of their stoneground flours and breads, there are minimal signs of other common pathologies in the Sedgeford population's dentition. Very little evidence of caries (tooth decay) and gum disease exists: there is a moderate amount of dental calculus (the hardened accumulation of dental plaque), but high levels in one individual are rare. The worst outcome for an individual was the loss of his or her teeth due to abscesses or extreme wear, which loosen the tooth socket and lead to the tooth falling out: all individuals of middle or older age show some degree of ante-mortem tooth loss.

Studying the bones themselves gives us another indication of how healthy the population was. In most cases bones are well formed with normal morphology (shape), and strong features suggesting well-developed musculature. Once again, this is evidence for good childhood nutrition, though continuation of that level of nutrition into adulthood is less easy to determine. The occurrence of some evidence for nutritional diseases like osteoporosis suggests that these conditions were difficult to prevent, then as now: other disease indicators (such as cribra orbitalia, the somewhat controversial indicator of anaemia) are rare in this population.[8]

---

[8] The low incidence of cribra orbitalis in this population was confirmed by a formal study carried out during the 2003 season.

The rate of infective disease is impossible to determine from skeletal remains, as acute disease will kill the individual before the skeleton shows any changes. However, if chronic disease, such as tuberculosis and osteomyelitis (infection of the bone tissue), is present, it will become apparent in the skeletal remains. Of the former, no evidence has yet been seen at Sedgeford: only one example of the latter has been noted to date. The lack of such infections is all the more surprising considering that medical knowledge and treatment would have been minimal by our standards, although we have no way of knowing what efficacious local remedies were to be had.

Degenerative disease – especially osteoarthritis – was, on the other hand, as common as it is now. Almost every individual shows evidence of joint changes which would have led to painful movement and perhaps loss of mobility. Some of these people would have lived for a very long time with their disease, and had it in many joints. This would probably be the most serious health problem to be found in this population, and was probably the highest cause of morbidity and loss of quality of life.

Rather surprisingly, evidence of healed injuries, in the form of bone calluses and other indicators, is very low, and those that do exist are relatively minor. Distinguishing peri-mortem (at the time of death) fractures from taphonomic (occurring post-burial from natural processes) fractures with any confidence is something we do not attempt, and so we cannot tell if major fractures that may lead to death in modern populations (eg fractured femur, hip) occur in this one. The minor fractures that we have noted provide us with the impression of a physically active, but relatively safe, working and living environment.

Having said that, evidence for violent death in this community has been noted in a number of individuals. Two of these were buried side by side in the Reeddam; both had died of violent blows to the head. S1018, or 'Cnut', had suffered a heavy blow across the top of his head, shattering his cranium, and another below his left ear that would have caused horrendous soft-tissue injuries. Another skeleton seems to have received a blow with a sharp weapon across the mouth. Sadly we have no way of knowing in what circumstances these individuals died, be it a scuffle or a fully-fledged battle. These few individuals show us that Anglo-Saxon north-west Norfolk may have been a healthy place to live, but could also be a dangerous one.

Childhood is also a critical and vulnerable period in survival. A discrete area of the Boneyard cemetery area has yielded a large number of mainly child burials. Until the time that this area was identified and explored (2000 onwards), we had been puzzled by the lack of evidence for infant (below the age of one year) and child mortality and had wondered what burial practices may have been favoured for children in the contemporary Anglo-Saxon community. A high rate of infant and child mortality would normally be expected in a population of this time. To date, the 'children's cemetery' has yielded evidence for a number of smaller children (three to four years of age) and traces of much younger ones. Although the numbers of identified child and infant burials may still not reflect the expected rate of mortality, the rate of preservation of very small bones is of course likely to skew the available evidence. It is also expected that more material will come to light in future seasons.

Mortality for those who escaped violent or childhood death seems to follow patterns displayed by other pre-industrial populations, with the majority of women dying during their child-bearing years, and men dying in the period of early old-age. Those adults who survived these periods often seem to have lived to a considerable age: rough estimates suggest ages of 70 or more for the most elderly.

Evidence for the status of women is sketchy, and notable mainly by the lack of evidence for poor status. Sexual dimorphism, or the size and growth difference between the sexes, is within normal ranges for this population, supporting the theory that there was no prejudice in the feeding and care of female children.[9] The ratio of male to female adult burials at 1:1 also strongly indicates that there was no survival advantage for either sex.

One individual raises the issue of violence against women. S0061, a woman of over 30, suffered an injury to her jaw which led to the formation of a bone spur on the hinge of her mandible, a condition which would have caused joint inflammation and considerable pain. The idea that this may have been caused by a blow to the head was raised on site at the time of studying this skeleton, and the issue of domestic violence within this community should certainly be kept in mind. However, any such interpretation must remain speculative, and it is difficult to make further comment on the presence of domestic violence without more evidence.

In conclusion, the archaeology of Sedgeford of the Middle-Saxon period gives us the impression of a small but thriving community, with literate and artistic elements, enjoying a high quality of life indicated by good health, minimal disease and injury, and only some evidence of violent death. SHARP continues to work at Sedgeford annually, and publication of our first research monograph should take place within the next 12 months.[10]

---

[9] A large difference between adult females and males would suggest restricted feeding of girls while boys received good nutrition.

[10] Three books are due to be published within the next year: the first will introduce a monograph series of *Sedgeford Papers*, the second is a set of conference papers, and the third is a popular summary of the aims, methods and results of the first seven years of excavation by SHARP on the Anglo-Saxon/medieval aspect of the project. Further information on SHARP and the site are available through the SHARP website: www.sharp.org.uk

Dimensions and distribution: aspects of Pictish sculpture

Pamela O'Neill

This paper does not consider the subject matter or style of Pictish sculpture, but rather some less commonly discussed aspects of that sculpture. By examining certain physical aspects, I hope to draw some conclusions about how we should consider the corpus of Pictish sculpture as a whole, thereby providing future research with a more secure basis for considering the all-important function and meaning of the sculpture. My examination centres on the dimensions of the stones which the Pictish sculptors prepared to receive their work, and on the distribution of the worked stones within the landscape.

In this paper consideration is restricted to a very small sample of the corpus of Pictish stone sculpture. First, I do not propose to consider Allen and Anderson's[1] Class I stones, that is the rough or unshaped boulders containing only those specific depictions which are referred to as Pictish symbols. Classes II and III are shaped and dressed stones containing relief carving including the Christian cross, the distinction being that while Class II stones also contain Pictish symbols, Class III stones do not.

Allen and Anderson[2] considered that the Class I and II stones belong to some sort of common group by virtue of the presence of Pictish symbols, whereas Class III stones are separate because of the absence thereof. However, the Class II and III stones are so similar in every other respect, where the Class I stones are so different, that it seems obvious to me that the function of the Class I stones is quite distinct from that of the Class II and III stones, which must serve a similar, if not identical, range of functions.

This conclusion is supported by the distribution patterns. It is quite unusual to find more than one Class I stone at a single site, whereas, as I shall demonstrate, Class II and III stones seem generally to have been grouped together at sites. Further, there is some evidence that Class I stones are distributed in a pattern which might reflect farm sites, homesteads or forts, whereas the Class II and III stones are not.[3] They concentrate at centres of population; I would suggest at centres of religious population.

---

[1] J Romilly Allen and Joseph Anderson, *The Early Christian Monuments of Scotland* (Edinburgh, 1903; new ed 2 vols Balgavies, 1993).
[2] Eg Allen and Anderson, vol 1, pp cv ff;
[3] M Barry Cottam and Alan Small, 'The Distribution of Settlement in Southern Pictland', *Medieval Archaeology* 18 (1974) 43-65, p60.

The second restriction of scope for this paper is that only the stones in Allen and Anderson's 'East Central' region[4] will be considered. The need for brevity dictates that only one region can be considered in any detail. The East Central region seems most appropriate because it has the highest concentration of Class II stones, and because Cottam and Small chose it for their interesting 1974 study of distribution patterns.[5] When Allen and Anderson completed their study (c 1900), this consisted of the counties of Kincardine, Forfar, Perth, Fife, Kinross and Clackmannan.

Distribution
The locations for sculpture recorded by Allen and Anderson are in general relied upon as the find-sites of the stones. The sites are remarkably easy to find when armed with Allen and Anderson and a road atlas from 1900,[6] which is a tribute to the standard of Allen and Anderson's work. However, the picture they give of distribution is somewhat skewed, and a close reading of their notes[7] might allow future researchers to learn more about the original or at least earlier distribution of the sculpture.[8]

In many cases, Allen and Anderson record the location of a sculptured stone as within a substantial private estate. It is my firm belief that in almost all of these cases the stone had been relocated prior to recording by Allen and Anderson. This is probably not the case with the Class I stones, whose original distribution pattern and purpose were very different. However, in the case of Class II and III stones, I would argue that in the era leading up to Allen and Anderson's great survey, these stones were considered very attractive by some landowners, and plundered from their original sites for the beautification of private estates. I believe that it is possible to postulate origin sites for the stones suspected of relocation, and further that it is possible to infer a pattern of distribution which reflects the circumstances in which the stones were originally erected.

The most striking sites in Allen and Anderson's study are the centres where large quantities of sculpture are found. Principal among these are St

---

[4] Allen and Anderson, vol 1, p10.
[5] Cottam and Small.
[6] John Bartholomew, *Bartholomew's Touring Atlas and Gazetteer of the British Isles* (Edinburgh, 1897-1903; repr London 1998).
[7] Allen and Anderson's entry for each stone gives notes (in more or less detail) concerning provenance and physical description.
[8] For simplicity I will refer to the stones in the present tense as if they are still where Allen and Anderson found them, and I will describe distances in miles as they did. References to sites are as listed in Allen and Anderson, various pages. I count multiple fragments which Allen and Anderson attributed to a single sculpture as separate pieces. In at least one case (St Vigeans 1 and 1a) I am certain that Allen and Anderson's attribution is incorrect (I am currently preparing an article on this subject).

Andrews with 32 pieces (This number has increased since Allen and Anderson's time; Hay Fleming in 1931 cited almost 70 pieces[9]), Meigle with 31 pieces and St Vigeans with 30 pieces. Each of these is at least 5 miles from its nearest neighbour in terms of sculpture sites, and all have ecclesiastical associations.

The next largest concentration is at Strathmartine. I believe that the nearby single stones on private property at Balluderon farm and at the church at Tealing should be associated with the centre of Strathmartine. I suggest that the stone at Balluderon might well have been relocated. The stone at Tealing stands on high ground about two miles to the north of Strathmartine. This is a pattern that is found elsewhere, so that it is possible that this location was originally significant to Strathmartine, possibly marking a boundary or route. Including Balluderon and Tealing, the centre at Strathmartine has 18 surviving stones.

I suggest a centre at Forteviot with nine surviving stones. These include the Dupplin Cross, whose location has a similar relationship with Forteviot to that of Tealing with Strathmartine. Also included is the stone at Invermay, which is situated on high ground just over a mile to the south of Forteviot. Again, it seems likely that the sites of Dupplin and Invermay marked boundaries or routes in relation to Forteviot.[10] I am also including a stone which Allen and Anderson found in the church at Dunning, about three miles away. I would suggest that as the settlement of Dunning was considerably larger than Forteviot by Allen and Anderson's time, and ancient stone sculpture added some prestige, the stone might have been relocated.

There are centres with six surviving stones at Abercromby, Abernethy and Kirriemuir. The Abernethy stones include one that had been reused in a well at Carpow, and one that had apparently been removed to decorate the grounds of Mugdrum house. Allen and Anderson noted that it stood 'on an elevation' near the lodge gates, and so the possibility arises that it may have been repositioned there for decorative purposes. Of the Kirriemuir stones, one is at Cossins, about two miles to the south. It is in the middle of a marsh, and so it is unlikely to have been removed there for decorative purposes. It was probably a route or boundary marker.

I associate four surviving stones with a centre at Brechin. Two of these are at Aldbar, about two miles from Brechin. Allen and Anderson

---

[9] Hay Fleming's 1931 catalogue of the St Andrews Cathedral Museum is cited in Isabel Henderson. 'Primus inter Pares: the St Andrews Sarcophagus and Pictish Sculpture' in Sally M Foster (ed), *The St Andrews Sarcophagus: a Pictish masterpiece and its international connections* (Dublin, 1998) 97-167, p165.
[10] This has been suggested by Leslie Alcock and Elizabeth A Alcock, 'The context of the Dupplin cross: a reconsideration', *Proceedings of theSociety of Antiquaries of Scotland* 126 (1996), 455-458.

note that one is said to have been brought from Brechin, and in that case I think it likely that both were. The ecclesiastical site at Monifieth also has four surviving stones.

Several centres have three surviving stones. These include the ecclesiastical sites at Kingoldrum and Inchbrayock. Aberlemno has two stones, and another was reused in the castle at Woodwray, about two miles away. If one stone from a site has been reused as building material, it is likely that others from that site were as well, so that Aberlemno may originally have had an even larger number of sculptured stones. The island abbey of Inchcolm has two stones, and it seems to me that another was moved to the nearby mainland town of Inverkeithing before being lost.

The church at Glamis has two stones, and another is located at Eassie, about two miles to the west. There are two stones at the ecclesiastical site at Invergowrie, and another at Benvie, about a mile to the north-west. Menmuir church has two stones, with another at Lethnott church, about a mile to the north-west. These last two have the outlier on higher ground, and all three of these might again represent some kind of boundary or route markers.

If we assume the stone on private property at Largo to have come from Scoonie, and that at Sauchope to have come from Crail, there are seven sites with two surviving stones: Scoonie, Crail, Aberlemno, Dunblane, Dunkeld, Logierait and St Madoes.

Fifteen sites with a single example of Class II or III sculpture remain. Of these, Allen and Anderson noted additional 'undecorated' freestanding crosses at Dull and Fowlis Wester,[11] so that these two sites can legitimately be considered as having multiple sculptured stones. The single slabs beside the road at Gask and in the street at Crieff may have been relocated from Fowlis Wester, to which they are fairly close.

I suspect that the slab in the churchyard at Farnell and the fragment built into the garden wall at Kinnell manse were relocated from Brechin, from where we have seen that sculpture was removed to Aldbar. The slab at Kettins had been reused as a footbridge, so had obviously been relocated, and although the origin site need not have been far away, I would suggest Meigle as a likely candidate. The slab in the 'old burying-ground' near Rossie priory may nave been brought from nearby Invergowrie. The cross at Camuston stands decoratively on a grassy knoll in the grounds of Panmure House, to which it was almost certainly relocated by the landowner, although no obvious origin site suggests itself.

The slab at Alyth was dug out of the manse garden, where I would suggest it was probably deliberately buried, most likely during the Reformation. Its origin site may well have been Meigle. Other pieces

---

[11] The possibility must be considered that these crosses had once been embellished with relief sculpture which had succumbed to the forces of nature or vandalism.

would undoubtedly have been relocated during the Reformation, as a result of efforts either to protect them or to dispose of them.

There remain only five sites with a single stone: Dogtown, Fordoun, Murthly, Tullibole, and Allen and Anderson's Dunfallandy (which they noted had been relocated from Killiecrankie). While three of these are in ecclesiastical contexts, there is no evidence to suggest either that they are in situ or that they have been relocated.

Bearing in mind the probable loss of sculpture due to plunder, quarrying and iconoclasm, I would suggest that the balance of probabilities is that most, if not all, sites originally had multiple sculptured stones. This preliminary survey can clearly not be taken as conclusive. Allen and Anderson's information is not always to be relied upon; further information has come to light since their publication, including the finding of additional sculpture. Nonetheless, I believe that the results give a sufficient basis to form hypotheses from which to pursue further research.

I would postulate that Pictish stone sculpture of classes II and III originated in clusters of several stones at each site. Therefore, any site which has a single sculptured stone ought to be approached as either probably not an original site, or a site from which much has been lost. In considering such questions as the decoration of stones or the conditions of their manufacture, or indeed their function, we ought to approach the question as though any stone existed in the context of a group, rather than as an isolated example.

There are other interesting points to be explored as a result of this preliminary survey. Of particular interest to me are the stones that appear to be boundary or route markers associated with the centres to which they are close. The idea of boundary markers has been much written about, but I believe that further empirical research of this nature would contribute to the debate. There is also an intriguing array of sites[12] following the course of the River Tay at fairly regular intervals, which would bear investigation.

Dimensions

One of the Pictish sculptures at St Vigeans is a cross-slab which has supposedly been reconstructed, but is actually pieces of two separate cross-slabs cemented together. They were joined in the late nineteenth century, it seems primarily because they could be joined together. In other words, they were roughly the same width and thickness.[13] The following preliminary survey of the dimensions of Pictish stone sculpture is designed to show that it might very well be entirely coincidental for two cross-slabs in the same

---

[12] Dull, Aberfeldy, Logierait, Dunkeld, Murthly; note also Killiecrankie on the River Garry, which eventually flows into the Tay only about 10 miles from Killiecrankie.

[13] One of these fragments (St Vigeans 1a) is excluded from the survey of widths in this paper, as I believe that only one edge can be accepted as unbroken.

location to have the same width and thickness. I do not investigate height, as it is most common for fragments to be joined along lateral fractures. I use the measurements recorded by Allen and Anderson to test the question.[14]

Of the 196 stones in the sample (see Table 1), Allen and Anderson failed completely to record the thickness of 60, almost one third of the sample. A further 37, almost one fifth of the sample, appear to have been broken or split through their plane, so that the original thickness is no longer evident. The extant thickness of these 37 items ranges from a mere 1.5 inches to 10 inches. There remain 99 stones whose original thickness survives more or less intact. Of these, 78 are cross-slabs, and it is these which will be the focus of my discussion here.

In many cases, Allen and Anderson recorded two thicknesses for a stone, which I have labelled minimum and maximum. This reflects in some cases an apparently deliberate graduation in the thickness, such as a narrowing towards the top of the stone, and in other cases the difference between the ground of the sculpture and the highest points of the relief. While both of these figures might be important, the maximum thickness would more or less reflect the size of the slab from which the sculptor began to create the monument.

Where Allen and Anderson recorded two thicknesses, the difference varied from 0.5 of an inch to 5 inches, but was generally around 1 inch. This is largely a reflection of the particularly deep relief carving favoured by Pictish sculptors. It also highlights a difficulty with modern measurements. All of these stones have suffered varying degrees of wear. Many are situated in the open air and many have been used as building material or pavement. Others have been deliberately defaced. In most cases, the thickness indicated for the ground of the sculpture should still be accurate, but it is difficult to assess how much of the relief has been removed.

Of our 78 cross-slabs, the thickest is 13.5 inches thick, and the thinnest only 2 inches. There is a concentration of eight stones at 7 inches thick, plus a single stone at 7.25 inches. Eleven stones are 6 inches thick, and another two 6.5 inches. Eight are 5 inches and two 5.5 inches. Nine stones are 4 inches thick and six are 4.5 inches thick. Nine are 3 inches and five 3.5 inches thick. The mean thickness is 5.5 inches, and the standard deviation is 2.4.

I would tentatively postulate that a thickness range of between 3 and 7 inches was very common, and so it should not surprise us if several distinct stones at any given site share those dimensions. Only five slabs are

---

[14] Allen and Anderson used inches for their measurements, and rather than convert to centimetres and obscure any rounding that had taken place in the figures, I too have used inches.

thinner than this postulated range, and only 13 are thicker. 60 stones, or 77% of the cross-slabs with complete recorded thickness, fall into this postulated thickness range.

Similar difficulties confront a study of the width of the stones. Allen and Anderson did not record widths for 14 stones. A further 65, approximately one third of the 196 stones recorded by Allen and Anderson, appear to have had some of their width removed by breakage. There is the added complication that a number of the stones are incorporated into buildings with only one face exposed, and while this face is recorded as a width it might well be a thickness. I have for this reason excluded the four narrowest stones from St Andrews for this calculation.

Again, there are frequently two widths for a stone. This is primarily because many of them are not precisely rectangular, but taper slightly towards either top or bottom. Again, I have chosen the wider measurement for primary consideration. The sample consists of the 91 cross-slabs with complete recorded widths.

The widest slab is 66 inches, and the narrowest complete slab only 10 inches. There are significant concentrations of eleven slabs at 21 inches wide, seven at 20 inches, six at 19 inches, seven at 18 inches and another at 18.5, and six at 17 inches. Taken together with the remaining 51 slabs, the mean width is 23.7 inches and the standard deviation is 10.5.

I would again postulate tentatively that these widths might indicate a commonly occurring range of 17 to 21 inches, including 38 or 42% of the stones. Thirty-five stones are wider, and 18 narrower.

There is a distinct concentration of the sample around the thickness and width ranges I have outlined. Sixty-three stones have both width and thickness intact and recorded by Allen and Anderson. Of these, 19 or 30% have both width and thickness within my postulated ranges.

This suggests that it is not necessarily likely that any two fragments which have similar or even the same thickness or width were originally part of the same monument. With cross-slabs, the nature and layout of the sculpture is of necessity similar from one piece to the next. That is, one face must work around the large central cross. This is arguably also true of the dimensions, which must be dictated by the practicalities of available material, structural integrity and intended site. This is reflected in the concentration of the sample around specific width and thickness ranges.

This means that many of the fragments that survive have similar dimensions or the remnants of similar dimensions. We should approach the corpus with this in mind, and not assume that any great significance attaches to apparent similarity between pieces.

Conclusion

This preliminary analysis of some aspects of the dimensions and distribution of Pictish sculpture gives some tentative indications for approaching the corpus of Pictish stone sculpture. The results cannot be considered conclusive, as the sample data do not reflect the extent of current knowledge and require further research and measurement. Nonetheless, on the basis of this analysis, I believe that it is reasonable to suggest, firstly, that Pictish stone sculpture of Allen and Anderson's classes II and III was primarily located in clusters at sites and not as individual isolated pieces, and secondly, that Pictish cross slabs tended to be made within certain width and thickness ranges. I believe that it is important that any study of Pictish sculpture be informed by these considerations. No monument or fragment should be studied as though it were the only item at its origin site, and importantly, no two fragments should be assumed to be from a single original monument unless there is definite evidence supporting such an assumption.

Table 1: Class II and III sculptured stones of 'East Central' region

Name	Class	Type	Max height	Min height	Max width	Min width	Max thickness	Min thickness
Fordoun	II	slab	63	63	36	36	4	4
Aberlemno 2	II	slab	b	90	50	35.5	11.5	8
Aberlemno 3	II	slab	111	111	40	40	11	8
Aldbar	III	slab	66	66	22.5	19	5	5
Balluderon	II	slab	b	48	27	27	7	7
Benvie	III	slab	36	36	23	23	5	3.5
Brechin 1	III	slab	b	38	36	36	6.5	6.5
Brechin 2	III	recumbent	b	57	18	18	9	9
Brechin 3	III	doorway	74.5	74.5	22	20	u	u
Camuston	III	cross	78	78	33.25	18	8	7
Cossins	II	slab	93	93	28	26.5	10	10
Eassie	II	slab	80	80	40	40	9	9
Farnell	II	slab	81	81	27.5	25.5	5	5
Glamis 1	II	slab	b	60	28	28	u	u
Glamis 2	II	slab	105	105	66	56	u	u
Inchbrayock 1	II	slab	29	29	19	16	2	2
Inchbrayock 2	III	slab	b	12	13	13	3	3
Inchbrayock 3	III	slab	b	13.5	12	12	b	b
Invergowrie 1	III	slab	33	33	21	16.5	u	u
Invergowrie 2	III	slab	b	17	17	17	u	u
Kettins	II	slab	110	110	48	39	10	10
Kinnell	II	slab	54.5	54.5	13	13	b	7
Kingoldrum 1	II	slab	b	24	15	15	3	3
Kingoldrum 2	III	slab	b	39	24	24	b	3
Kingoldrum 3	III	slab	b	9	b	8	u	u
Kirriemuir 1	II	slab	30	23	19	18	u	u
Kirriemuir 2	II	slab	36	33	22	21	4	4
Kirriemuir 3	III	slab	b	26	b	20	4.5	4.5
Kirriemuir 4	III	slab	b	24	b	18	b	3
Kirriemuir 5	III	slab	18	18	16	14.5	3.5	3
Lethnott	III	cross	b	9	b	4	2	2
Menmuir 1	III	slab	41	41	18.5	18.5	6	4.5

Name	Class	Type	Max height	Min height	Max width	Min width	Max thickness	Min thickness
Menmuir 2	III	slab	b	14.5	12.5	12.5	2.5	2.5
Monifieth 1	II	slab	30	30	14.5	14.5	6	6
Monifieth 2	II	slab	18	18	b	12	3.5	3.5
Monifieth 3	II	slab	b	18	23	23	3	3
Monifieth 4	III	shaft	b	46	11	11	7	7
Strathmartine 2	II	slab	51	51	21	20	7	7
Strathmartine 3	II	slab	b	16	20	20	u	u
Strathmartine 4	II	slab	b	16	20	20	u	u
Strathmartine 5	II	slab	b	15	b	15	2	2
Strathmartine 6	II	slab	b	13	b	10	u	u
Strathmartine 7	II	slab	u	u	u	u	u	u
Strathmartine 8	III	cross	b	10.5	b	12	4.5	4.5
Strathmartine 8a	III	cross	b	18	b	10	4.5	4.5
Strathmartine 9	III	u	u	u	u	u	u	u
Strathmartine 10	III	u	u	u	u	u	u	u
Strathmartine 11	III	u	u	u	u	u	u	u
Strathmartine 12	III	u	u	u	u	u	u	u
Strathmartine 13	III	u	u	u	u	u	u	u
Strathmartine 14	III	u	u	u	u	u	u	u
Strathmartine 15	III	u	u	u	u	u	u	u
Strathmartine 16	III	u	u	u	u	u	u	u
St Vigeans 1	II	slab	b	43	21	21	7.25	7.25
St Vigeans 1a	II	slab	b	24	b	21	7	7
St Vigeans 2	II	slab	b	44	20	19	u	u
St Vigeans 3	II	slab	b	7	b	8	b	2
St Vigeans 4	II	slab	b	8	b	11	2.75	2.75
St Vigeans 5	II	slab	b	12	10.5	10.5	b	2.5
St Vigeans 6	II	slab	b	4	b	10	3	3
St Vigeans 7	III	slab	b	66	b	36	u	u
St Vigeans 8	III	slab	b	66	b	10	u	u
St Vigeans 9	III	cross	b	13	b	22	u	u
St Vigeans 10	III	slab	25	25	14	11	3	3
St Vigeans 11	III	slab	b	37	18	17	4	4
St Vigeans 12	III	slab	b	30	11	11	u	u
St Vigeans 13	III	slab	b	42	b	15	u	u
St Vigeans 14	III	slab	60.5	60.5	18	14	7	7
St Vigeans 15	III	cross	b	9.5	14	14	u	u
St Vigeans 16	III	slab	b	40	b	12	b	10
St Vigeans 17	III	slab	b	12	b	13	4	4
St Vigeans 18	III	slab	b	14.5	b	14	4	4
St Vigeans 19	III	slab	b	12	b	8	u	u
St Vigeans 20	III	slab	b	11	b	15	b	4.5
St Vigeans 21	III	slab	b	7	b	9.5	3	3
St Vigeans 22	III	slab	b	11.75	12	12	3	3
St Vigeans 23	III	slab	b	12	b	14	u	u
St Vigeans 24	III	slab	b	6.5	b	6.5	u	u
St Vigeans 25	III	slab	b	15	b	17	u	u
St Vigeans 26	III	slab	b	5.5	b	4	u	u
St Vigeans 27	III	slab	u	u	u	u	u	u
St Vigeans 28	III	slab	u	u	u	u	u	u
St Vigeans 29	III	recumbent	71	71	21	21	6	6
Tealing	II	slab	b	31	b	10.5	u	u
Woodwray	II	slab	b	69	40	33	5	5
Abernethy 2	III	slab	b	15	b	9.5	b	3
Abernethy 3	III	slab	b	9	b	12	u	u

between intrusions

Name	Class	Type	Max height	Min height	Max width	Min width	Max thickness	Min thickness
Abernethy 4	III	shaft	b	20	15	15	b	6
Abernethy 5	III	shaft	b	17	13.75	13.75	b	6
Alyth	II	slab	54	54	19	19	6	6
Carpow	III	slab	b	29	b	20	6	6
Crieff	III	slab	75	75	24	22	6	6
Dull	III	slab	b	15.5	b	32	b	3.5
Dunblane 1	III	slab	74	74	32	21	8	7
Dunblane 2	III	slab	b	33	20	20	b	8
Dunfallandy	II	slab	60	60	26	25	5	5
Dunkeld 2	III	slab	58	58	30	30	13.5	13.5
Dunkeld 3	III	slab	b	39	b	26	u	u
Dunning	III	slab	46.5	46.5	19	19	b	5.5
Dupplin	III	cross	103	103	37	18	13	7
Forteviot 1	III	slab	b	24	18	18	7	6
Forteviot 2	III	doorway	78	78	18	18	13	13
Forteviot 3	III	cross	b	12	b	10	b	6
Forteviot 4	III	slab	b	16	b	14	b	6
Forteviot 5	III	slab	b	6	b	12	u	u
Forteviot 6	III	u	u	u	u	u	u	u
Fowlis Wester	II	slab	124	124	33	21	6	4.5
Gask	II	slab	b	76	49	49	9	9
Invermay 1	III	cross	b	18	b	24	b	6
Invermay 1a	III	cross	b	22	b	17	b	5
Invermay 1b	III	cross	b	14	b	11	b	4.5
Logierait	II	slab	49	49	23	23	4.5	4.5
St Madoes 1	II	slab	69	69	36	30	8	7
St Madoes 2	III	slab	b	34	21	21	4	4
Meigle 1	II	slab	72	72	40.5	40.5	7	6
Meigle 2	II	slab	97	97	39	39	6	6
Meigle 3	II	slab	b	16	14	14	2.5	2.5
Meigle 4a	II	slab	b	b	35	35	6	6
Meigle 4b	II	slab	b	b	35	35	6	6
Meigle 5	II	slab	30	30	21	19	6.5	5
Meigle 6	II	slab	b	22	17	14	4.5	4.5
Meigle 7	II	slab	b	17	21	21	3	3
Meigle 8	II	slab	b	8	b	8	b	2.75
Meigle 9	III	recumbent	71	71	13	8	12	12
Meigle 10	III	slab	b	18	b	36	u	u
Meigle 11	III	recumbent	68	65	27	19.5	19	11
Meigle 12	III	recumbent	b	57	19	19	11	10
Meigle 13	III	slab	b	6	b	12	u	u
Meigle 14	III	slab	b	8	b	9	u	u
Meigle 15	III	slab	b	9	b	12	b	1.5
Meigle 16	III	slab	b	7	b	9	u	u
Meigle 17	III	slab	b	7.5	18	18	u	u
Meigle 18	III	slab	b	7	b	8.5	u	u
Meigle 19	III	slab	b	15	11	11	u	u
Meigle 20	II	slab	b	12	b	b	7	7
Meigle 21	III	slab	b	30	14	14	4.5	3.5
Meigle 22	III	slab	b	10	b	32	b	3.5
Meigle 23	III	slab	31	31	21	21	5	5
Meigle 24	III	slab	b	14	21	21	u	u
Meigle 25	III	recumbent	60	60	24	24	11	11
Meigle 26	III	recumbent	60	60	20	19	9	7
Meigle 27	III	slab	b	22	b	19	3	3

Name	Class	Type	Max height	Min height	Max width	Min width	Max thickness	Min thickness
Meigle 28	III	slab	b	16	19	19	b	2
Meigle 29	III	slab	b	18	b	13	b	4
Meigle 30	III	slab	b	10	b	7	b	3.5
Murthly	II	slab	b	24	44	44	b	4
Rossie	II	slab	66	66	46	39	12	9
Abercromby 1	III	slab	b	22	17	17	8	8
Abercromby 1a	III	slab	b	21	17	17	8	8
Abercromby 2	III	slab	42	42	21	21	u	u
Abercromby 3	III	slab	51	51	17	17	u	u
Abercromby 4	III	slab	b	26	b	14	5	5
Abercromby 5	III	slab	b	13	b	9	u	u
St Andrews 1	III	recumbent	69	69	35	35	28	28
St Andrews 2	III	slab	b	56	18	18	b	6
St Andrews 3	III	slab	b	16.5	17	17	6	6
St Andrews 4	III	slab	b	15	18	18	5.5	5.5
St Andrews 5	III	slab	b	20	20	20	5	5
St Andrews 6	III	cross	b	12	b	20	6	6
St Andrews 7	III	slab	b	20	21	21	5.5	5.5
St Andrews 8	III	slab	b	21	18	18	4	4
St Andrews 9	III	slab	23	23	14	9	b	3
St Andrews 10	III	slab	b	17	b	18	b	5
St Andrews 11	III	slab	b	11	21	21	3.5	3.5
St Andrews 12	III	slab	b	23	20	20	b	3.5
St Andrews 13	III	slab	b	23	22	22	b	4.5
St Andrews 14	III	shaft	b	74	17	15	9	9
St Andrews 15	III	slab	b	14	13	13	4.5	4.5
St Andrews 16	III	slab	b	10	b	7	b	2
St Andrews 17	III	slab	b	9.5	b	7	b	3.5
St Andrews 18	III	slab	19	19	19	19	3.5	3.5
St Andrews 19	III	shaft	b	95	11	11	u	u
St Andrews 20	III	shaft	b	11	4.5	4.5	u	u
St Andrews 21	III	shaft	b	23	4	4	u	u
St Andrews 22	III	shaft	b	19	6	6	u	u
St Andrews 23	III	shaft	b	21	4	4	u	u
St Andrews 24	III	shaft	b	24	4	4	u	u
St Andrews 25	III	shaft	b	24	b	4	u	u
St Andrews 26	III	shaft	b	30	6	6	u	u
St Andrews 27	III	recumbent	45	45	22	22	12	12
St Andrews 28	III	slab	b	12	b	10	b	6.5
St Andrews 29	III	slab	b	16	b	12	b	7.5
St Andrews 30	III	slab	b	17	16.5	16.5	4.5	4.5
St Andrews 31	III	slab	b	21	10	10	3.5	3.5
St Andrews 32	III	shaft	b	8	7	7	5	5
Crail	III	slab	75	75	30	27	u	u
Dogtown	III	cross	b	59	21	21	1	1
Dunino	III	slab	b	11	b	19	b	5
Inchcolm 1	III	slab	b	26.5	b	12	4	4
Inchcolm 2	III	recumbent	60	60	21	21	12	12
Inverkeithing	III	slab	u	u	u	u	u	u
Largo	II	slab	b	78	30	30	6	6
Mugdrum	III	shaft	b	11	29	29	16	16
Sauchope	III	slab	72	72	33	33	u	u
Scoonie	II	slab	b	42	b	28	4	4
Tullibole	III	slab	51	51	20	18	7	6

Note: u = unrecorded, b = broken

A sense of place:
sacred sites and assembly sites in Pictland

Kristen Erskine

Gathering together can be a ceremonial reaffirmation of community across time and space, a natural and spiritual communion with the past and with the land. The process of assembly can assert ownership, celebrate, release tensions, redress grievances or give sanctuary. Bringing the extended community together on traditional land is a process whereby the place of each individual within the community and within the world is re-established and reinforced.

Pictland, the kingdom of northern Scotland which flourished between the fifth and ninth centuries CE, sprang from a fusion of the indigenous tribes of the region. Its citizens probably gathered for all of the reasons just listed. The Picts left little written explanation for their choice of sites for gathering. Theirs was an oral culture that prided itself on memory skills, genealogies recited at length, and landscapes described in epic tales. Literacy was embraced only in the later stages of the Pictish kingdom, along with Christianity and the monastic tradition.[1] Although the burial of the Pictish king, Bridei mac Bili, on Iona around 593CE is indicative of Christian influence, the first verifiable acceptance of Christianity, and with it the written recording of activities, was Nechtan mac Derile's proclamation of compliance with the Roman Church in 710.[2]

Applying a multi-disciplinary approach to the search for assembly sites in the Pictish region has yielded a clearer picture than relying on history or archaeology alone. Examining archaeological, historical and onomastic data together allows us to build on current theories by highlighting hitherto neglected aspects of Pictish culture. In recent years the field of onomastics has illuminated the Picts' shared cultural heritage with the wider Celtic milieu whilst highlighting the indigenous marks left in the placename record. So while *nemeton* links the Picts with Celtic-speakers across Europe, *pett* (a parcel of land) sets them apart.

The placename sites, unless accompanied by documentary and/or material evidence, were relatively neglected as sites of interest by researchers until recent years when onomastics proved a rich vein for investigating some of the sacred and celebratory functions of the Pictish

---

[1] K Hughes, *Celtic Britain in the Early Middle Ages: Studies is Scottish and Welsh Sources* (Suffolk, 1980).
[2] Bede, *Historia Ecclesiastica Gentis Anglorum* (trans L Sherley-Price, 1955, rev ed 1990) V.21, p 320.

community. The combination of the study of the etymological derivation of placenames with their topographical study can aid in revealing elements of sacred and administrative importance within the landscape. Pinpointing these sites of assembly is a beginning, for as Barry Raftery pointed out, 'the complexity of religious beliefs and practices often defies easy reconstruction from material remains ... [as] archaeology tends to uncover only the end-products of ... ritual activities ...'.[3] Similarly, archaeologist Ian Armit noted that 'archaeology can give only a fragmentary reflection of prehistoric life'.[4]

Pictland did not experience the large-scale physical incursions by alien cultures that the southern part of the island endured (although there was trade and cultural exchange at similar levels to the rest of Britain). This means that the sacred places of assembly had the opportunity to remain relatively constant over a substantial period. Foremost among these were the *nemeta*, which according to Watson 'were holy places, often in groves, used as meeting-places for purposes of judgement ... [and over time] they remained the objects of superstitious reverence ... sometimes [becoming] the site of Christian churches'.[5] There are many placenames which can be translated in part as places of assembly, either sacred or purely administrative, in Pictland but I have limited discussion in this paper to a few, namely the *nemeton*, the *cuthill*, the *annat* and briefly the *comraich*.

The conversion to Christianity was initially piecemeal, but as the Dalriadan and Ionan influence grew stronger, Gaelic made inroads into the language and thus the placenames of the Picts. Monasteries and mother churches were established in some parts of Pictland and the Old Irish word *comairce* (modern Scottish Gaelic *comraich*) was applied to some of these to indicate 'the privilege of sanctuary enjoyed by certain churches within a definite radius'.[6] The two greatest were those of Applecross founded by the seventh-century saint Máel Ruba and that of Tain in Ross and Cromarty. The latter encompassed Newmore Wood, which translates as '*Neo' Mhòr*', the 'great *nemeton*'[7] and is part of a cluster of sites with *nemeton*-derived names just north of the River Averon. There is also an historical record of sanctuary at Navidale (dale of the *nemeton*) on the east coast of Sutherland.

As some assembly places like the *nemeta* were appropriated by the church, relatively secular sites of assembly and judgement arose, in particular sites identified by the word *cuthill*. The word is perhaps derived from the Old Irish *comdál* (modern Scottish Gaelic *còmhdhail*) meaning 'meeting' or 'parliament'. The distribution pattern, as revealed by historical

---

[3] B Raftery, *Pagan Celtic Ireland* (London, 1994) p 179.
[4] I Armit, *Celtic Scotland* (London, 1997) p 100.
[5] W J Watson, *Celtic Placenames of Scotland* (Edinburgh, 1926) p 245.
[6] Watson, p 259.
[7] *ibid*, p 249.

and placename records, shows that there was a popular court 'for each area approximating to the size of an average medieval parish', and that there appears to be virtually only one *cuthill* per parish.[8] Of particular interest is the siting of these *cuthills* close by hills and often by megalithic remains. If, as has been suggested, these courts were imposed by the new Dalriadan rulers, the sites might have been deliberately chosen to draw authority from the past and to enable administration of secular laws 'under God's open sky', from which the process derived much of its validity.[9] It would have also been a practical decision to use sites like these that would have been well known locally. The distribution of surviving placenames derived from *cuthill* is remarkably similar to the distribution of surviving *nemeton* placenames, being almost exclusively confined to the north-east. This is not to claim a similar antiquity for *cuthill* as a placename, but to draw attention to the evidence for changes in society which can be found in the placename record. As the English language arrived, and with it another code of law, the intrusive Gaelic term *cuthill* would have hardened into a placename, 'turning what was a mere description, well understood by all, into the permanent name for a locality'.[10]

As well as the ancient word *nemeton*, the Picts used a number of other placenames for important sites of community ceremonies and gathering. The *annat* and *comraich* sites had numinous qualities while the *cuthill* sites were more prosaic. However, the line between the sacred and the mundane was blurred. Most daily business in the early medieval period had sacred overtones. Judgements were not only administered by the king, local chieftains, and their designated agents: the Christian church may have played a role, and this role may have previously been played by the druids.

Eliade described the appearance of sacred sites as 'an irruption of the sacred that result[ed] in detaching a territory from the surrounding cosmic milieu [which made] it qualitatively different' from the rest of the landscape.[11] In the word *nemeton* we have the idea of such a sacred place. Although Rivet and Smith suggested that the word could be applied both to 'natural sacred groves' and to 'artificial constructions',[12] all available information indicates that the *nemeton* placename referred exclusively to natural sites in pre-Christian Pictland.

The sixth-century saint, Columba, whose ministry extended to parts of Pictland from his base in Iona, recognised the need to retain a sense of cultural continuity. He was recorded as being more fearful of the sound of

---

[8] G W S Barrow, 'Popular Courts in Early Medieval Scotland: Some Suggested Place-Name Evidence', *Scottish Studies* 25 (1981) 1-24, p 10.
[9] ibid, p 9.
[10] ibid, p 12.
[11] M Eliade, *The Sacred and the Profane* (Florida, 1959) p 26.
[12] A Rivet and C Smith, *The Place Names of Roman Britain* (New Jersey, 1979) p 254.

an axe in the woods of Derry than of death and hell, which suggests in light of 'his austere attitude to superstition' that 'he was fearful not so much of vengeful spirits as of breaking the sense of continuity that was so important to his people's way of life'.[13] It appears that it was church policy to rehabilitate sacred sites.[14]

One of the miracles ascribed to Columba in his *Vita* consists of turning a 'noxious well' in the province of the Picts into a healing fountain. He did not demand that the people desist from their belief that the well had some supernatural quality, but rather ensured through his actions that his god was credited with the newly apparent healing qualities of the water.[15] Watson's discussion of the *annat* placename notes the regularity with which the placename adjoins a 'fine well or clear stream'. He quotes lines from Duncan MacIntyre's poem 'the wine of the burn of the *Annat*, its taste was of honey to drink it' to argue 'that the water of the burn received virtue from the *annat* by which it flows'.[16] Bearing in mind Columba's transformation of the well, perhaps the recurrence of the name *annat* in association with water sources is due in part to the Christianising of water sources spiritually significant to the pre-Christian Picts. Professor Barrow has described the Christian practice of co-opting established pagan traditions as 'a desire ... to put some much-frequented spot, some commonly used well or spring, under the invocation and blessing of a revered saint'.[17]

There are also holy wells at the *nemeton* sites of Newdosk, St Bennet's on Navity Moor and Ben Newe. In the case of the latter, the village of Newe to the south of the mountain on the bank of the River Don was probably the actual site of the assembly ground. I have found that many of the other *nemeta*, namely Eilean Neave, Navidale, Navity Moor, Strathnoon, Nevie, Duneaves, Newtyle and Finavon are juxtaposed with water, both coastal and riverine, which would have benefited from the dual purposes of access and sanctity. Given Columba's and perhaps his contemporaries' concern for continuity we can surmise a little of what might have been happening at that 'early cultural seam that marked the point at which pagan concepts, and the places connected with them, were taken over by the Church'.[18]

---

[13] M Beith, *Healing Threads: Traditional Medicines of the Highlands and Islands* (Edinburgh, 1995) p 124.
[14] V Flint, *The Rise of Magic in Early Medieval Europe* (Oxford, 1991) p 254.
[15] Adomnán, *The Life of Saint Columba* (ed W Reeves, 1874, facsimile ed Llanerch, 1988) book II ch X p 78.
[16] Watson, p 437.
[17] G W S Barrow, 'The Childhood of Scottish Christianity: a Note on Some Place-Name Evidence', *Scottish Studies* 27 (1983) 1-24, p 1.
[18] W Nicolaisen, 'Early Christianity in Pictland' in D Thomson (ed), *The companion to Gaelic Scotland* (Oxford, 1983) p 228.

When Christianity was eventually fully embraced by the secular authorities in Pictland, the missionaries wisely celebrated their sacraments at the sacred sites, and transformed wells and stones into dwelling places of the Christian divine. Where the Pictish divinities could not be demonised and exorcised, they would likely have been appropriated by being afforded saintly status like Brigit of Ireland. The Early Christians built their chapels within the *nemeta*'s precincts, the placename melding over time in some places with saints' names. It has only been through the efforts of two researchers in particular, W J Watson in the early part of the twentieth century and G W S Barrow in the second half of the same century that we are beginning to appreciate the antiquity of the term and its relevance to the field of Pictish studies.

The sites themselves remained the one constant in the Picts' lives. The *nemeta* were rededicated to the new faith and their use continued. All but five of the twenty-two *nemeton* sites we can still locate in the Pictish region of Scotland had chapels added in the early medieval period. People continued to meet there to worship and celebrate, and sanctuary was afforded those who came within the boundaries. The historical Picts, while unified to an extent with an externally recognised over-king, a common language, and the use of symbol stones, would probably have maintained their own localised rituals and sites of spiritual significance. This would explain, in part, the seemingly haphazard appearance of the *nemeton* placename in geographically diverse sites. *Nemeton* was a general word, meaning 'place of assembly, judgement and sanctuary',[19] not a specific word such as 'high rocky hill where we whoop it up on *Samhuinn*' or 'well in a low lying valley where we get together to vote'. This meant that it could appear anywhere there was space for the local population to gather, celebrate, hear proclamations or judgements or seek sanctuary. Its importance to the community is emphasised in the continuing use of the name for nearby sites. In Ross and Cromarty the church and village of Nonikiln are surrounded by Cnoc Navie, Newmore Wood, Inchnavie and Dalnavie. In Angus, Kirkton of Nevay, East Nevay, West Nevay and Nevay Park all lie within a two-kilometre radius of Nevay Chapel.

According to Thomas Clancy, placenames with *annat* frequently appear as compounds and 'they need not be the places referred to ... they may express their relationship...to the mother church'.[20] In the case of *nemeta*, also, the placename attaches to surrounding locations. One example of this is *Eilean Neave*, which stands less than 500 metres off the Sutherland coast. The name translates as 'Island of the *Nemeton*'. There are traces of two enclosures but the island lacks the fresh water sources necessary to support a permanent settlement. *Cnoc Phobuill*, a flat-topped

---

[19] Watson, p 245.
[20] Clancy, p 102.

hill, lies directly opposite the island on the mainland. The name means hill of the assembly, tribe or people, and I have proposed that this is the site where the bulk of the community might have gathered. There are both Irish and Cornish parallels to suggest possible uses of these two linked sites. The lack of fresh water and the blowhole on the island invite comparison with *Tech Dunn* (House of Donn), an island off the southwest coast of Ireland which 'has a natural archway under which the sea flows with tremendous force'.[21] Medieval Irish texts mention the belief in an offshore island where the lord of the dead resided, and that the 'heathen' believed that their souls would there go to Donn.[22] The site of Lammana in Cornwall looking out onto Looe Island parallels the suggested use of Cnoc Phobuill as a gathering place. Records from 1290 CE describe what happened in Cornwall. Looe Island was 'where ... monks celebrate[d] Divine Service [but] ... many ... people ... want[ing] to visit the ... chapel ... often lost their lives in the stormy sea, [so] a ... chapel ... was constructed upon the coast opposite the ... island'.[23] A similarly practical decision could have been made centuries earlier by the community near Eilean Neave.

I have suggested above that sanctuary was one of the *nemeta*'s roles and in Newmore Wood we find one of the two great sites of sanctuary or *comraich* of early Christian Pictland. No traditions for that site survive but they do for the other, Applecross on the west coast. Máel Ruba's grave was, according to Watson, still revered in modern times, 'and the person who takes earth from it is ensured safety in travelling and return to Applecross'.[24]

In addition to dirt providing security we also see dirt as providing judgement, another vital part of the *nemeta*'s functions. A sod taken from an island by Fuat mac Bile to Ireland was placed at Nemed in the Fews Mountains 'and on it dooms were pronounced: if the judgement was false the sod turned upwards'. Patrick transformed the site into a Christian one by claiming it as 'the sod of the Land of Promise'.[25] In Ireland the word *nemed* meant 'holy place, sanctuary, church' preserving the earlier Indo-European *nemeton* under a Christian gloss. Judgement too remains part of the folklore of the *nemeton* sites, especially in St Bennet's on Navity Moor, which was believed by the local people to be the eventual site of the Final Judgement as predicted in the Book of Revelation.

---

[21] D O'hOgain, *The Sacred Isle Belief and Religion in Pre-Christian Ireland* (Wiltern, 1999) p 58.
[22] *ibid.*
[23] W M M Picken, 'Light on Lammana', *Devon Cornwall Notes and Queries* 35/8 (1985) 281-286, p 283.
[24] Watson, p 287.
[25] Watson, p 245.

Gathering places provide a focus for community. Unlike fortified sites which were the focus of hostile attention and risked destruction, the *nemeta* required only a clearing large enough for the local population to assemble. Using a site as a *nemeton* or another assembly or sanctuary site did not exhaust the soil as farming does. We could regard the use of *nemeta* as a static, stablising presence over generations. *Nemeton* was an ancient word from the Picts' Indo-European past, but it continued to have a functional place in the language of the Picts well after they accepted Christianity. It lives on even now in the placenames they have left for us. As needs changed within the community and new ideas were welcomed, the use of existing sites changed and new places were added to the inventory.

Knowing the locations of assembly sites, especially in relation to settlement sites, royal residences and later Christian foundations, expands our knowledge of the evolution of community interactions. Our knowledge of the Picts remains patchy, but as Barry Raftery said 'while we may never know the answers with absolute certainty, in trying to unravel the shadowy ritual world of the Celts the archaeologist [and others] must at least ask questions and offer tentative suggestions'.[26] The survival of ancient sites of assembly and sanctuary in the placename record provides us with a wonderful opportunity to better understand the contribution of such sites to the 'sense of place' in Pictish culture.

---

[26] Raftery, p 179.

Aspects of kingship in Pictland and early Scotland

Julianna Grigg

The beginnings of a cohesive nation in Pictland, and later Scotland, appear historically with the Roman incursion into the regions beyond the Antonine and Hadrianic walls. Tacitus mentions the Caledonii massing to remove the Roman armies, and perhaps here we see the beginnings of a new kind of kingship necessitated by a joint desire of the regional rulers to retain lordship of individual tribal regions. Their leader, Calgacus (meaning swordsman), is given a stirring speech by Tacitus, who describes Calgacus as courageous and of a high lineage.[1] With the withdrawal of the Romans there was a further need to instil a sense of national awareness, as settlers from Ireland established a foothold on the west coast and the Strathclyde Britons and later the Northumbrians inched across the borders. The archaeology emphasises that Pictland was not an isolated rural backwater, but participated fully within the cultural milieu of Europe, Ireland and the rest of Britain. Instead of treating the Picts as a people in *illo tempore*, due to the paucity of documentary evidence, they should be considered as participants in the great trade, both intellectual and material, that was occurring on the North and Atlantic seaboards.

The most useful documentary evidence of a system of kingship in Pictland is found in the Pictish regnal lists. These come from around seven manuscripts and Marjorie Anderson has published an authoritative edition of the lists which provides a useful discussion on their provenance and where they diverge.[2] The regnal lists and associated origin tales have been broken down into three basic sections. The first section includes the heroic and legendary origins of the Picts and their division of Scotland into territories. At least one version of these tales was known to Bede and they are primarily found in Irish sources. The next section is referred to as 'pseudo-historic' and contains an extensive list of kings until Bridei mac Máelchon (around 550 CE) who, as the first identifiably historic king, begins the historic section of the Regnal lists. The authenticity of the historic section of the regnal list is supported by Irish annal entries, Bede and hagiographic sources such as the *Life* of Columba. The bareness of the regnal lists is offset by documentation primarily coming from the Picts' neighbours. Recent investigation of those manuscripts has yielded excerpts

---

[1] Tacitus, *The Agricola and The Germania*, Agricola ch 29.
[2] M O Anderson, *Kings and Kingship in Early Scotland* (Edinburgh, 1973).

that may have come directly from Pictish sources.³ Most scholars agree that Pictish society shared much in common with other Celtic-speaking regions. It is therefore possible to use the information we have from these contemporary societies and, with the native archaeology, art history and verbal record, illuminate some of the possible systems and belief structures of Pictland.

The study of kingship in Ireland has benefited from relatively early documentation, whether hidden in saga literature or described in legal texts and hagiography. Scholars have found a common heritage shared by Irish kingship customs, which dates back to the earliest horizons of Celtic-speaking settlement in Ireland. Comparative analysis traces these to a common Indo-European pattern. McCone found parallels linking the 'king's major functions as leader in war, presider over his assembled people ... and judge or lawgiver' to Hittite, Spartan Greek and Roman customs.⁴ The responsibilities of Irish kingship are enumerated in the legal tract *Críth Gablach*. McCone summarises these as:

> acting for his túath in various external legal dealings, giving them a righteous judge, upholding the material support *(folog)* due under certain circumstances, and providing a duly constituted and conducted assembly *(óenach)* for the proper promulgation of a military hosting *(slógad)*, or special ordinance *(rechtge)* in the three crucial areas of armed expulsion of foreigners ..., preparation of crops ... and 'faith that illuminates'.⁵

War Leader

One of the primary duties of the king was to be a war leader. With the Northumbrian and Dalriadan expansions, the occasional aggression from Strathclyde as well as the Picts' own internal feuds, a strong leader was required to ensure Pictish territories were safeguarded. The requirement for a great battle leader may have been the origin of a high king of Pictland. Perhaps the great Calgacus, with whom Tacitus empathised, was the first great leader to found the role of overlord in Pictland. However, contemporary sources do not assign the title of high king until the first verifiable historical figure Bridei mac Máelchon, who is described by Bede as *rex potentissimus*.

---

³ K Forsyth, 'Evidence of a lost Pictish source in the *Historia Regnum Anglorum* of Symeon of Durham' in S Taylor (ed), *Kings, Clerics and Chronicles in Scotland, 500-1297* (Dublin, 2000) 19-32.
⁴ K McCone, *Pagan Past and Christian Present in Early Irish Literature* (Kildare, 1990) p 108.
⁵ *ibid*, p 122.

Most societies at this time required a strong leader in warfare. This is seen throughout Britain and Ireland with annal entries confirming Anglo-Saxon, Irish and Pictish kings leading their troops into battle, often at their own risk. Binchy found that in Ireland '[v]alour in battle was the supreme test of rightful kingship'.[6] It may have been a requirement of leadership to first lead a successful raid or war. The Irish king Dathí, whose reign is attributed to the early third century, was, according to Watson, 'inaugurated by a great raid on Strathclyde'.[7] A much later inauguration rite of a chieftain in the Western Isles of Scotland, recorded by Martin Martin in the seventeenth century, required the potential chieftain to give proof of his valour before being accepted as chief or lord. This usually required him to lead his men on a cattle-raiding expedition.[8] Of interest is the almost Fenian imagery that describes Somerled's rise to power. Somerled was the founder of the Lordship of the Isles in the twelfth century and his historians spin a wonderful tale about his cunning rout of Norse forces as a reason for his promotion to leader.[9]

The Irish sources also list failure in war as one of the reasons for a king to be deposed.[10] Certainly the annals list a number of Pictish kings who are exiled or 'bound', which may have been a legal term for the enforced abdication of leadership rights. Failure in war may be the reason for the exile in 672 of Drust, who failed to expel the Northumbrians. It has been speculated that he was in league with Northumbria to keep Pictland as a vassal state.[11] Other kings, such as Taran who was expelled around 697, may have been similarly removed for being ineffectual leaders. Furthermore, short reign lengths may represent a highly competitive system relying on more than popularity and birth to retain the leadership of the loose federation of Pictland.

Right to rule
The king lists, as we have them, indicate that the succession was limited to a small group of noble families. It has been postulated that kingship may have been shared systematically amongst the regional kings.[12] Such a system could explain some instances of dual sovereignty but this is not clear

---

[6] D A Binchy, *Celtic and Anglo-Saxon Kingship* (Oxford, 1970) p 17.
[7] W J Watson, *The History of the Celtic Place-Names of Scotland*, (Edinburgh, repr 1993) p 217.
[8] M Martin, *A Description of the Western Islands of Scotland*, (Edinburgh, 1999) p 71.
[9] D J Macdonald, *Clan Donald* (Loanhead, 1978) pp 19f.
[10] McCone, p 122.
[11] A O Anderson, *Early Sources of Scottish History: AD500 to 1286* vol I (Edinburgh, 1922) p 181 n 6.
[12] see Smyth ch 2 pp 36-83 for a discussion on this and a non-matrilinear theory of Pictish succession.

from the available evidence.[13] Any system of succession which is not based on primogeniture would require support from the regional leaders and at least a majority agreement on the succession. It is, therefore, not surprising that the annals describe various internal battles, particularly after the death or abdication of a stable or successful monarch.

This was the case when Nechtan abdicated in 724. Two years later Nechtan may have been promised support from a faction of his nobles to recover his sovereignty, as the annals of Tighernach for 726 note that he is bound by Drust, the current king. Drust quashes this possible rebellion only to be expelled from the kingdom by Alpin. The annals of Ulster, Tighernach and Clonmacnoise all relate that in 728 there are a number of battles based around Moncrieff Hill or Caislen-Credi (presumed to be Moot Hill at Scone). Onuist mac Urguist (Oengus mac Fergus) fights a 'pitiful battle' against Alpin, and Nechtan is offered the kingship. According to the annals of Clonmacnoise 'Eolbeck the son of Moydan and the rest of the nobles and people of the Picts turned their backs to Alpin, and did receive Nechtan the son of Derile as king into the kingdom again'.[14] However, it seems that Onuist may have rebelled against Nechtan's reinstallation, as the annals of Ulster for 729 describe a battle between the armies of Onuist and Nechtan. A number of men who are named amongst the fallen may have been the immediate family and supporters of Nechtan. The annal entry states that 'the family of Angus triumphed'. Onuist then faced Drust, who no doubt had been busy gaining support from his place of exile, and killed Drust. Many other Pictish kings faced succession disputes and, as can be seen in the medieval inaugurations such as that of Alexander III in 1249, there may have been some rush to inaugurate the next king after the death of his predecessor.

The Pictish regnal lists may, on occasion, have been compiled to assert a king's genealogical right to gain the succession. According to Marjorie Anderson, most of the extant manuscript versions of the lists appear to come from a single exemplar, or tradition, up to 724 CE. After this date, which correlates with Nechtan's abdication, the lists have differing reign dates and, in a few cases, successions.[15] This implies that the Pictish regnal list was written down and may have been used to confirm the succession. The political implications of the manipulation of the genealogies cannot be avoided. Foundation myths for the beginning of the Pictish peoples were current in Bede's time and by the middle ages the

---

[13] The rules for succession may have altered depending on the power and allegiances of the reigning king. A very interesting analysis of the fluid nature of succession during the Pictish period is given by A A M Duncan, *The Kingship of the Scots, 842-1292: succession and independence*, (Edinburgh, 2002) p 12.

[14] A O Anderson, pp 221-26.

[15] M O Anderson, p 88.

origin legends were being written into Irish manuscripts and were used to assert the primacy of the Irish/Scottic dynasties. The regnal lists traditionally begin with the reign of Cruithne, who ruled over Ireland and Alba and whose seven sons divided Pictland between them. Their reign was followed by the reigns of thirteen kings, some having distinctly Irish names. Miller emphasises that the extant scribal history came from an oral tradition that was prone to 'continuous reorganisation and rectification of history ... and the selection and organisation of those memories useful for retention'.[16] This is a useful point as there is some doubt about whether the Pictish succession system required the degree of genealogical assertion seen in the Irish agnatic system.

The church became the literate body responsible for writing down the regnal lists. This can be seen in the conscious re-working of the chronology of the regnal lists to conform to an 84-year Easter cycle, which superseded the 95-year cycles in 710.[17] Royal patronage of the church would have been essential, with dedications and enshrinements a form of political propaganda similar to that seen in Mercia in the middle ages.[18]

Columba is the first clergyman known to have taken an active part in the inauguration process. He blessed and consecrated Áedán mac Gabráin into the Dalriadan kingship (before the convention of Druim Cett in 575). Of course his actions may have reflected the secular ambitions of a member of the Uí Néill ruling family from which Columba came. Consecration of a king by the clergy became very popular from the eighth century in Europe, Britain and Ireland, and appears to have been based on the Old Testament ritual anointing. Around 786, in a report to Pope Hadrian, the papal legates in England write about the ordination of kings, implying that they were chosen by priests and elders and were born from legitimate marriages.[19]

Exactly how much power the church had to confirm succession in Pictland and later in Scotland is difficult to ascertain. There are the remains of a chapel near Moot Hill at Scone, and another on the summit of the hill, but no date has been established for their foundation.[20] According to Fordun's account of Alexander III's investiture, the inauguration stone was in the keeping of Scone monastery. The bishops of St Andrews and Dunkeld and the abbot of Scone were all present at the ceremony. While

---

[16] M Miller, 'The Last Century of Pictish Succession', *Scottish studies* 23 (1979) 39-67, p 57.
[17] M Miller, 'The disputed historical horizon of the Pictish king-lists', *Scottish Historical Review* 58 (1979) 1-34.
[18] S J Plunkett, 'The Mercian Perspective' in Sally M Foster (ed), *The St Andrews Sarcophagus: A Pictish Masterpiece and its International Connections* (Dublin, 1998) 202-26, p 225.
[19] F J Byrne, *Irish Kings and High-Kings*, (2nd ed, Dublin, 2001) p 159.
[20] See RCAHMS online catalogue http://www.rcahms.gov.uk/canmore (registration required).

this is a late reference it cannot be doubted that the involvement of the church in the process of approving and inaugurating a monarch in Pictland would have followed a similar pattern to that of Ireland and Britain. It may be important to note, however, that the final blessing Alexander III receives is from a *Seannachie*. This may also be seen in the Irish inauguration ritual on the mound of Carn Fraoich (Co Roscommon), of Féilim Ó Chonchobhair in the fifteenth century where, despite the presence of bishops and coarbs, the person who gives the rod of kingship to Ó Chonchobhair is a *fili* [poet].[21] In 906, Constantine II and his bishop Cellach proclaimed, from Moot Hill, that 'the rights in churches and gospels should be kept in conformity with [the customs of] the Scots'.[22] While a secular and ecclesiastic partnership was not uncommon at this time, it may not mean that the church had appropriated the entire inauguration process. The claim that the church merely took over the role in the ritual that was fulfilled earlier by druids is impossible to verify.

There are indications that succession came through the maternal line in Pictland. Bede is our earliest authority for this, but it is a contentious issue. There have been numerous attempts to create genealogies showing matrilineal succession, but at this stage it is a subjective exercise. The Irish agnatic succession system was allegedly introduced by Kenneth mac Alpin. However, Giric (with no patronymic) appears to have ruled from 878-89, and if his succession relied on the possession of 'royal blood' it seems that he could have established that inheritance only through a maternal line.[23] His appearance is repressed in later versions and there is confusion over whether he was merely a foster-father to Eochaidh ap Rhun, but Miller is inclined to see this as 'a resurgence of Pictishness.'[24] As Byrne has noted,[25] Malcolm II ensured that his daughter's son, Duncan, inherited the kingship, and there was a clear attempt to renew the succession debate with Lulach, the son of Gruoch, granddaughter of Kenneth III. Moray provided more cause for dispute with Lulach's daughter's son Oengus rising against David I in 1130.

A curious feature of the historic regnal lists is the patronymics of Northumbrian, Dalriadic, Strathclyde and Cumbric nobles. Some of these patronymics may be explained by exiled princes, such as Eanfrith who fathered the Pictish king Talorcan mac Eanfrith; others may have been added later from an oral tradition. There is an interesting mythological theme of a euhemerised goddess spurning suitors from nearby to bestow her

---

[21] Byrne, pp 15f.
[22] M Lynch, *Scotland: A New History*, (London, repr 1992) p 28.
[23] Duncan, p 12.
[24] Miller, 'Last Century', p 50.
[25] Byrne, p xli.

affections on a stranger.[26] This can be seen in a number of Irish sagas as well as in the Mabinogion, where Pwyll chases a strange woman who claims she loves him as a result of hearing of his exploits.[27] The patronymics indicate that the Picts had a tradition of securing royal alliances with their neighbours, and a foreign father was no bar to succession to kingship. On balance, this practice would have inspired closer ties with the Picts' neighbours and may have aided their eventual assimilation with the Scots.

Administration
To ensure the co-operation of the regional lords there would have been a sophisticated system of hostage, fosterage and fealty. Certainly, this is the situation described in the *Life* of Columba. Here Bridei mac Máelchon is described as holding court with a number of subordinate kings from the Orkneys. Columba requests safe passage for his brethren in Orkney and he addresses Bridei to 'command this chieftain earnestly, since his hostages are in thy hand ...'.[28]

The king would have had the support of a number of councillors and advisors (as documented for the court of Bridei mac Máelchon) to promote the rule of the king and the ordinary operation of society. There is a clear indication that the king issued various edicts and decrees; his role may also have included passing judgement. When Domnall mac Alpin came into power he asserted the laws of Áed Find, confirming continuity with Dalriada. His brother Kenneth had previously re-established the cult of Columba at Dunkeld, thus conforming secular and religious society to the dominant political group now in control of Pictland.[29] Bridei mac Derile signed the *Cáin Adomnán* [Law of the Innocents] along with Curitan, bishop of Rosmarkie.[30] This law, with signatories from the Pictish, Scottic and Irish clerical and royal houses, was ratified at the Synod of Birr, County Offaly, in 697. As a piece of social legislation it shows the extent of diplomatic unity possible amongst the Picts, Dalriadans and Scots/Irish. According to Anderson, Adomnán's law included the payment of tax to Iona by the Irish daughter houses.[31] As signatories to this law, Columban houses in Pictland would also have been liable for payment of the tax to Iona. When Nechtan was finally removed from the kingship in 729 (as previously described) the Annals of Ulster mention the death of his tax

---

[26] McCone, p 110.
[27] J Gantz (trans), *The Mabinogion*, (London, 1976) pp 53f.
[28] A O Anderson, pp 58f.
[29] Miller, 'Last Century', p 48.
[30] Watson, p 233; see also M Ní Dhonnchadha, 'The Guarantor List of the *Cáin Adomnán*', *Peritia* 1 (1982) 178-215.
[31] A O Anderson, p 223, n 5.

gatherers (*exactores*), which confirms a secular system of taxation.[32] In later times we find the term *mormaer* used as the title of a district official (or leader), whom the Book of Deer describes as the 'king's deputy in his district ... collecting the royal revenue'.[33]

According to Bede, Nechtan made considerable changes to religious life in Pictland. This appears to have been presaged by a request to Ceolfrith, abbot of Monkwearmouth and Jarrow, to confirm the Roman doctrine on such matters as the dating of Easter and the tonsure. Bede gives us a version of the letter that was read out to Nechtan and his assembled chieftains. Nechtan then proclaimed the new Easter dating and tonsure in public with his 'royal authority' and decreed that all the churches in Pictland would adopt his proclamation.[34] There was clearly a system in place to disseminate the new ecclesiastical systems throughout the region.

The Pictish Class I stones may represent part of a system of administration. Isabel Henderson has evaluated the possible origin centre of these landscape markers and found it to be the Moray Firth area.[35] The erection of the stones appears to coincide with the reign of Bridei mac Máelchon, whose palace was near the mouth of the River Ness. The stones are distributed along the coasts of Sutherland, Caithness, Orkney and Shetland and followed populated inland routes along rivers and at the heads of glens. They appear in the sixth century across most of Pictland. The symbols used on the stones had become fixed, implying a long period of design in other media. The rapid appearance of the stones would most likely occur if an edict were made for the stones' erection, with the symbols a legible code to the inhabitants. If Bridei was the leader who erected the symbol stones, he was implementing a system that connected all parts of his kingdom. The stones may have been gathering points and useful for administering taxation, issuing decrees and laws and mustering warriors.

Inauguration sites

While the rituals of inauguration may only be guessed at, the sites used for ceremonies are still traceable in the landscape. The Pictish sites of ritual importance appear to have much in common with the ceremonial sites in parts of Ireland. Bede and Adomnán indicate that the Picts' territory may have formed two separate regions separated by the mountain range known as the Mounth. The sparse references available could indicate changes to the importance of various regions over the centuries. This may have been

---

[32] *ibid*, p 225.
[33] I Henderson, 'Pictish Territorial Divisions' in P McNeill and R Nicholson (eds), *An historical Atlas of Scotland c.400-c.1600* (St Andrews, 1975) 8-9, p 9.
[34] Bede, *Ecclesiastical History of the English People*, 2.1.
[35] I M Henderson, 'The Origin Centre of the Pictish Symbol Stones', *Proceedings of the Society of Antiquaries of Scotland* 91 (1957-58) 44-57.

the result of the fluctuation in their borders, or have been inherent in their system of succession.[36] The court of Bridei mac Máelchon appears to have been located at the mouth of the Ness. Over a hundred years later, in 685, Bridei mac Bili removed the Northumbrians at Dunnichen Moss in Angus and claimed Fortriu as his power base.[37] He was called the King of Fortriu in the annals, and it is clear that Fortriu is a designation for the whole of Pictland.

Mounds and hills appear to be of primary importance in ceremonies. In Ireland they are often associated with the sacred tribal tree known as *bile* and the mounds often appear to have been in use in the neolithic or the bronze age, sometimes as burial cairns.[38] Warner confirms that the use of mounds 'for the rituals of kingship in the Early Medieval or Christian period is now a matter of general agreement'. He sees the mounds as representing a 'conduit between the Otherworld and the Real-world, mediated by the king-priest'.[39] Many mounds retained their symbolic and mythological function into the later medieval period. The importance of the mounds lay not only in their position as a landscape feature but in their archaic value as sacred sites. The deliberate adoption of neolithic and bronze-age sites legitimised ceremonies by incorporating the past into the present. This may not represent continuity, but the appropriation of the perceived mysteries and power of the ancients.

Scone was the primary focus of inauguration ceremonies from at least the medieval period. The area around Scone is full of ancient landmarks, standing stones and place-names with very early Christian attributes. The main focus of the medieval inaugurations was Moot (or Boot) Hill. This is a mound with a flat top near the old Scone palace, on which a mausoleum and church now stand; it is unclear whether it is a natural or man-made feature. Skene identified the first reference to the hill, in the annals of Tighernach, as the site of a battle between factions attempting to gain supremacy in 728.[40] The hill is apparently referred to in the annals as *Caislen credi*, although some scholars disagree with the suggestion that this

---

[36] Duncan has suggested that Forteviot became the principal seat of kings in the ninth century, with a possible inauguration site at Dunning nearby. In Ireland medieval inauguration occurred on the land of the principal inaugurator and this may have been the situation in Pictland; Duncan, p 11.

[37] Lynch, p 19.

[38] Byrne, p 27.

[39] R B Warner, 'Keeping out the Otherworld: The Internal Ditch at Navan and other Iron Age "Hengiform" Enclosures', *Emania* 18 (2000) 39-44, p 41.

[40] W F Skene, *Chronicles of the Picts, Chronicles of the Scots* (Edinburgh, 1867) p 280 n 5. See also S T Driscoll, 'Political Discourse and the Growth of Christian Ceremonialism in Pictland: the Place of the St Andrews Sarcophagus' in Foster (ed) 168-78. Driscoll notes that royal sites were legitimate targets during tribal warfare in Ireland, and this may be paralleled in Pictland; p 173.

is a reference to Moot Hill.⁴¹ However, there is general agreement that Moot Hill is the platform from which Constantine and Bishop Cellach issued their decrees on a united church in 906.⁴² It is unlikely that Constantine was the first to use the hill for this purpose. It would have been advantageous for the king to use a traditional site to proclaim new statutes and laws, thereby giving the decrees further legitimacy and authority. It is possible that it was from Moot Hill that Nechtan announced his church's conversion to the Roman dating of Easter after 710. The hill is later recorded as the site of parliaments.

Previous scholars have emphasised the position of Scone as being on the boundary between north and south.⁴³ This implies that Scone was the *axis mundi* of the kingdom, with all the cosmological attributes that this would in turn imply.⁴⁴ Scone stands at the confluence of the river Tay and the river Almond. Confluences were a favoured position for many Pictish settlements. The area is surrounded by a number of standing stones and stone circles, and a nearby site is called Schianbank (derived from the Irish *sídh* meaning ancient burial mound). This site overlooks Annaty burn; *annat* is a place-name element that indicates the presence of a Christian site, usually from the earliest period of Christianity in Pictland.⁴⁵ Further up the Tay is Dunkeld, the ecclesiastical capital under Constantine (d 820).⁴⁶ The name Dunkeld has been interpreted as meaning Fort of the Caledonians and the nearby site of Schiehallion [fairy hill of the Caledonians] may have been perceived as sacred.⁴⁷

As to the most famous relic from the inauguration rituals, the Stone of Scone, Skene has made a credible analysis of the texts to disprove the widely held view that Kenneth mac Alpin introduced the stone from Dalriada.⁴⁸ While there is no notice of Kenneth's inauguration on the Stone of Scone, it is notable that the annals still refer to Kenneth, and his two sons who succeed him, as kings of Pictland. Kenneth may well have seen himself as continuing the Pictish succession, despite later historians categorising him as the first Scottish king. Exactly when and why the Stone became a focus for kingship ceremonies is impossible to confirm. It may have represented the land, and certainly seemed to be accepted as the

---

[41] RCAHMS online catalogue.
[42] Lynch, p 28.
[43] Skene, *Chronicles*, p 210; *Ordnance Gazetteer: Scotland* (London, 1885) vol 6 PET-ZET.
[44] cf M Eliade, *The Sacred and The Profane: The Nature of Religion* (Florida, 1959).
[45] T Clancy, 'Annat in Scotland and the origins of the parish', *The Innes Review* 46 (1995) 91-115, p 91.
[46] M Dillon and N Chadwick, *The Celtic Realms*, (London, 1967) p 113.
[47] Watson, p 21.
[48] W F Skene, 'The Coronation Stone', *Proceedings of the Society of Antiquaries of Scotland* 8 (1869) 68-99.

receptacle of kingship by Edward I when he appropriated it in 1296. While it bears some similarities to the stones used in Irish inauguration rites, it may be one of the shared stock of ritual objects from an Indo-European past.

In Ireland the stones used for inauguration rites often have incised footprints. Byrne relates the story of the inauguration of Fedhlimidh son of Aedh mac Eoghan who has a shoe placed on his foot by a sub-king 'in the manner remembered by old men and recorded in old books'.[49] The most renowned incised footprint from Scotland is at Dunadd. This fort was firmly in the control of the Dalriadans, although there is an incised Pictish boar symbol alongside it.[50] However, recent excavation on the broch site of Clickhimin on Shetland uncovered an incised footprint on a slab at the beginning of the causeway.[51] Shetland was part of the northern Pictish culture as its brochs and other material finds such as painted pebbles reveal.[52] Martin Martin described a seemingly deliberate adoption of the incised footprint at Finlaggan on Islay. Martin states:

> There was a big stone of seven feet-square, in which there was a deep impression made to receive the feet of Macdonald; for he was crowned King of the Isles standing in this stone, and swore that he would continue his vassals in possession of their lands, and do exact justice to all his subjects: and then his father's sword was put into his hand.[53]

Heroic names

In one of the versions of the pseudo-historic regnal lists there is an interesting late reference to the thirty Bruidhes, or Brideis, who ruled over both Ireland and Alba for 150 years. Anderson has noted that this name may be a title rather than personal name.[54] Binchy believed that the Celtic term for a king, *rhi*, was replaced with a brythonic title, in Welsh *Breenhin*, in Cornish *Brentyn*, derived from Old Welsh *bryeint* meaning 'privilege, status'.[55] The equivalent of *bryeint* in Irish is *brigit*, 'the exalted one'. This may have been related to the widespread tribal name Brigantes, found in Ireland, Britain and continental Europe. Binchy suggested that this name change represented a new political system with the new king responsible for the cohesion of a range of tribes rather than simply ruling a single tribe.[56]

---

[49] Byrne, p 17.
[50] I Armit, *Scotland's Hidden History* (Gloucestershire, 1998) p 131.
[51] *ibid*, p 101.
[52] A Ritchie, 'Painted Pebbles in early Scotland', *Proceedings of the Society of Antiquaries of Scotland* 104 (1971-72) 297-301.
[53] Martin, p 148.
[54] M O Anderson, p 81.
[55] Binchy, pp 12f.
[56] *ibid*, p 14.

While Binchy's argument may be problematic, the list of 30 Bruidhes is a curious tradition.

The first Bridei we come to in the historic section of the list is Bridei mac Máelchon, who was a major force in gathering tribes to quash Scottic expansion. Bridei mac Máelchon appears to have been given the patronymic of a Welsh warrior king. Máelchon, or Maelgwyn, was the butt of Gildas' polemic, particularly as Gildas viewed him as apostate. The name Máelchon suggests a link with its linguistic parallels, Conmáel, a heroic figure in Irish literature, and Cunomaglos, a British divinity.[57] These heroic figures are associated with hunting and warriors. The Irish and Welsh tales speak of mythic hunts, and the Picts must have viewed hunting in a similar way, given the prevalence of hunting scenes on the Class II stones. Bridei came into power around 550, after a period of environmental upheaval. According to tree ring records from Ireland, a major climatic event caused extremely narrow growth cycles in 540 to 542. Ice-core samples from the same period reveal very large acid signals, while contemporary documentary evidence from Byzantium and China speak of the sun being blocked out and severe frosts in summer.[58] It is likely that this environmental event would have impacted on society with widespread famine, pestilence and possibly religious changes. Bridei may have adopted a ritual title to emphasise his reign bringing back the glories of the mythic past and environmental stability.

Possibly the most famous Bridei is Bridei mac Bili. His patronymic has the Irish meaning of sacred or tribal tree (often an oak) and according to Ó hÓgáin 'was also a common metaphor for a champion or a protector'.[59] Bridei was buried on Iona and may have been a close friend of Adomnán's. In a poem attributed to Adomnán, he watches over Bridei's body and laments:

> It is strange,
> After ruling a kingdom:
> A small ruined hollow of oak
> About the son of Dumbarton's king[60]

Other names in the king list reveal mythological elements, such as Taran which resembles the Gaulish and British thunder-god Taranis.[61] Nechtan reflects the name of a river deity[62] and Forsyth has recently noted that the

---

[57] R Warner, 'Navan and Apollo', *Emania* 14 (1996) 77-81, p 79.
[58] M G L Baille, 'Patrick, Comets and Christianity', *Emania* 13 (1995) 69-78.
[59] D Ó hÓgáin, *The Sacred Isle: Belief and Religion in Pre-Christian Ireland* (Cork, 1999) p 168.
[60] T O Clancy and G Márkus, *Iona: The Earliest Poetry of a Celtic Monastery* (Edinburgh, 1994) p 167.
[61] M O Anderson, p 90.
[62] P Jones and N Pennick, *A History of Pagan Europe*, (London, 1995, repr 2003) p 81.

name Onuist or Oengus is derived from a pan-Celtic source meaning 'unique choice, vigour, ability'.[63]

One particular aspect of the historic king lists is the regular use of patronymics from Bridei mac Máelchon onwards. The earlier parts of the list are more fragmentary and may contain names from Pictish mythology.[64] While some of the patronymics are confirmed by annal entries and hagiography, it is important to remember that surnames, and indeed first names, were not treated in the same way as they are today. For instance, Byrne finds that the gentilic formula *'mocu'*, which was used on some of the early ogham inscriptions in Ireland, could be followed just as easily by a mythical name as by a real one.[65] Judging by the name changes and multiple names given to the clergy at this time, names could be altered to suit new situations and status.[66] The Irish *Matyrology of Oengus*, devised around the early ninth century, provides information on clerical nicknames including Columba's original name *Cremthann*.[67] It is also clear from the Irish saga literature that there are situations where a warrior would adopt a new name as part of a coming of age rite.[68]

A glance at the king lists from the historic period reveals a relatively small stock of names. Miller has postulated that when Constantine mac Fergus named his son Drest it was with the possibility in mind that his son would gain the kingship.[69] And Kenneth mac Alpin was deliberately emphasising his continuity with the Pictish and Scottic succession by naming his sons Constantine, after the founder of Dunkeld, and Áed, after the Dalriadic king Áed Find.[70] This would imply a codified system of king-names by the early medieval period and the wish to harness the legitimacy of an ancestral name.

Conclusion

We must consider Pictland as being a loose federation of regional authorities and kings. These regional kings would need to be in agreement as to who would be their high king, perhaps not only in battle but also in a religious sense. With enemies and allies encroaching from at least three borders, the inauguration of a Pictish high king took on strategic importance. The inauguration ritual would provide a unity of sorts, with the

---

[63] Forsyth, p 23.
[64] M O Anderson, p 85.
[65] Byrne, p xxxii.
[66] Watson, p 169; St Kentigern (translated as 'first lord') is also known as St Mungo (translated as 'dear friend').
[67] W Stokes (ed), *The Martyrology of Oengus the Culdee*, (London, 1905) p 147.
[68] This is seen in the Fenian tale of 'Duan na Ceárdaich' (The Lay of the Smithy); G Murphy, *Dunaire Finn*, Part II (Irish Text Society 28, London, 1933) 7-15.
[69] Miller, 'Last Century', p 55.
[70] *ibid*, p 52.

new king elected by his contemporaries. Ultimately, the use of a significant sacred site and ancient ritual would provide legitimacy to the king's right to rule.

Valkyries in Caithness: an exploration of *Darradarliod*

Katharine Burke

The late Viking-age poem *Darradarliod* is preserved in the thirteenth-century Icelandic text *Njal's Saga*.[1] *Darradarliod* contains a tantalisingly enigmatic vignette of valkyries weaving the fates of men at a loom in Caithness. Here we find Odinn's spear maidens, dripping with the gore of warfare, combined with bizarre domestic cues. The iconoclasm of this juxtaposition warrants an investigation of pagan imagery in Viking literature. The poem mingles domesticity with religion, brutality and invasion, within the interior of the *dyngja*, the women's quarters of the Viking home, and the site for textile production.[2] *Darradarliod* provokes discussion of the socio-economic implications of women's textile work in early Norse society, the division of labour between women and men, and the roles that women played in Viking warmongering.

Darradarliod sets a scene where death is as inevitable as weft on warp. Early on Good Friday morning in Caithness, 1014, a Scandinavian man named Dorrud leaves his home and witnesses 12 valkyries riding furiously towards a *dyngja*. The valkyries enter the building, and Dorrud peers through the window from outside. The 12 begin to weave, and sing a song that *Njal's Saga* links with the battle of Clontarf, in Ireland. Dorrud watches the valkyries weave each man's fate on their extraordinarily grisly loom, and he sees that its construction is the debris of war:

> The warp is woven
> with warriors' guts,
> and heavily weighted
> with the heads of men
> Spears serve as heddle rods,
> spattered with blood;
> iron-bound is the shed rod,
> and arrows are the pin beaters;
> we will beat with swords
> our battle web.[3]

---

[1] *Njal's Saga* (trans Magnus Magnusson and Hermann Pálsson, Harmondsworth, 1960, repr 1983).

[2] Nanna Damsholt, 'The Role of Icelandic Women in the Sagas and in the Production of Homespun Cloth', *Scandinavian Journal of History* 9, 75-83.

[3] *Njal's Saga*, p 304.

After their song, the valkyries tear their gruesome fabric to shreds, and flee the *dyngja* on horseback, six to the north, and six to the south. Another character in the saga witnesses a similar event in the Faroe Islands. The gender of the valkyries is not specified, but presumably the Scandinavian audience did not need this clarification – textual and archaeological evidence indicates that the valkyrie was always female, and that only women used the *dyngja* to weave *vadmal* (homespun cloth) for the family.[4] Traditional depiction of Odinn's spear maidens ranged from terrible goddesses and wise women, to their most recognisable incarnations as psuedo-masculine, Amazonian figures.[5] These valkyries accessorised their blonde, female forms with the iconography of war, were armed to the teeth, and rode bareback into battles, in groups of six or twelve, where they chose who would live and who would perish.[6] In the afterlife, they were revered as the maidens of Valhalla, receiving fallen warriors with goblets of mead and infinite personal service. Arguably, these manifestations of Norse archetypes indicate a thirteenth-century Christian Icelandic interpretation of early Scandinavian belief. *Njal's Saga*'s valkyries recontextualise an ancient idea, and their presence in the saga evokes old songs, poems and carvings.

Darradarliod's *dyngja* internalises the valkyries, feminises and domesticates them. Why are they so far from the fighting, in the women's quarters on a Scottish farm? Why are they not hovering over the bloody Irish battlefield, as tradition would have them? They are an elaboration of the traditional image of the three Scandinavian mythological Norns, *Urd*, *Verdandi* and *Skuld* (Past, Present and Future), who measured and cut the thread of a man's life, not unlike the three Greek Fates.[7] Feminist scholars have argued that the valkyries' active presence in the *dyngja* legitimises and glorifies women's work at the loom.[8] It is also possible that the praise-poet and saga-writer mirrored women's prosaic tasks to highlight the archaic, fierce, pagan power of the warrior maidens. He certainly complicated their image.

Perhaps Christianity drew the valkyries indoors, as a metaphor for the shift in Norse beliefs. Significantly, Christians produced *Njal's Saga* in the thirteenth century, and the Battle of Clontarf took place on Good Friday. Pagan mythology infused many Scandinavian texts, indicating that the thirteenth-century Christian audience was keen to preserve old beliefs and songs, but as muted background music rather than centre-stage. The domestic scene might also signify 'tamed' Vikings, hundreds of years after

---

[4] Judith Jesch, *Women in the Viking Age* (Woodbridge and Rochester, 1991) pp 130-39.
[5] Jenny Jochens, *Women in Old Norse Society* (Ithaca, 1995) p 138.
[6] Jesch, p 39.
[7] Damsholt, p 87; Jochens, *Women*, p 139.
[8] Jochens, *Women*, p 137.

their violent invasions, more concerned with maintaining their farmsteads than raiding for gold and glory. The valkyries' ferocity is definitely maintained with their control over the outcome of the war, the climactic tearing of the fatal fabric, and the presence of their traditional steeds. Utilising textile work, however, to manoeuvre a war across the sea renders their roles more interesting.

As Klaus von See has emphasised,[9] war is undoubtedly the poem's main focus. The poem is possibly named after the weaving of the pennants, *vefr darradar*,[10] as the armies clash. Feminist scholars Anne Holtsmark and Nanna Damsholt have canvassed the idea that *Darradarliod* was a women's work song, or *Arbejdssange*,[11] and have emphasised the importance of the site of women's work: the *dyngja*. Studies have suggested, however, that weaving at vertical looms was usually a solitary activity, definitely not undertaken in groups of 12, more awkward than rhythmic, and therefore not particularly conducive to work songs.[12] However, most early Anglo-Scandinavian households contained more than one woman, and, as historians and archaeologists agree that every woman in Viking society wove, inevitably some exchange was made between the textile workers: perhaps song, certainly gossip, storytelling and chatter. It seems most likely, however, that men sang *Darradarliod* as a praise poem for the young King, winning land and reputation:

> Our pronouncement was good
> for the young prince;
> sound of mind
> we sing victory songs.
> May he who listens
> learn from this
> the tones of the spear-women
> and tell them to men.[13]

Darradarliod is one of only two literary references to the Viking vertical loom. No medieval loom has been excavated intact, so *Darradarliod's* description provides invaluable clues towards an understanding of material culture.[14] Evidence of the *dyngja* was demonstrated at Stöng, in Iceland,

---

[9] *ibid.*
[10] *ibid.*
[11] Anne Holtsmark, 'Arbejdssange' in *Kulturhistorisk Leksikon for Nordisk Middelalder fra Vikingetid til Reformationstid* Vol 1 (Copenhagen, 1956) cited in Damsholt, p 89.
[12] Jochens, *Women,* p 139.
[13] *Njal's Saga,* p 302.
[14] The loom described in the first paragraph of this paper is based on the vertical loom. In Darradarliod, 'blood rains from the beam's cloud', like warp threads, and 'the warp...is heavily weighted with the heads of men' instead of the stone weights commonly used by Icelanders. (*Njal's Saga,* pp 303f). This description does not

where excavations revealed a Viking-age house, almost intact, preserved by the volcano's eruption.[15] One room contained whalebone weaving batons, spindle whorls, and warp weights. Similar sites with a high density of textile tools have been excavated at Coppergate, in York,[16] and throughout Northumbria, Scotland and Ireland, leading scholars to believe that *dyngjas* were common throughout Norse society. It seems most likely that the loom was permanently set up in the *dyngja*, and that the length of cloth was limited only by the height of the roof beam. In smaller homes, the loom was set up against one wall of the room where the household slept and ate.

The contents of Scandinavian women's graves have shaped historians' understanding of Viking textile work. Excavations throughout Scandinavia, the British Isles and Iceland have revealed tools of clay, stone, glass, lead, amber and antler in women's graves.[17] Fortunately for archaeologists and historians, women were buried wearing metal brooches, which have preserved precious textiles. Ferrous oxide, released when the brooch corrodes, replaces the textile fibres, mineralising and preserving the fabrics.[18] Garments made from wool and animal fibres have been best preserved, in particular the woollen diamond-twill found in graves throughout the Viking world.[19]

Excavations at the Viking site of Coppergate indicate a shift from a self-sufficient, exchange economy, to a commercial, manufacturing society. Anaerobic conditions (waterlogged soil with no oxygen) preserved large quantities of material evidence of Scandinavian textile production.[20] The adoption of the horizontal loom in the eleventh century particularly enabled this socio-economic shift – more fabric could be produced efficiently, because the length of the weft was less restricted. This was a move away from home-based work, to a division of labour historically recognisable as medieval guilds.[21]

---

match a horizontal loom, where gravity did not play such a significant role in the production of cloth.

[15] Damsholt, p 77.
[16] Nina Crummy, 'From Self-Sufficiency to Commerce: Structural and Artifactual Evidence for Textile Manufacture in Eastern England in the Pre-Conquest Period' in Désirée G Koslin and Janet Snyder (eds), *Medieval Textiles and Dress: Objects, Texts, Images* (New York, 2002) p 26.
[17] Jesch, p 19.
[18] Crummy, p 27.
[19] Margareta Nockert, 'A Scandinavian Haberget?' in N B Harte and K G Ponting (eds), *Cloth and Clothing in Medieval Europe: Essays in Memory of Professor E.M. Carus-Wilson* (London and Edington, 1983) p 104.
[20] Crummy, p35.
[21] Crummy, p 37.

Labour within the Viking household, *hjòn*, was strictly divided by Norse law.²² The production of homespun was the responsibility of the landowner's wife as part of her duties *fyrir innan stokkr*, or *fyrir innan gordr*, ('within the threshold' work), alongside dairy preparation, childbearing and acquiring and cooking food.²³ Men usually fulled and dyed the fabrics, in keeping with their labours *fyrir utan stokkr*, or *fyrir utan gordr*, ('outside the threshold' work)²⁴ The mistress of the *hjòn* probably standardised the cloth production, and supervised the fulling and dyeing. Wool was dyed in fleece or on the skein, so that stripes and patterns could be woven.²⁵ Gudrun's garments, as described throughout *Laxdaela Saga*, match the techniques and patterns achievable with vertical looms (stripes, chevrons etc): 'Gudrun was wearing a tunic with a tight-fitting woven bodice, and a tall head-dress, and round her waist she had tied a fringed sash with dark blue stripes.'²⁶ These patterns are simple, and are also achievable with horizontal looms. However, horizontal looms typically create more complicated patterns than stripes and chevrons. Given that *Laxdaela Saga* contains detailed descriptions of lavish clothing, and that this and other Viking narratives reveal that Icelanders were preoccupied with potlatch and out-doing, Gudrun's clothing must reveal the most impressive textile work of her time. Therefore, these patterns, lacking the complexity achievable with the horizontal loom, suggest work from the vertical loom. This indicates that the sagas can be interpreted as evidence of early Scandinavian material culture, as well as of thirteenth-century desires for a good story.

Clothing the Scandinavian family demanded significant daily ritual. Men and women were sewn into their layers of garments each morning for a tighter fit.²⁷ Which begs the question: who sewed Viking men into their clothes when they were away raiding and trading? Textual evidence suggests that Norwegian sailors took sheep, needles and thread to sea for darning purposes.²⁸ Women made undershirts, caftans, tunics and coats for the family, usually from worsted wool and pleated linen.²⁹

---

[22] Jochens, *Women*, p 116.
[23] *ibid*, p 117.
[24] Fulling was the process of beating cloth to cleanse and thicken it and alter its texture. This is explained in more detail in Françoise Piponnier and Perrine Mane, *Dress in the Middle Ages* trans Caroline Beamish (New Haven, 1997) p 16.
[25] Crummy, p 37.
[26] *Laxdaela Saga*, translated Magnus Magnusson and Hermann Pálsson (Harmondsworth, 1969) p 188.
[27] Jochens, *Women*, pp 125-28. Jochens itemises the types of personal body services provided by women, usually to men, sometimes to women of higher social status.
[28] *ibid*, 142.
[29] Inga Hagg, 'Viking Women's Dress at Birka: A Reconstruction by Archaeological Methods' in N B Harte and K G Ponting (eds), *Cloth and Clothing in Medieval*

The localised power of the mistress of the household, as family seamstress, is exemplified in the sagas. In *Laxdaela Saga*, Gudrun Osvif's-daughter, at her lover's suggestion, makes her first husband a woman's shirt that will allow her to divorce him, if he wears it. The narrative is in keeping with early Icelandic law, which declared that transgressive dress was grounds for divorce.[30] Her lover then divorces his wife Aud for wearing trousers, but Aud, truly wearing the pants in the relationship, wreaks her revenge, not from her loom, but man-style: with a blade.[31]

In *Laxdaela Saga*, the gendered nature of domestic tasks is seen when Bolli returns from killing Kjartan. Gudrun, the mistress of the household, says to her husband: 'Great *vadaverk* have taken place today: I have spun twelve ells of yarn and you have killed Kjartan.'[32] This is a play on the intriguing Old Norse word *vadaverk*, which means both violent action and producing homespun cloth,[33] perhaps revealing the extensive physical exertion of textile work. Certainly, the fulling process involved beating fabric for optimum results. Gudrun implies that slaughter and vengeance are men's work, and that spinning is for women.[34] Vikings would have acknowledged that producing homespun was no benign task. *Vadaverk* indicates that the Old Norse language was conducive to imagining the valkyries' violent spinning.

Both vengeance and textile production were demonstrably significant in shaping narratives and prompting action in the sagas. Throughout the sagas, female characters use cloth and textiles, as objects within their control, to instigate action, frequently by whetting masculine aggression. In these incidents, clothing and textile work are metaphors for female power, tangled with men's actions, emphasising the cooperative division of labour. Bloodstained clothing is rarely unaccompanied by a female voice demanding revenge. She impugns masculinity and goads men to avenge the unjustly slain with further bloodshed. This is called *eggja*, or *hvòt*. In *Laxdaela Saga*, Gudrun preserves the fringed sash that Helgi used to wipe

---

Europe: Essays in Memory of Professor E M Carus-Wilson (London and Edington, 1983) p 349.
[30] 'If women deviate so far from custom and tradition that they wear men's clothes or adopt any male practice whatsoever in order to be different from others, and also if men adopt any female practice of whatever kind, then the punishment will be banishment for the person, whether man or woman, who does so.' *Grágás. Laws of early Iceland: the Codex Regius of Grágás* Vol I ch 155, p 46, cited in Damsholt, p 84.
[31] *Laxdaela Saga*, p 125.
[32] *Laxdaela Saga*, p 176.
[33] Jochens, *Women*, pp 159f. See also Damsholt, p 84. Ólafur Halldórsson suggested this interpretation of the element 'vada' in 'Morgunverk Gudrúnar Osvifsdóttir', *Skirnir* (1973), pp 125-28.
[34] Damsholt, p 84.

Bolli's blood from his blade, so she can show Bolli's son when he is old enough to avenge his father. Helgi is familiar with the role that the child inside Gudrun will play when he says, 'Under this very sash lies the one who will take my life.'[35] In early Scandinavia, women had no political rights through their own persons.[36] Men carried out justice on their behalf; this is reflected throughout the sagas. Female characters use objects within their control to prompt retaliation. A prime example of *hvöt* comes from Hildigunn in *Njal's* Saga: 'This cloak, Flosi, was your gift to Hoskuld, and now I give it back to you. He was slain in it. In the name of God and all good men I charge you, by all the powers of your Christ and by your courage and manliness, to avenge all the wounds which he received in dying – or else be an object of contempt for all men.'[37] Flosi's response echoes the teachings of the Christian church, that women who encouraged revenge were manifestations of evil[38] and embodied dangerous female power: 'Flosi flung off the cloak and threw it into her arms and said, 'You are the worst monster and want us to take the course which will be worst for us all. Cold are the counsels of women.'[39]

Weaving has been associated extensively with early medieval women's magic throughout Europe. Valerie Flint has discussed the fact that Viking women's magic included incantation at the loom, usually to the detriment of the wearer of the cloth woven, and writing magical curses into fabric with runes from the futhark. A woman's weaving tablet, found at Lund, was engraved with what seems to be a curse on her ex-lover.[40] Her voice was preserved on the object that was closest to her hand, the weaving tablet. The fabrics woven with the tablet were therefore connected with her curse. The relationship between women's magic and textile work has also been preserved in less impromptu texts: Eddic poetry associated the word *skript* (meaning writing and representation) with women's embroidery in *Gudrun's Second Lay*[41] and *Volsunga Saga*.[42] In the law text *Codex Regius*, the word *bók* was used for embroidery and weaving.[43] If textile work was perceived as a type of writing, then patterns and clothing were manifestations of ideas, a visual code, like a language. A more formidable reading suggests that the association between women's textile work and

---

[35] *Laxdaela Saga*, p 188.
[36] Damsholt, p 79.
[37] *Njal's Saga*, p 195.
[38] Birgit Sawyer and Peter Sawyer, *Medieval Scandinavia – From Conversion to Reformation, circa 800-1500* (Minneapolis, 1993) p 189.
[39] *Njal's Saga*, p 195.
[40] Jenny Jochens, *Old Norse Images of Women* (Philadelphia, 1996) p 46.
[41] Carolyne Larrington (ed and trans), 'The Second Lay of Gudrun' in *The Poetic Edda* (Oxford, 1996) Gdr2 str15.
[42] R G Finch (ed and trans), *The Saga of the Volsungs* (London, 1965) ch 34 v 86.
[43] Jochens, *Old Norse Images*, p 127.

cursing was widespread, and that the links between inscribed or cursed fabric were recognised by medieval law. Medieval literature allowed for both beneficial and malevolent interpretations of women's textile work.

Significantly, women enabled men to brave the elements, not only by clothing them, but also by producing the distinctive Viking rhomboid sails from homespun woollen cloth. Production of sails by women is widely accepted by historians, because of a lack of evidence of Viking-age weavers' long sheds for mass production of sails. A praise poem from Ottarr the Black sings of the role of women in equipping ships, enabling their men to go raiding and trading, far from the hearth:

> You scored with planed rudder
> the splash-high waves; the sail
> spun by women played on
> the launch-reindeer's mast-top[44]

A small longship's sail required sixty-two square metres of homespun. Nearly 126,000 metres of woollen yarn were essential, which would take four women an entire winter to spin.[45] It is not unlikely that women sang songs like *Darradarliod*, about their men's victories overseas, whilst making the homespun to carry them across there.

Darradarliod is a sophisticated example of thirteenth-century Icelanders investing their heritage with images of *vadaverk*, victory and settlement in the British Isles. Valkyries are adopted by the saga-writer from the cultural currency of an ancient religion. Dorrud, the Scandinavian everyman, is placed where he can watch females watching men, an imitation of Scandinavians observing their histories. The home was the meeting point between men and women, where men boasted of their wild achievements to women, the site where wars lingered in song and memory. *Darradarliod's* valkyries perform their terrible work in the women's space of the home. Their powerful hands at the loom embody notions of textile work and sorcery, and the balance of gendered tasks, on a grand and catastrophic scale.

---

[44] Jesch, p 152.
[45] *ibid*.

Wésten: the birth of 'The Waste Land'

Chris Bishop

I sat upon the shore
Fishing, with the arid plain behind me
Shall I at least set my lands in order? ...
These fragments I have shored against my ruins ...[1]

When Eliot utilised the image of 'The Waste Land' to represent his own feelings of despair and hopelessness he was, by his own admission, self-consciously borrowing from a literary tradition that traced its genesis through romantic poetry and medieval romance, back into the songs of his Insular ancestors. Eliot's poetry, however, was informed by a range of subjectivities unknown to the Anglo-Saxons and his wasteland, therefore, differs from the wastelands of these ancestors in significant ways. Eliot, for example, contrasts the wasteland with the arable whereas the Anglo-Saxon juxtaposition lay between the inhabited land and the empty — between the mead-hall and the ruin.

The motif of ruin — ruined cities, ruined halls — and of the *wésten*, or 'wasteland', in general, was of deep significance to the Anglo-Saxons judging by its prevalence in the extant poetry. Modern perceptions of the heroic nature of Anglo-Saxon society have rested on no more than five poems — several of them fragmentary and only three of them surviving in medieval manuscripts. The *wésten*, on the other hand, appears in a good many Anglo-Saxon poems, yet its power as sign to these early peoples is still relatively unexplored. The purpose of this paper is to explore the importance of the *wésten* motif — and in particular the image of ruin — to the Anglo-Saxons and to examine the ways in which an appreciation of this theme augmented the Anglo-Saxon perception of *wyrd* (fate) and modified their philosophic consolations of community and honour.

The Ruin of Britain
The literary function of the ruin may be obvious enough, but this is not to say that its genesis lay in allegory alone; to the Anglo-Saxon audience the

---

[1] T S Eliot, 'The Wasteland' lines 424-431 in *The Complete Poems and Plays: 1909-1950* (New York, 1962). Subsequent quotations from poetry in this paper are from the following editions: *Beowulf*: F Klaeber (ed), *Beowulf and the Fight at Finnsburg* (3rd ed, Boston, 1950); *The Ruin*, *The Wanderer*, *The Seafarer* and *The Wife's Lament*: G P Krapp and E Van Kirk Dobbie (eds), *The Exeter Book* (New York, 1936); *Gnomic Verses*: D Whitelock (ed), *Sweet's Anglo-Saxon Reader* (Oxford, 1967); *Voluspa*: Guðni Jónsson (ed), *Eddukvæði* (Akureyri, 1954). Translations are my own.

79

motif must have represented a tangible reality. Almost every inhabited space of the Anglo-Saxon world must have evidenced the physical phenomenon that engendered the poignancy of the *wésten*.

During the third century of the Common Era, the population of Roman Britain rose to three or four million.[2] This enormous population, perhaps three times the Doomsday reckoning, was a result of improved farming practice including the introduction of new cereal species from the continent, optimal climatic conditions and, possibly, the *Pax Romana*.[3]

The Peace of Rome was established and maintained by the Roman army, and by the second century Britain was barracks to one-eighth of all Rome's forces. Added to these 40 000 troops were considerable numbers of administrators, servants, slaves and family members all of whom served to make Britain a thoroughly Romanised province.[4]

Rome established 100 or more provincial towns in Britain and these towns were ordered according to Roman specifications and enjoyed all the amenities essential to Roman life — temples, administrative centres, substantial houses and, of course, baths. Baths needed water, which was supplied by means of aqueducts and disposed of by efficient sewers. Such baths were also common features in Roman forts, of which there were considerable numbers, especially after the construction of the Antonine and Hadrianic walls.

As the province grew in wealth and the material trappings of civilisation, all this military and civil administrative infrastructure was augmented by the works of British potentates. During the third and fourth centuries, provincial magnates began to build extensive villas in the countryside. The architecture of these villas was self-consciously Roman — utilising hypocaust (heating) systems — and the ruins that survive into the present day clearly indicate the magnitude of the stonework and the intricacy of the ornament involved.[5] After four centuries of Roman rule, the total effect of these villas, forts, cities and walls — combined with the large-scale road system built to service them — can only have served to create a deeply Romanised provincial civilization. This civilization, however, was not the world of the Anglo-Saxons.

It is impossible to determine with any certainty the population of the Anglo-Saxon kingdoms in the centuries before the Norman conquest. It was certainly nowhere near the population of Britain during the Roman occupation. This pattern of decline began with the reduction of the Roman garrison in Britain during the fourth century and was no doubt exacerbated

---

[2] Nicholas Higham, *Rome, Britain and the Anglo-Saxons* (London, 1992) p 20; Richard Hodges, *The Anglo-Saxon Achievement* (London, 1989) p 15.
[3] Higham, pp 18f.
[4] Troop strengths and ratios from Higham, pp 39, 50.
[5] Stephen Johnson, *Later Roman Britain* (London, 1987) pp 24-27.

by both the subsequent invasions and various Insular rebellions. Complete Roman withdrawal from the province during the first decade of the fifth century ushered in a period of economic collapse followed by a fiscal stagnation that was to last for several centuries. Added to all this was a series of plagues during the fifth and sixth centuries and an abrupt climate change during the mid-sixth century.[6]

Whether the population decrease occurred as a natural downturn in fertility generated by socio-economic conditions,[7] or as a result of some catastrophe, the result in terms of this paper remains the same. Anglo-Saxon Britain contained only a fraction of the population of Roman Britain and the people who inherited the Roman province lived lives quite different from those of their Latin antecedents.

Between the Britannic provincial zenith of the second and third centuries and the rise of the Anglo-Saxon hegemony in the seventh, the pattern of settlement in Britain changed dramatically. The villas were gradually abandoned. Roads were left to ruin. The frontier walls and the garrison forts decayed.

In the Roman towns, populations declined steadily and many settlements were abandoned altogether. Large-scale industry ceased to function,[8] sewers collapsed,[9] roofs fell in, courtyards were filled in and cultivated.[10] Outside the towns fields were left fallow, wheat disappeared as a crop,[11] grazing land reverted, forests and bogs began to spread.[12]

At what point the Anglo-Saxons came into this landscape is of little consequence to the argument at hand. If they came in as Roman mercenaries and looked on as the province fell apart; or if they came in as conquerors or as refugees after the Roman withdrawal; or if they migrated wholesale in the wake of British civil war, famine and plague, the result was still the same. By the time in which the *wésten* poems were being composed — the eighth century at the earliest — the Anglo-Saxon poets must have found themselves in a landscape littered with the remnants of a distant and monumental past.

---

[6] See M Baille, 'Do Irish Bog Oaks Date The Shang Dynasty?', *Current Archaeology* 117 (1989) 310-13; C Burgess, 'Volcanoes, Catastrophe and the Global Crisis of the Late 2nd Millenium BC', *Current Archaeology* 117 (1989) 325-329.

[7] There had been widespread economic collapse throughout the Empire under the Emperor Diocletian (d 337); see Higham, p 28 and also P J Fowler, 'The countryside in Roman Britain: a study in failure or a failure in study', *Landscape History* 5 (1983) 5-9.

[8] Hodges, p 17.

[9] David A Hinton, *Archeology, Economy and Society: England From the Fifth to the Fifteenth Century* (London, 1990) p 10.

[10] *ibid*, p 6.

[11] Higham, p 127.

[12] Higham, p 78; Hinton, p 10.

The impact of this landscape on the people cannot be underestimated. The scope of Roman settlement and the scale of their architecture must have been mesmerising to the tribal Anglo-Saxons. Broken statues, fallen walls, and ruinous cities must have been apparent almost everywhere. Anglo-Saxon children driving their pigs into the forest for pannage must have stumbled across old milestones. Women must have beaten out their washing by the streams against pavers worn smooth by centuries of Roman use. Apothecaries must have gathered herbs from the fugitive gardens of decrepit Roman courtyards.

Early Christian ascetics sought out places of isolation in which to perfect their practice of religion, and these places of isolation included ruined Roman forts. The Irish hermit Fursa established himself in just such a *burh* in East Anglia,[13] and the first permanent Anglo-Saxon mission to the Frisians was based initially in the ruined Roman fortress of Traiectum, now Utrecht.[14]

Among the West-Saxons this practice may have been encouraged, to produce monastic buffer zones between themselves and their enemies.[15] When Cynegils entered into an alliance with Oswald of Northumbria in 635, he converted to Christianity and, with Oswald's permission, granted the old Roman fort at Dorcic [Dorchester] to Bishop Birinus in order that he might establish a monastery there.[16] An alliance with Oswald, cemented by Cynegils's marriage to Oswald's daughter, immediately placed the West-Saxons in contention with Mercia, and Dorcic lay on the Mercia-Wessex border. Similarly, a half-century later, Ine established another monastery at Abingdon. Again the house he endowed lay strategically between himself and his Mercian enemies.[17]

It is well to remember that the monastic institutions in which the Anglo-Saxon poems were transcribed, if not composed, lay close to or within Roman ruins and that these ruins played a seminal part in the genesis of many such houses. These are the material realities that occasioned the Anglo-Saxon vision of the *wésten*.

The poetic record

It may be possible to dismiss the *bitre burgtunas brerum beweaxne* [l 31 — bitter citadels infested by brambles] of *The Wife's Lament* as poetic hyperbole. Perhaps the citadels are metaphoric — nothing more than mountains transformed by the poet's imagination. If they were the only

---

[13] Bede, *Historia Ecclesiastica Gentis Anglorum* III.19 in J E King (ed and trans), *Opera historica* (London, 1930).
[14] Bede, *EH* V.11; Alcuin, *Vita Villibrodi* 5.
[15] Hodges, p 52.
[16] Bede, *EH* III.7.
[17] Hodges, p 52.

example in Anglo-Saxon poetry of the ruined city motif then such an opinion might carry weight, but the casual nature of this reference informs us that this theme was familiar to the *scópas'* audience and leads us to expect its common employment in other poems. Even a cursory glance at the remaining corpus shows that this is indeed the case.

The intention of the opening lines of the *Cotton Gnomics*, for instance, is nowhere near so ambiguous.

> 1   cyning sceal ríce healdan ceastra béoð feorran gesyne
>   orðanc enta geweorc þá þe on þysse eoðan syndon
>   wrætlic weallstána geweorc wind byð on lyfte swiftest
>   þunar byð þrágum hlúdast þrymmas syndan crístes myccle
> 5   wyrd bið swíðost ...

[The king holds the land. The city is seen far distant — the skilful work of giants who, when on this earth, wrought splendid mansions. Wind aloft is fastest, thunder at times the loudest. Glorious is Christ's might. *Wyrd* is strongest ...]

The *Cotton Gnomics*, unlike their counterparts in the Exeter manuscript, form a single coherent unit whose theme is constant and whose instruction is unwavering. The poem is a skilful discourse on what is and what must be and how one is to act in the world in the light of this information.

Through a series of thematically and metrically connected passages the poet juxtaposes what is inherent in nature with what is created by humans, and consistently delineates this juxtaposition through the use of contrasting participles of the same verb *beon* [to be]. Thus *byð* [the third person singular] indicates what is inherent while *syndon* [the present plural indicative] signifies what has been created. This subtle contrast is a feature of Anglo-Saxon Gnomic poetry[18] and is seen by some as a delineation between the natural world and the artificial world or, perhaps, between what is and what should be. The comparison is clear even in the brief quote given above with the present plural indicative being used for both Christ and the giants, while the third-person singular is reserved for natural phenomena: the wind, the thunder, and, significantly, *wyrd*. It may be possible, also, that the language used implies a belief on the part of the *scóp* that Christ's might is itself subject to *wyrd*.

The *scóp*, having spoken briefly in the opening of the poem about kings and kingdoms, then returns to a series of *byð* gnomes about seasons and the weather. So the king holds the land, but the king is not all-powerful; in the one line the poet shows both the power of the office and the weakness of the man. Here is the city of the giants, a race who held the

---

[18] See C Larrington, *A Store of Common Sense: Gnomic Theme and Style in Old Icelandic and Old English Wisdom Poetry* (Oxford, 1993).

land before, fallen to ruin. The winds blow through the ruins and on into the sky; time marches on. The ruler's empire swells and eclipses all others, as powerful and as fleeting as the thunder. The thunder here is compared not only to the wind and the giant's work but also, perhaps surprisingly, to Christ's glory, described here as *myccle*, a word that also carries connotations of noise and clamour in Anglo-Saxon.

The poet leaves the audience in no doubt as to the author of change through each of these scenarios. Christ's might may be glorious, but *wyrd* is the strongest. These brief lines are expanded upon in *The Wanderer*.

The poet of *The Wanderer* was similarly impressed by the *eald enta geweorc* [1 87 — ancient giant's work] that fell idle, and this poet, too, saw in that fall the machinations of *wyrd*. The subtlety and complexity of this poem continue to appeal to modern audiences, and rightly so. The debt of its author or authors to Isidore of Spain[19] and the pagan philosopher Boethius[20] has already been explored by other scholars, as have its literary links to Pliny[21] and the *Book of Lamentations*,[22] and its location within a complex body of pagan Germanicism is also no new idea.[23] It is perhaps this last area of correlation that will interest us most in the context of this paper.

The text of the poem is unambiguous about the role played by *wyrd* in the downfall of the ancient city, and the preconceptions underpinning that supposition have been rightly identified as fundamentally non-Christian.[24] The civilisation that shaped the great city of *The Wanderer* fell through the whim of fate; there is no implication of impropriety or evildoing in any descriptions of the city-builders. Furthermore *wyrd*, in destroying the city, has acted in malice. The poem serves as a poignant elegy for a fallen people, and as a warning for its intended audience.

> 95 *eala þeodnes þrym hu seo þrag gewat*
> *genap under nihthelm swa heo no wære*
> *stondeð nu on laste leofre duguþe*
> *weal wundrum heah wyrmlicum fah*
> *eorlas fornomon æsca þryþe*
> 100*wæpen wælgifru wyrd seo mære*
> [Alas! The tribe's glory! How that time has vanished — darkened under night's helm as if it never was. The

---

[19] J E Cross, 'Ubi Sunt Passages in Old English', *Vetenskaps-societetens i Lund Årsbok*, (1956, 1958-59).
[20] J E Cross, 'On the Genre of *The Wanderer*', *Neophilologus* XLV (1961).
[21] *ibid.*
[22] S I Tucker, 'Return to *The Wanderer*', *Essays in Criticism* VIII (1958).
[23] I L Gordon, 'Traditional Themes in *The Wanderer* and *The Seafarer*', *Review of English Studies* (1954) 1-13.
[24] B F Huppé first points this out in 'The Wanderer: Theme and Structure', *Journal of English and Germanic Philology* XLII (1943) 516-538.

towering wall, serpent carved, stands now as a shrine to that
dear brotherhood, the people destroyed by the ash-spear's
power — the slaughter-greedy weapon. *Wyrd* is glorious.]

The hall and the *duguðe*, bulwarks of Germanic society, have failed to save the people. Nor has the supernatural come to their aid.

There is good reason to believe that the entwined serpents so prevalent in Germanic art were intended to serve as protective talismans and there is reason to believe that this practice continued well into the Christian period amongst the Anglo-Saxons. Even with the gradual move away from the animal imagery of early Anglo-Saxon ornamentation towards the more stylised and geometric patterns of the illuminations of the latter period, the Anglo-Saxons may well have continued to impart protective connotations to decorative knot-work, especially when the finials were serpentine. It has been proposed that the intertwining serpents on the entrance of Benedict Biscop's chapel at Monkwearmouth bear witness to the continuance of this practice into the Christian period, and indeed into Christian architecture.[25] If this is so, then the message of doom within *The Wanderer* is even more dire, for here the poet informs us that not even such powerful talismans could protect these ancient peoples; the serpent walls are in ruins and neither the strength of their arms nor the power of their magic has saved these ancient peoples from destruction. They have been erased from the earth and no-one even knows who they might have been.

The Ruin combines the features expressed in both the *Cotton Gnomics* and *The Wanderer* into a single, thematically cogent, whole. The extraneous is stripped away to reveal a single powerful meditation on the ruins themselves and on the nature and meaning of ruin. There are no characters to talk to us or to explain the purpose of the poem, no points to be laboured. The text, astonishing in its modernity, is a simple set piece, a musing upon a broken city, a city broken by *wyrd*. The poem starts:

1 wrætlic is þes wealstan wyrde gebræcon
2 burgstede burston brosnað enta geweorc

[Beautiful is this building broken by *wyrd* — the city ruined,
the giant's work decays]

Alain Renoir's incisive comments on the power of this first line are worth recounting here.[26] The modern audience is prepared for the contents of this poem by the title which it now bears, but no such title appears in the manuscript. An Anglo-Saxon audience, more used to praise-songs, would have expected the theme that followed from *wrætlic is þes wealstan*

---

[25] See Ernst Kitzinger, 'Interlace and Icons: Form and Function in Early Insular Art' in R Michael Spearman and John Higgitt (eds), *The Age of Migrating Ideas: Early Medieval Art in Northern Britain and Ireland* (Edinburgh, 1993) p 4.

[26] See Alain Renoir, 'The Old English *Ruin*' in Martin Green (ed), *The Old English Elegies: New Essays in Criticism and Research* (London, 1983), p 155.

[beautiful is this building] to be one of eulogy rather than elegy, but the only glory to be sung of here is the glory of *wyrd*.

The comparison between *wyrde gebræcon* in line 1 of *The Ruin* with *wyrd seo mære* in line 100 of *The Wanderer* and *wyrd byð swiðost* in line 5 of the *Cotton Gnomics* is obvious, as is *brosnað enta geweorc* (*The Ruin*, l 1), *eald enta geweorc idlu stondon* (*The Wanderer*, l 87) and *orðanc enta geweorc* (*Cotton Gnomics*, l 2). Obvious too is the correlation of *The Ruin*'s *wrætlic is þes wealstan* (l 1) with the *wrætlic weallstána geweorc* (l 3) of the *Cotton Gnomics*. If these poems are not directly referring to each other, then they are clearly utilising the same poetic formulae; either way, the indications are of the thematic importance of the ruin motif to the Anglo-Saxons.

It is tempting, also, to think that the description of the building's foundations at line 20, bound by the mason *wirum wundrum togædre* [wondrously together by wires] might describe a talismanic process similar to that alluded to in *The Wanderer*. Indeed, if *wirum* [by wires] were a scribal error for *wirmum* [with serpents] then the reference would be, in effect, identical. Beyond these similarities, though, *The Ruin*, partly because of its extended exploration of a single theme, evidences several elaborations not found in the other works.

The Ruin, more than any of the other works discussed in this paper, makes explicit the virtue of the city dwellers whose civilisation has come to an end. These inhabitants were *hygerof* [l 19 — stout-hearted] and *secgrofra* [l 26 — brave], as well as *glædmod* [l 33 — happy] and *wlonc* [l 34 — splendid]. This amounts to significant praise in Anglo-Saxon. It is also clear from the text that warfare was not the bane of these people as it was to the giants of *The Wanderer*.

Rice æfter oþrum [l 10 — one kingdom after another] called this city home, *ofstonden under stormum* [l 11 — persisted beneath the storms]; the *heah horngestreon* [l 22 — high abundance of pinnacles] in the *meodoheall monig* [l 23 — many meadhalls] resounded to the *heresweg micel* [l 22 — great martial sound]. The bane of these people was not warfare; it was pestilence.

Wyrd seo swiþe [l 24 — *wyrd* is great], writes the poet of *The Ruin*, another direct correlation with the *Cotton Gnomics*, and continues:

    25 *crungon walo wide cwoman woldagas*
          swylt eall fornom secgrofra wera
    27 *wurdon hyra wigsteal wésten staþolas*
[The dead fell wide. The plague came. Death took away all the brave ones and these ramparts became ruins.]

It is unlikely that this poem was composed earlier than the eighth century,[27] so it is impossible that the poet who created it was an eyewitness to the plagues that ravaged Britain in the fifth and sixth centuries, although historical records of such events might have been available at that time.[28] What is more likely is that the *scóp* who composed the poem, whenever that might have been, used the agency of pestilence to illustrate more dramatically a dominant theme of the ruin poetry — the whim of fate. Plague is an indiscriminate killer, caring neither for virtue nor position, and as such it dramatises the arbitrary and unfair nature of *wyrd*, in stark contrast to the mercy and justice of God.

God is nowhere mentioned in *The Ruin*, yet its composition was clearly well after the conversion of the Anglo-Saxons to Christianity. It is a poem written down by a cleric in a book donated to a Cathedral by a Bishop — a poem that deals with the transience of the earthly — but the only moral the audience is impressed with is that *wyrd seo swiþe*.

The final examples of poetic reference to ruin come from *Beowulf*. As stated previously, Beowulf ventures twice into a *wésten*, the first time to confront the Grendel-dam and the second time to battle the dragon. The visual differences enumerated between those two regions by the *scóp* serve to indicate the breadth of the Anglo-Saxon sense of *wésten*.

The *wésten* of the Grendel-kin is a realm of deep mystery:

1357... *hie dygel lond*
warigeað wulfhleoþu windige næssas
frécne fengelád ðær fyrgenstréam
under næssa genipu niþer gewíteð
flód under foldan nis þæt feor heonon
mílgemearces þæt se mere standeð
ofer þæm hongiað hrinde bearwas
1364 *wudu wyrtum fæst wæter oferhelmað*
[They guard a hidden land of wild-slopes, wind-swept headlands (and) deadly fen paths, where cold torrents grow dark under cliffs (and) streams plunge into the earth. It is not that far hence that this mere stands, to measure it by miles, overhung by icy woods, the water overshadowed by thick vegetation]

This *wésten* is markedly at odds with the dragon's wilderness of barren rocks *glédum forgrunden* [l 2335 — blasted by fire]. The visual incongruity, one wilderness of water and the other of fire, serves to illustrate that the primary purpose of the word *wésten* was to denote not a description of landscape, but a landscape devoid of people.

---

[27] See Roy F Leslie (ed), *Three Old English Elegies* (Manchester, 1961) p 35.
[28] The tenth century *Annales Cambriae*, for example, record a *mortalitas magna* in the entry for 547.

There is some comparison made between the *wésten* of the dragon and that of the Grendel-kin. The abode of the Grendel-kin is referred to as a *níðsele* [l 1513 — hall of conflict] and its roof as the *hrófsele* [l 1515 — roofed hall]. The use of the element *sele* may be meant to imply that the structure was crafted rather than a cavern. Similarly the dragon's lair, which we know to have been made by an ancient race, is referred to as a *dryhtsele dyrnne* [l 2320 — hidden princely hall] and an *eorðsele* [l 2515 — subterranean hall], although most commonly (some ten times) as a *beorh* [barrow]. An ancient race, once again giants, also features in the *ælwihta eard* [dwelling place of monsters] of the Grendel-mere, for while evidence of their hands upon the chamber beneath the flood is conjectural, their crafting of certain artefacts within that chamber is elsewhere explicitly stated [l 1679].

Thus the *wésten* is still thematically present in *Beowulf*; the fallen ancient races persist and the ruins remain. Broad thematic similarities are thus established across five poems collected from three Anglo-Saxon manuscripts, all of them in the West-Saxon dialect. In terms of material survival, this would seem to make ruin as important a motif as heroism — but what did it mean to the audience who first heard these poems?

A singular vision
Although many other cultures have given expression to the concept of transience — including some societies that may have informed the Anglo-Saxons *scopes* — there remains something unique in the Anglo-Saxon representation of this phenomenon. Before that representation is explained, however, it should be made clear that the Anglo-Saxon motif of ruin was culturally specific and, therefore, owed less to Christianity than some scholars might want to believe.

By the tenth century, when the ruin poems were first written down, Anglo-Saxon poets as well as audiences would have been well versed in their scriptures. Bede tells us that Benedict Biscop decorated the north wall of his church at Monkwearmouth with images of the Apocalypse brought back from Rome.[29] An ivory carving of the Last Judgement from the late eighth or early ninth century[30] and several similar manuscript drawings of the early eleventh century[31] would seem to indicate that this theme remained as focal for Insular Christians as it did for their continental brethren. This, combined with the evidence of visual images such as the tower of Babel,[32] attests to a Christian Anglo-Saxon understanding of transience.

---

[29] Bede, *Lives of the Abbots*, ll 369-370.
[30] C R Dodwell, *Anglo-Saxon Art* (Manchester, 1982) p 89, plate 17.
[31] Dodwell, pp 104f, plates 23 a and b.
[32] Dodwell, p 71, plate 12.

Continental, predominantly Christian, scholarship must also have made itself felt within the Insular church. Clerical poets such as Alcuin, whose Latin poetry also explores the ephemeral nature of material existence, drew inspiration from continental sources such as Venantius Fortunatus, to whose *De excidio Thoringiae* Alcuin's own *De clade Lindisfarnensis* has been compared.[33] So too, the literary similarities between, for instance, Isidore of Spain's *ubi sunt* passages and those of *The Wanderer* have been understood for quite some time.[34] There is, however, a substantial difference between these Christian works and those which form the focus of this paper.

When Alcuin lamented the ruin of Rome, or the fall of Jerusalem, or indeed the expulsion from paradise, he was quick to draw a lesson from calamity, and this lesson was clear in its orthodoxy. '*Redemptio uiri proprie diuitie*' ['redemption is man's eternal reward'] he wrote in his letter to Bishop Higbald, therefore '*amemus eterna et non peritura*' ['love the eternal and not the perishable'].[35] Nor were the calamities of which poets like Alcuin wrote accidents of nature, for churchmen like him saw in the wrath of nature the hand of God.

The tower of Babel is cast down by God to punish impudence. Sodom and Gomorrah are incinerated to burn away their iniquity. Rome is prophesied to fall during the End of Days because of wickedness. But in none of the Anglo-Saxon poems at hand is any sort of judgement implied. The language throughout each of the poems that deal with ruin as motif clearly attributes the fall of the ancient races to the machinations of *wyrd* and no attempt is made to justify or explain the arbitrariness of that machine. This perception of ruin and its interrelationship with *wyrd*, then, is neither Christian nor continental, and yet neither is it a common Germanic affectation.

Even the Eddic poetry of Scandinavia, to which we might turn for some comparison, evidences little similarity to the ruin poems of the Anglo-Saxons. The *Voluspa* — possibly betraying a significant Christian contribution to early Scandinavian thought — deals explicitly with the destruction of the world at Ragnarok, but this destruction is succeeded by regeneration and life's insatiable desire for itself:

> 57 *sól tér sortna sígr fold í mar*
> *hverfa af himni heiðar stjörnur*
> *geisar eimi ok aldrnari*
> *leikr hár hiti við himin sjalfan ...*
> 59 *sér hon upp koma öðru sinni*

---

[33] Christine Fell, 'Perceptions of transience' in M Godden and M Lapidge (eds), *The Cambridge Companion to Old English Literature* (Cambridge, 1993) p 178.
[34] See footnote 20, above.
[35] Fell, p 177.

> *jörð ór ægi iðjagræna*
> *falla forsar flygr örn yfir*
> *sá er á fjalli fiska veiðir*
> [The sun grows black. The earth sinks gently into the sea.
> The heavens turn, bright stars choked by smoke and fire.
> Terrible flames leap into the sky ... Afterwards, I see the
> earth rising from the sea, forever green. An eagle soars over
> rushing fall, hunting for fish from the fells.]

The only similarity between the ruin poems of the Anglo-Saxons and the Eddic poetry of the Scandinavians lies in the Germanic preoccupation with fate, but fate as perceived by the Anglo-Saxons was quite different from fate as perceived by their non-Insular brethren, and for good reason. There are no stone-age megaliths or Roman cities to be found in greater Germany or Scandinavia. The Germanic tribes who peopled these lands looked out over a physically and temporally continuous landscape and must have seen in those fields and forests the same homeland they might have imagined their distant ancestors enjoying. The Anglo-Saxons, however, operated within a landscape made claustrophobic by the material survivals of ruined civilisations and to them, unlike their Viking neighbours, fate was entropic. In this belief lies the key to understanding the significance of ruin as sign in Anglo-Saxon literature.

To the tribal Anglo-Saxons, *wyrd* was an axiom. Scholars of Anglo-Saxon poetry previously argued that the emphasis placed on this *wyrd* in the Anglo-Saxon poems indicated their early composition, but the current trend in scholarship is to press for later origins. If this is true, then the great bulk of Anglo-Saxon literature evinces the failure of Christianity to erode that axiom to any real degree.

Attempts by the Church to subordinate the power of *wyrd* to that of God are also evident, although not in any of the *wésten* poems, but the logical failure of that hypothesis was clearly apparent to thinking Anglo-Saxons and it is certainly dealt with explicitly in poems such as *The Fates of Men*. If God wields *wyrd*, the poet seems to ask, then why do the innocent suffer?

Anglo-Saxon literature, however, also evinces another, probably indigenous, attempt to ameliorate the entropic certainly of *wyrd*, the reassurance of *eorlscipe* [honour]. *Wyrd* was powerful, but the Anglo-Saxons took comfort in community and in the sure knowledge that through the performance of duty or the achievement of honour, some form of immortality might be gained, albeit the immortality of name. This immortality of name, the *æftercweðendra*, would be celebrated within the mead-halls where the community gathered and the power of *wyrd* was, at least momentarily, checked. It was this belief that made the horror of ruin so palpable to the Anglo-Saxons.

The poems of ruin take from the audience even that last hope, for in them not only are the mead-halls destroyed and the fraternities dead, but even their memories are erased. No-one remains to tell of these people, to recite their king-lists, or to praise their heroes.

The landscape of the ruin poetry is barren, stark and — most significantly — uninhabited. Apart from the *ðyrs* [giant, demon ?] and a number of serpents, nothing lives in the Grendel-mere. So powerful is this *wésten* injunction against habitation that deer, we are told, fleeing from hounds, prefer to take their chances with the baying pack rather than enter the swamp.[36] Nor are the *wésten* of *The Wanderer*, *The Wife's Lament* or the *Cotton Gnomics* inhabited. In *The Ruin* even the voice of the narrator is absent; the poem is told without human agency in any form.

The images of these poems, like those used to describe *wyrd* itself, are redolent with ice and frost and bitter winds. In *The Wanderer* the buildings stand *winde biwaune ... hrime bihrorene hryðge* [ll 76–77 — wind blown, frost covered, storm swept], while *The Ruin* talks of *hrim on lime* [l. 4 — frost on the mortar]. There is no coincidence, either, in the poet's choice of half-lines in the section that finishes the description of the ruins in the *Cotton Gnomics* — *wyrd byð swiðost winter byð cealdost* [l 5 — *wyrd* is strongest, winter is coldest]. The metaphoric winter threatens and nothing will survive it.

The deep, dead sea
In turning to the metaphoric winter, the reader is pressed to make one final observation about the Anglo-Saxon motif of *wésten*, and that relates to the comparison that might be made between the wasteland and the deep, dead sea. Keeping in mind that the primary horror of the *wésten* for the Anglo-Saxon audience lay not in its climate but in its solitude, we find several points of similarity between *wésten* and *sæ* [sea].

Both *The Wanderer* and *The Seafarer* describe a sea that is fiercely cold, vast and overpowering. This marine landscape is as barren as any terrestrial *wésten* — indeed the poet of *The Seafarer* juxtaposes the verdancy of the fields with the barrenness of the ocean — and just as uninhabited. Save for a few solitary birds, there are no other life forms on the waves' surge, and the sailors who venture out upon it are tormented constantly by memories of the homes and families they have left ashore. There are also ruins in the sea.

Both poems mourn the lot of a lone seafarer in an open boat subject to the ocean's whims. Alone and psychologically naked, these men sort constantly — almost compulsively — through the things that brought them happiness once, but which exist no longer. They remember generous lords

---

[36] *Beowulf*, ll 1368-1372.

and warm halls, but they remember too how these lords passed under the earth and how the halls fell, and they can trace the genesis of their present hardships back to that moment. The ruins of the sea are ruined memories — the mead-halls are transformed into *cearselda* [halls of sorrow] *gecunnad in ceole* [explored — but also understood — in a boat].[37]

Both poems also employ an identical description of this oppressive landscape: in both the sea is *hean*.[38] *Hean* is not an easy word to understand and any attempt to explain it must rely heavily on context. It carries with it both the sense of lowly, abject or despised or, paradoxically, raised or exalted. The first meaning is possibly the elder, as evidenced by the Gothic *hauns* (also meaning abject or despised) but in the poems at hand the word carries a sense both of depth and of oppressive power.

It must be understood that the early Germanic sense of being despised rested intrinsically upon the actions of the subject of the verb as well as the object. Thus *heannes*, as used in the Northumbrian Gospels, carried as much a sense of treading down as it did of being downtrodden.

Subsequently, the boatmen of *The Seafarer* and *The Wanderer* struggle against the depth and power of the ocean — a power whose oppressive nature is apparent in the text. This power produces in the narrator of *The Wanderer* a state of mind described in identical terms to the sea itself:

23 ... *ond ic hean þonan*
wod wintercearig ofer waþema gebind
24 *sohte sele dreorig* ...
[... and I, abject, thence departed in the grief of winter over
the waves' expanse, sought halls of sorrow ...]

It is this sentiment which leads to one final comparison between the *wésten* and the *sæ*. Compare the lines above to those of *Beowulf*, describing the fear experienced by the thief as he leads Beowulf into the dragon's *wésten*. The thief:

2408 ...*sceolde héan ðonon*
wong wísian hé ofer willan going
2410 *tó ðæs ðe hé eorðsele ánne wisse*
[... must, abject, thence guide them to the plain against his
will, to the very barrow ...]

These similarities are not coincidence. They are evidence of the indelible link between the wasteland and the deep, dead sea in the poetry and in the minds of the Anglo-Saxons.

---

[37] *The Seafarer*, l 5. See also *seledreorig* in *The Wanderer*, l 25.
[38] *The Wanderer*, l 82; *The Seafarer*, l 34.

Conclusion

Ruin stood as a potent metaphor in the Anglo-Saxon mind. The origin of the motif lies in an historical and material reality — the ruined cities of Roman Britain — but the metaphysical reality that it came to embody struck much deeper at the core of Anglo-Saxon society. In the Anglo-Saxon mind, the ruins that littered their physical landscape served to represent the certainty that their civilisation would one day also collapse and that everything their culture had achieved would stand as nothing.

This *wésten* must have created, in the minds of those who embraced it, a considerable existential dilemma, invalidating as it does the primary institutions of early Germanic tribalism: the importance of appropriate action and the cohesiveness of the people. Just how the Anglo-Saxons dealt with this dilemma, however, remains to be illuminated.

The absorption of Cornwall into Anglo-Saxon England

Lyn Olson

There is a sort of methodological envelope around this paper, which will take us to rather unexpected places in the first part, but rest assured that most of it is about Cornwall. I liked the theme of the conference 'Between Intrusions' not least because it could be related to my favourite lecture for my favourite undergraduate course 'The World Turned Upside Down'. I liked it still more when I realised that the first intrusion was the Roman conquest rather than the coming of the Saxons, because this problematises the so-called Age of Migrations, the *Völkerwanderungszeit*, 'folks'-trekking-time', the period of maximum transition examined in the aforementioned course. In the aforementioned lecture I propose two models of cultural contact and change: the 'intrusive' model and the 'ethnogenesis' model. These are illustrated by a fortunate coincidence: that in 1988 when we celebrated the Australian Bicentennial, the government of Austria, not Australia, marked the many-times-over centennial of the origin of the Bavarians, in a period rather arbitrarily put between 488 and 788.[1]

The European settlement of Australia is an extreme case of the intrusive model. There was a time when Bennelong and all his ancestors looked out into what would be Sydney Harbour and saw no European ships, until one day the ships were there and European settlement began. This sort of radical intrusion brought devastating disease, as also to the Americas, but not in the so-called barbarian invasions of Europe. The case of the Bavarians of that time is very different. They lived across the Danube from the great Roman fortress of Regensburg and helped to garrison the Danubian defences. With the disintegration of these in the fifth century, the Bavarians made Regensburg the centre of their power, expanding their control over all sorts of people, who ultimately took on their identity. This is a striking case of ethnogenesis where identity grows up on the spot, is set by the ruling group, and is fluidly taken from it by others.[2] Now if, I tell my students, the intrusive model on the one hand and the ethnogenesis model on the other are borne in mind when considering the Migration Period of

---

[1] *Die Bajuwaren* (Hefte zur bayerischen Geschichte und Kultur 6, Munich, 1988).
[2] My understanding of ethnogenesis owes a lot to what Edward James has to say about ethnic formation in *The Origins of France: From Clovis to the Capetians, 500-1000*, (New Studies in Medieval History, Houndmills and London, 1982) ch 1 'The Peoples of Gaul'. Cf Andrew Gillett (ed), *On Barbarian Identity: Critical Approaches to Ethnicity in the Early Middle Ages* (Turnhout, 2002).

European history, then the reality of ethnic change will often lie in between the two, but on the whole closer to the ethnogenesis model.

We turn here to Cornwall, but will return to these concepts at the end of the paper in drawing conclusions about Cornwall's absorption into Anglo-Saxon England. This paper will present fragments of evidence that when taken together indicate that the Cornish 'establishment' — landed layfolk and leaders of the church — was absorbed into the English system, and in the process re-oriented itself to the new English power. This happened back in the ninth and tenth centuries, so that by the Norman conquest of England in the second half of the eleventh century, Cornwall was another English county, although one with distinctive features including first and foremost its occupation by a distinctive ethnic group: the Cornish.

These people had Celtic roots in southwest Britain, where in the pre-Roman Iron Age lived the Dumnonii, on whom the Romans typically based a large unit of local/regional government, the *civitas Dumnoniorum* with its urban centre at *Isca Dumnoniorum* or Exeter. When the Roman Empire crumbled in the fifth century, the western *civitates* (city territories) of Roman Britain went it alone. In the sixth century according to Gildas[3] and the beginning of the eighth century in a letter of Aldhelm[4] — these are contemporary references — there was a kingdom of Dumnonia ruled respectively by Kings Constantine and Gerent (Gerontius). There are a few more Latin loans to Cornish personal nomenclature which can be seen in place-names such as Trevillian, the farmstead of Milian from Latin Aemilianus, and in the name of the Cornish king Entenin from Antoninus.[5] Such names represent an earlier accommodation with Rome, which after its conquest offered Celtic aristocracies a place in at least local power, opportunities which the Celtic aristocrats took up. So did the English to the Cornish establishment, but with, I will argue, more respect for Cornish institutions admittedly similar to their own.

---

[3] *De Excidio Britanniae* II.28-9 (ed and trans M Winterbottom, History from the Sources 7, London and Chichester, 1978) pp 29f (English) and 99f (Latin).

[4] *Epistolae* 4, ed R Ehwald, *Aldhelmi Opera* (Monumenta Germaniae Historica, Auctores Antiquissimi 15, Berlin, 1919) pp 480-86.

[5] J E B Gover, 'The Place-names of Cornwall' (unpublished typescript, 1948, deposited in The Royal Institution of Cornwall Library, Truro) p xvii, lists several; the entry for Trevillian is on p 90 and cf O J Padel, *Cornish Place-Name Elements* (English Place-Name Society 56/57, Nottingham, 1985) p 232. 'Milian clericus' witnessed a manumission by King Edmund (d 946) recorded in the Bodmin Gospels (ed M Förster, 'Die Freilassungsurkunden des Bodmin-Evangeliars' in N Bøgholm *et al* (eds), *A Grammatical Miscellany offered to Otto Jespersen on his Seventieth Birthday* (Copenhagen and London, 1930) p 85). For Entenin see L Olson, 'Saint Entenyn', *Cornish Studies* 3 (1975) pp 25-28.

In the course of the English conquest of southwest Britain the Celticity of Devon — the name derives from Dumnonia — but not of Cornwall was lost. The eighth century was remembered in the Anglo-Saxon Chronicle for great fights against the West Welsh, which is what the southwest Britons were called from the point of view of Wessex, as opposed to the North Welsh, those of Wales. The first reference to the Cornish people (in Latin) in the later eighth century is specifically as enemies of the English.[6]

By the reign of Egbert in the early ninth century the English were definitely in the ascendancy. 'King Egbert ravaged from east to west against the West Welsh' in 815.[7] In the year 838,

> a great ship army came to the West Welsh, and they joined together and were fighting against Egbert king of Wessex; then he heard that, and went with a force, and fought against them at Hingeston Down, and there put to flight both the Welsh and the Danes.[8]

Back in 825, 'There was a battle of the Welsh and the men of Devon at Galford'.[9] This is a very old and long-standing distinction. I have heard in Cornwall someone from Devon say that Sir Francis Drake was 'a Devon man' and of course people refer to themselves as Cornish. By 981, we read that 'Padstow was ravaged, and the same year much damage was done everywhere near the coast, both among the Devon men and among the Welsh'.[10] The Vikings were now the common enemy, but the distinction

---

[6] Grant by King Cynewulf of Wessex of land in Somerset to the church at Wells '*pro amore Dei, et pro expiatione delictorum meorum, necnon, quod verbo dolendum est, pro aliqua vexatione inimicorum nostrorum Cornubiorum gentis*' (ed Walter de Gray Birch, *Cartularium Saxonicum: a Collection of Charters relating to Anglo-Saxon History* I (London, 1885) no 200). This paper owes a great deal to an unpublished timeline of documented events in the Saxon Conquest of Cornwall assembled by Oliver Padel, whose translations I often follow.

[7] '7 þy geare gehergade Ecgbryht cyning on Westwalas from easteweardum oþ westewearde' (ed Janet M Bately, *The Anglo-Saxon Chronicle* 3: MS A (Cambridge, 1986) p 41).

[8] '*Her cuom micel sciphere on Westwalas, 7 hie to anum gecierdon 7 wiþ Ecgbryht Westseaxna cyning winnende wæron. þa he þæt hierde 7 mid fierde ferde 7 him wiþ feaht æt Hengestdune 7 þær gefliemde ge þa Walas ge þa Deniscan*' (ed. cit., pp. 42-3). Alliances of British both with and against the Vikings are paralleled in later ninth-century Brittany (see N S Price, 'The Vikings in Brittany', *Saga-Book* XXII.6 (1989) 319-440).

[9] '*Her wæs Wala gefeoht 7 Defna æt Gafulforda*' (ed cit, p 41).

[10] '*Her on þys geare wæs Sancte Petrocesstow forhergod; 7 þy ilcan geare wæs micel hearm gedon gehwær be þam særiman ægþer ge on Defenum ge on Wealum*' (ed Katherine O'Brien O'Keeffe, *The Anglo-Saxon Chronicle* 5: MS C (Cambridge, 2001) p 84).

between the men of Devon and the Welsh, that is the Cornish, was still made. We will go on to see how it was preserved.

In the middle of the ninth century comes the first indication of the incorporation of the Cornish establishment into the English system in the absorption of Cornwall into Anglo-Saxon England. Sometime between 833 and 870 a profession of obedience to the archbishop of Canterbury was made by 'the humble Kenstec, elected though unworthy to the [or 'an'] episcopal seat among the people in Cornwall in the monastery which in the language of the Britons is called Dinuurrin'. (This is the first use, again in Latin, of the name 'Cornwall'.) It was normal for bishops in England to profess obedience to the archbishop of Canterbury, but the description of the see here is not normal and the names of the bishop and his base are Cornish. The Latin is *'humilis licet ad indignus episcopalem sedem in gente Cornubia in monasterio quod lingua Brettonum appellator* [sic] *Dinuurrin electus'*.[11] A *gens* is not just a band of people, it is an ethnic group.

At the end of the ninth century King Alfred the Great was influential but peripheral in Cornwall. He hunted there and had lands in the northeast. In 891 three of what one is tempted to call 'retro' Irishmen set themselves adrift to go where God would take their boat and thus landed 'among the Cornish, and then went immediately to King Alfred'.[12] For our purposes it is interesting that they went to him, and this is the first occurrence of *Cornwalas*, that is 'Welsh' combined with a regional name only seen before in Latin forms. (It is also very interesting that these Irish fetched up in Cornwall to provide concrete and contemporary evidence of contact across the Irish Sea culture-province.) Alfred's son King Edward at the beginning of the tenth century established the see of Crediton and gave its bishop three Cornish manors, Pawton, *Cællincg* (the place is not certainly identified) and Lawhitton, 'that there every year he should visit the Cornish race, to stamp out their errors, for previously as much as they could they resisted the truth and did not obey papal decrees'.[13] The errors are unspecified; it is very late for problems over the date of Easter or form of the tonsure.

---

[11] Canterbury, Cathedral Library, Register A, fo 292; see L Olson, *Early Monasteries in Cornwall* (Woodbridge, 1989) pp 51f. As I pointed out in note 6 there, an interesting parallel with the language of Kenstec's profession is the following entry at the end of a list of Galician sees and parishes in the late sixth-century Spanish *Parochiale*: '*Ad sedem Britonorum ecclesias que sunt intro Britones una cum monasterio Maximi et que in Asturiis sunt*' (ed P David, *Études Historiques sur la Galice et le Portugal du VIe au XIIe Siècle* (Lisbon, 1947) p 44). Both concern fringe British areas of a regular diocesan church.

[12] '*7 þa comon hie ymb .vii. niht to londe on Cornwalum 7 foron þa sona to Elfrede cyninge*' (ed Bately, p 54).

[13] '*ut inde singulis annis visitaret gentem Cornubiensem . ad exprimendos eorum errores . Nam antea in quantum potuerunt veritati resistebant . et non decretis apostolicis*

Athelstan is the English king traditionally associated with really bringing Cornwall under English control.[14] We hear no more of Cornish kings after Dungarth, king of Cornwall, who drowned in 875 according to the *Annales Cambriae* (not yet a contemporary source)[15] and who may indeed be the Doniert on an inscribed stone from east Cornwall.[16] An entry for 927 in the Anglo-Saxon Chronicle says that King Athelstan 'brought under his rule all the kings who were in this island: first Huwal, king of the West Welsh', but this is certainly Hywel Dda of Wales, the usage of 'Westwala' here perhaps reflecting the perspective of England rather than just Wessex, for which Wales really was to the north.[17] 'King Ricatus', thought to have been the last known Cornish ruler, has recently been dismissed by Professor Charles Thomas as an incorrect reading of the Penzance Market Cross![18]

In 936 Athelstan was responsible for the second indication of the incorporation of the Cornish establishment into the English system in the absorption of Cornwall into Anglo-Saxon England. Again, this concerns the church: quoting from a contemporary charter, 'Therefore I restore and willingly bestow into perpetual possession all the territory of the episcopate, that is of Blessed Germanus, bishop of the region of Cornwall'.[19] Athelstan, according to the record of another charter, made Conan bishop in the church of St Germans,[20] or as what may be an interpolation in a late tenth-century letter of Archbishop Dunstan of Canterbury put it, 'gave to Conan the

---

oboediebant' (ed Birch, *Cartularium Saxonicum* II (London, 1887) no 614, a tenth-century forgery).

[14] A forthcoming publication by Oliver Padel on this elusive subject is eagerly awaited.

[15] '*Dungarth rex Cerniu, id est Cornubiae, mersus est*' (ed and trans J Morris, *Nennius. British History and The Welsh Annals* (History from the Sources 8, London and Chichester, 1980) pp 46 [English] and 90 [Latin]); the phrase offset by commas is not in the earliest manuscript.

[16] R A S Macalister, *Corpus Inscriptionum Insularum Celticarum* II (Dublin, 1949) no 1054; cf H O'Neill Hencken, *The Archaeology of Cornwall and Scilly* (London, 1932) pp 268, 271.

[17] '*7 ealle þa cyngas þe on þyssum iglande wæron he gewylde, ærest Huwal Westwala cyning, 7 Cosstantin Scotta cyning, 7 Uwen Wenta cyning, 7 Ealdred Ealdulfing from Bebbanbyrig*' (ed G P Cubbin, *The Anglo-Saxon Chronicle* 6: MS D (Cambridge, 1996) p 41). But for William of Malmesbury in the passage cited below, 'Occidentales Britones' are the Cornish and 'Aquilonalibus Britannis' are the Welsh.

[18] *And Shall These Mute Stones Speak? Post-Roman Inscriptions in Western Britain* (Cardiff, 1994) pp 298-300; cf Macalister, no 1051, and Hencken, p 268.

[19] '*Omne igitur territorium episcopatus uidelicet Beati Germani Cornubiae regionis Episcopi ... restituo et in diocesi[m] perpetuam libenter offero*' (an immunities clause has been omitted here). See O J Padel, 'Two New Pre-Conquest Charters for Cornwall', *Cornish Studies* 6 (1978) 26-27.

[20] '*Ex charta donat. Æthelstani. Erexit in Ecclesiam S. Germani quoddam Conanum Episcopum anno Dni. 936 nonis Decembris*' (Leland, *Collectanea* (ed Hearne, 3rd ed, London, 1774) I.75).

bishopric as far as the Tamar flowed'.[21] Finally, at the end of the tenth century the endorsement of an important charter specifies that the diocese is 'in the province of Cornwall', '*bisceoprice in to Wielcynn*', literally the Welsh people.[22] In other words, the designation of the diocese is, like that in the profession of Kenstec, tied to an ethnic group. Likewise the name of Bishop Conan is Cornish. So too of his base of operations as we know from other tenth-century documents that the Cornish name for St Germans was *Lannaled* or *Lanalet*.[23] There is evidence that this was a well-established Cornish religious house near the English border rather than an English outpost inside Cornwall.[24]

Athelstan's charter speaks of restoration but not of Dinuurrin where Kenstec's see was, which is probably to be located at Bodmin, site of the monastery of St Petroc.[25] Now Dunstan's (interpolated?) letter says that Conan was given all Cornwall, and the aforementioned charter from the end of the tenth century says specifically that the place and governance of St Petroc was to be in the power of the bishops of Cornwall at St Germans. So there was an English fiddle here perhaps, but if so one using Cornish institutions. That the Cornish bishopric was eventually ended when Cornwall was placed under the bishop of Exeter in the eleventh century[26] only proves my point that for a while space was made for the Cornish ecclesiastical establishment within the English system. There will be a little more to say about the names of the bishops presently.

The third indication of the incorporation of the Cornish establishment comes in the middle of the tenth century, when a few property charters suggest that a place was also made for Cornish landed gentry within the English system. In the time of King Athelstan Count Maenchi gave Lanlovern (modern Lanlawren) to St Heldenus (that is, Hyldren): the gift of Cornish property to a Cornish saint by a nobleman with a Cornish or Breton name, but done in the Saxon land at Athelney (an Anglo-Saxon royal site)

---

[21] '*þa gelamp hit þæt æpestan cing sealde cunune bisceoprice ealswa tamur scæt . þa gelamp þæt eadræd cyng het daniel 7 betæhte þa land swa him witan ræddun . inn to sce germane to þam bisceopstole*' (ed A S Napier and W H Stevenson, *The Crawford Collection of Early Charters and Documents now in the Bodleian Library* (Oxford, 1895) 19). On this and the two previous documents see Olson, *Early Monasteries*, p 63f, and K Jankulak, *The Medieval Cult of St Petroc*, (Studies in Celtic History 19, Woodbridge, 2000) pp 61f.

[22] A W Haddan and W Stubbs (eds), *Councils and Ecclesiastical Documents relating to Great Britain and Ireland* I (Oxford, 1869, repr 1964) p 683. On this charter of King Æthelred the Unready, dated 994, which is also referred to in the next paragraph, see Olson, *Early Monasteries*, pp 74-78, and Jankulak, pp 62-65.

[23] See Olson, *Early Monasteries*, pp 60-63.

[24] See Olson, *Early Monasteries*, pp 60-66.

[25] See Olson, *Early Monasteries*, pp 52-56, 73; Jankulak, chs 2, 4.

[26] J M Kemble (ed), *Codex Diplomaticus Aevi Saxonici* IV (London, 1846) no 791.

as the charter states, which shows a perception of difference. The deed also contains a phrase, 'into perpetual possession', which is characteristic of Cornish charter form.[27] Of a number of other charters for property in Cornwall from the Anglo-Saxon period, two deserve especial mention. Both are grants in the late 960s by King Edgar, the first to Wulfnoth Rumuncant of land at Lesneage and Penare in the parish of St Keverne and the second to Ælfeah Gerent and his wife Moruurei of land at Lamorran, and Trenowth in Probus parish.[28] The men have double names, English followed by Cornish; the wife has a Cornish name, and serves to confirm that Ælfeah Gerent is just one person, besides being a typical example of the participation of women in landholding in the tenth century.

These are Cornish gentry orienting themselves to the new, English power. Their double names are highly significant; another example is Wulfsige Cemoyre, Bishop of Cornwall in the same period,[29] who followed Bishop Daniel, himself likely a Cornishman given that Old Testament names seem to be characteristic of the British. In the next generation, the names would be just English. This undermines traditional statements about the replacement of Cornish by English landholders based on the presence of very few with Cornish names in all of Domesday Book, which, it must be remembered, indicates tenure at the end of the Anglo-Saxon period as well as in 1086.[30] In other words, the names have changed but not the families, strongly contrasting with the result of the Norman conquest which really did see a nearly complete replacement of the English landholding aristocracy by the Normans, a few Bretons and so forth.

The fourth and final indication of the absorption of Cornwall into Anglo-Saxon England is the fate of the early monasteries of Cornwall on which I did my doctoral thesis.[31] The Domesday Book also shows Cornish landholding religious establishments assimilated to English minster churches. However, their distribution, mostly toward the west and

---

[27] See Padel, 'Two New Pre-Conquest Charters', pp 20-26; Olson, *Early Monasteries*, pp 63, 78-84. 'Menki vicecomes' signed a Redon charter in tenth-century Brittany (P-H Morice (ed), *Mémoires pour servir de preuves à l'histoire de Bretagne* I (Paris, 1742)).

[28] Ed Birch, *Cartularium Saxonicum* III (London, 1893) nos 1197, 1231. See Padel, 'Two New Pre-Conquest Charters', p 23 and especially p 25, note 22; Olson, *Early Monasteries*, p 108; L Olson and O J Padel, 'A Tenth-Century List of Cornish Parochial Saints', *Cambridge Medieval Celtic Studies* 12, (Winter 1986) pp 68f.

[29] See W M M Picken, 'Bishop Wulfsige Comoere: an Unrecognised Tenth-Century Gloss in the Bodmin Gospels', *Cornish Studies* 14 (1986) 34-38.

[30] Caduualant (Cadwallon) is an example right where one would be expected: holding a manor on the north coast of Cornwall from St Petroc before the Norman Conquest (Exchequer Domesday, fo 120d, ed C and F Thorn from a draft translation by Oliver Padel, *Domesday Book* 10: Cornwall (Chichester, 1979)).

[31] Olson, *Early Monasteries*, esp the Conclusion. The map reproduced in this article is from p xiv.

especially along the mid-section of the north coast of Cornwall, but also thinly in the east and north where English settlement was most intensive and influence most readily exerted, shows their different origin (see map).

By the time of the Norman conquest, the conference's second intrusion, Cornwall was another English county, but with distinctive features from its Celticity going back before the Roman conquest, the conference's first intrusion. It had become a Celtic part of England. This had advantages: as Charles Thomas pointed out,[32] 'Cornwall is the most fully documented region of "Celtic" Britain' in the period under consideration, which can be seen from evidence cited in this paper. It also, as Oliver Padel has shown, had an important and little-recognised role in transmitting the Arthurian legend to the Normans and beyond.[33]

I conclude with reference to the intrusive and ethnogenesis models of cultural contact and change, presented at the outset of this paper. There was an undoubted English intrusive presence in Dumnonia and Cornwall. 'Ravaged from east to west' is pretty intrusive. On the other hand, the taking on of English names by the landowning Cornish is activity characteristic of ethnogenesis — it's the way the process worked. It seems to me that people of some means who know what side their bread is buttered on and naturally gravitate to power are most apt to identify with the ruling group. Yet the Cornish identity was preserved. Why? This paper has presented evidence that a place was made for the Cornish 'establishment' and even Cornish institutions as Cornwall was absorbed into Anglo-Saxon England, at just the time to have made a crucial difference in how people thought of themselves and how they were regarded by others.

To the harder question of why this policy was followed, which of course was asked after the conference paper, a couple of tentative answers may be made. First, Cornwall may not have been considered worthy of a lot of trouble. The Romans perhaps felt the same way, as we are singularly uninformed about their conquest of the region and have evidence that its romanisation was very limited.[34] William of Malmesbury's statement in the twelfth century that King Athelstan had expelled the Cornish — *contaminata gens*! — from Exeter and set the River Tamar as their boundary comes to mind: beyond the Tamar, compromises could be

---

[32] C Thomas, 'The Character and Origins of Roman Dumnonia' in C Thomas (ed), *Rural Settlement in Roman Britain* (London, 1966) p 97, note 151.

[33] O J Padel, 'Geoffrey of Monmouth and Cornwall', *Cambridge Medieval Celtic Studies* 8 (Winter 1984) 1-28; *idem*, 'Some South-Western Sites with Arthurian Associations' in R Bromwich *et al* (ed), *Arthur of the Welsh* (Cardiff, 1991) 229-48; *idem*, 'The Nature of Arthur', *Cambrian Medieval Celtic Studies* 27 (Summer 1994) 1-31.

[34] Thomas, pp 74-98; H Quinnell, 'Cornwall during the Iron Age and the Roman Period', *Cornish Archaeology* 25 (1986) 111-34.

made.[35] Second and more positively, Viking-Age Britain was a multicultural place. Asser testifies to how welcoming King Alfred was to foreigners[36] and King Athelstan not only gave refuge to Bretons driven out by the Vikings but gave vital assistance to them in recovering their homeland.[37] In contrast to the nation-building of early Wessex,[38] the policy of the later English kings of necessity may have been more inclusive of difference.

Map: Sites of early monasteries in Cornwall

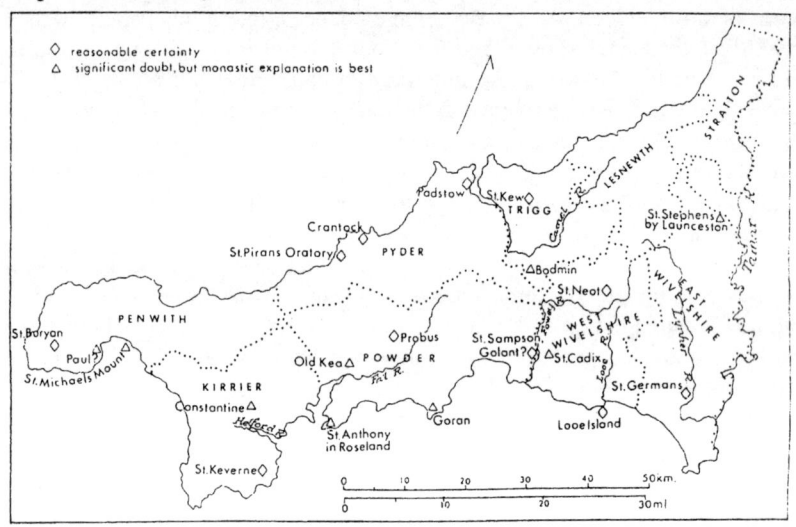

---

[35] *Gesta Regum Anglorum* 134.6 (ed and trans R A B Mynors, completed by R M Thomson and M Winterbottom, Oxford and New York, 1998) pp 216f.

[36] 'He similarly applied himself attentively to charity and distribution of alms to the native population and to foreign visitors of all races, showing immense and incomparable kindness and generosity to all men, as well as to the investigation of things unknown. Wherefore many Franks, Frisians, Gauls, Vikings, Welshmen, Irishmen and Bretons subjected themselves willingly to his lordship, nobles and commoners alike, and, as befitted his royal status, he ruled, loved, honoured and enriched them all with wealth and authority, just as he did his own people' (*Life of King Alfred* 76, trans S Keynes and M Lapidge, *Alfred the Great* (Harmondsworth, 1983) p 91).

[37] See Price. Evidence for cultural links between Cornwall and Brittany around this time may somehow be relevant. The List of Cornish Saints (Olson and Padel) is added to texts written in Breton Caroline script, and the Bodmin Gospels is a Breton manuscript brought to Cornwall.

[38] Martin Grimmer made this suggestion after my conference paper, with specific reference to King Ine.

The metalworking tradition in medieval Irish law

Neil McLeod

The medieval Irish law texts distinguish between the blacksmith (*goba*), who worked with iron, and the metal-wright (*cerd*), who worked with copper, bronze, silver and gold. No doubt most metal-wrights worked (at least most of the time) with copper and its alloys (all covered by the word *uma*),[1] and so were frequently referred to simply as *umaidi* (basiers). Sometimes the word *cerd* is used in a narrow sense[2] to distinguish workers in precious metal (the gold- and silver-smiths) from those making humbler, more utilitarian products of copper and bronze (the *umaidi*).[3]

A judge was expected to be an expert in the laws relating to the proper payment due to craftsmen for their work. The Old Irish law-text *Uraicecht Becc* states that even the lowest-ranking judge 'is competent to give decision for the folk of arts and crafts in regard to justice, in the estimation and measurement of the work and the remuneration of every product.'[4] There was an Old Irish text which dealt with the law relating to metal-working. This text was called *Bretha Creidini*. Unfortunately, no copy of it now exists.

This lost law-book is referred to in a Middle Irish text[5] which lists the areas of law in which a judge should be competent. This list is composed largely of the titles of legal texts. Among these are the titles of four texts which deal with the law relating to specific professions. These four texts are *Bretha Déin Chécht* ('the Judgements of Dian Cécht'), *Bretha Goibnenn*

---

[1] The term *uma* covers copper, bronze, and brass. See B G Scott 'Varia II', *Ériu* 32 (1981) 153-57, p 156.

[2] On the other hand, *cerd* is also used more generally to mean 'artisan'. Much the same is true of the word *sáer* (a word with a very wide range of meanings). *Sáer* could be used of artisans generally, or in a specific sense restricted to master-builders. (The latter had noble status - in other contexts *sáer* means simply 'noble'.)

[3] A section of the Old Irish status-text *Uraicecht Becc* awards the same noble honour-price to 'blacksmiths (*gobainn*) and brasiers (*umaidi*) and whitesmiths (*cerda*) and physicians (*leigi*)': cf D A Binchy (ed), *Corpus Iuris Hibernici [CIH]* (Dublin, 1978) Vol v 1613.9f. The translation is that of Eoin MacNeill in 'Ancient Irish Law: the law of status or franchise', *Proceedings of the Royal Irish Academy* 36 C (1923) 265-316, p 278. (An inferior translation of *Uraicecht Becc* may be found in Vol v of R Atkinson, W N Hancock, T O'Mahoney and A G Richey (eds), *Ancient Laws of Ireland [AL]* (Dublin, 1865-1901). This particular passage occurs at p 94.19f.)

[4] The translation is by Eoin MacNeill in 'Status or franchise', p 278.

[5] This text is known as *Urcuilte Bretheman*. It is to be found in *CIH* Vol vi 2102.31-2103.32. See Fergus Kelly, *A Guide to Early Irish Law* (Dublin, 1988) p 268.

('the Judgements of Goibniu'), *Bretha Creidini* ('the Judgements of Creidine'), and *Bretha Luchtaini* ('the Judgements of Luchtaine').[6]

Each of these texts is named after a mythical exponent of a particular profession. Dian Cécht was the chief physician of the *Túatha Dé Danann*, Goibniu was their master blacksmith, Creidine their master metal-wright, and Luchtaine (sometimes called Luchta) their master wood-wright.[7]

It is likely that these four texts all belonged to the third and final part of the great Old Irish legal collection called the *Senchas Már*.[8] Of these four texts, only one remains intact. This is *Bretha Déin Chécht*, which deals with the regulation of the medical profession.[9] It concentrates mainly on the fees that a doctor should charge for treating various injuries. These fees vary with the nature of the injury, the area of the body injured, and the status of the victim.

Only a few scraps of *Bretha Creidini* have survived. However, we have good evidence that it took much the same approach as *Bretha Déin Chécht*. That is, it dealt with the legal standards for manufactured metal items, and the way in which the fees for metal-work were to be calculated. In this paper I will sketch out the information currently available on these topics. First, however, some notes on the status of the metal-wright.

Status and duties of metal-wrights

It is no coincidence that the physician, the wood-wright, the blacksmith and the metal-wright are singled out for particular treatment in the laws. These four professions were considered to be high-status callings, sometimes mentioned in the same breath as those of ecclesiastical learning and of poetry. (In his book *Pagan Past and Christian Present*, Kim McCone discusses two examples in which all these arts are closely linked. In the Latin Life of St Daig of Inishkeen, Mochtae predicts that the young saint has the power of healing, and that he will 'artistically make very many utensils of iron and bronze as well as gold and silver' and that he will 'write very many volumes most excellently'. In Cormac's Glossary the goddess Brigit is represented in the form of three sisters who are respectively the

---

[6] *CIH* Vol vi 2103.11-12.
[7] Cf T F O'Rahilly, 'The Three Gods of Craftsmanship' in *Early Irish History and Mythology* (Dublin, 1946) 308-317.
[8] See Liam Breatnach, 'On the original extent of the *Senchas Már*', *Ériu* 47 (1996) 1-43, p 33.
[9] The text is edited and translated by D A Binchy in *Ériu* 20 (1966) 1-66. For a discussion of its provisions see Neil McLeod, 'The Not-so-exotic Laws of Dian Cécht' in G Evans, B Martin and J Wooding (eds), *Origins and Revivals: Proceedings of the First Australian Conference of Celtic Studies* (Sydney, 2000) 381-99.

goddess of poetry, the goddess of medicine, and the goddess of smithcraft.[10])

We know from the Old Irish status text *Uraicecht Becc* that blacksmiths and metal-wrights had an elevated status in Irish society (though their status was less than that of master-builders,[11] and far short of that achievable by poets and ecclesiastics).

Many craftsmen had a lowly status, equal to that of the small farmer known as the *ócaire*. This was true, for example, of the 'chariot-wright and house-carpenter' and even of decorative craftsmen such as the 'cloth-figurer and relief carver'.[12] The master blacksmith and metal-wright, on the other hand, enjoyed noble status, being ranked on a par with the lowest grade of the nobles, the *aire déso*.[13]

The metal-wright attained the status of 'master' (*ollam*) when he was recognised as being an expert in his trade. In his 1923 translation of *Uraicecht Becc*, Eoin MacNeill suggested that the popular assembly of each kingdom would officially recognise one of its metal-wrights as being at the head of his profession in that kingdom, and that it was only this person who attained the status of *ollam* and with it the same rank as the *aire déso*.[14] However, the glosses to *Uraicecht Becc* assume that all proficient metal-wrights attain noble status, and this seems also to be the import of a passage in the Old Irish text of *Uraicecht Becc*. That passage declares that all 'blacksmiths and bronze-wrights and metal-wrights and physicians' are entitled to the same honour-price 'even though it be an *ollam* of those [crafts]'.[15]

Master craftsmen normally passed on their art by taking on apprentices. The master-apprentice relationship was similar to the relationship between a fosterer and their foster-child: where the training was given in return for a fee, the master became liable for the crimes of the apprentice.[16]

In Irish society, status as a metal-wright required more than the possession of the requisite skill, just as the status of a farmer required more than the possession of the requisite amount of land. The farmer lost his

---

[10] Kim McCone, *Pagan Past and Christian Present in Early Irish Literature* (Maynooth, 1990) pp 161f. For the role of the carpenter see *ibid*, pp 163-65.
[11] See Kelly, *A Guide to Early Irish Law*, pp 61f.
[12] See MacNeill, 'Status or franchise', p 280.
[13] The passage translated by MacNeill at 'Status or franchise', p 278 (§39) appears to give the master metal-wright an honour-price slightly higher than that of the *aire déso*. However, MacNeill was working from the published transcription of a single manuscript which happens to be defective at this point (compare *CIH* v 1613.12 with *CIH* ii 706.29 and iv 1234.33).
[14] MacNeill, 'Status or franchise' p 281 note 3.
[15] *CIH* v 1613.11f; cf MacNeill, 'Status or franchise', p 278 §39 [= *AL* v 94.19f].
[16] See *CIH* iv 1433.37-43 [= *AL* iv 236.15-24].

status if he did not make productive use of his land,[17] and likewise the metal-wright was required to make productive use of his skill in order to maintain his status. So, for example, the commentary to *Uraicecht Becc* notes that a smith is entitled to his noble honour-price if someone steals his tools; but there is a proviso to this. He is only entitled to the honour-price due to a smith if he accepts and performs work for everyone in the surrounding area, or as the commentary puts it, 'only if he has performed work for each neighbour of the four neighbours who surround him'.[18] The smith was required to take work from the public at large. The refusal to perform such work deprived him of his honour-price.

The normal expectation appears to be that metal-working (in precious metals and copper alloys) on the one hand, and blacksmithing on the other, were distinct trades.[19] This emerges, for example, from a passage of commentary which is found in the law-text known as *Bretha Étgid*. That commentary[20] explains that visitors cannot be held liable for accidentally damaging items of gold or silver or copper, if those precious items are left where one would not expect to find them. The commentary quotes directly from another Old Irish text, *Críth Gablach*. *Críth Gablach* points out that one would not expect to find such objects strewn about the floor of a house.[21] The commentary to *Bretha Étgid* states that one would not expect to find objects of gold or silver or copper in a blacksmith's forge. No compensation can be sought by those foolish enough to leave such precious objects there, or in a mill, or a kitchen or a drying kiln.

The commentary goes on to say that one *would* expect to find items of gold or silver or copper in the forge of a metal-wright (*cerd*). And so the person who damages such items is liable for that damage. This suggests that the trades of the blacksmith and of the metal-wright were usually distinct.

The same impression arises from another commentary dealing with the names for vessels of various sizes. These names varied according to whether they were made of iron or of copper. This commentary declares that

> the blacksmith in his trade does not make a bright-metal vessel like the silversmith, but he makes a dark-metal vessel.

---

[17] See Neil McLeod, 'Property and honour-price in the Brehon law glosses and commentaries', *Irish Jurist* 31 (1996) 280-95, p 284.
[18] *CIH* v 1593.18-19: '*acht mo dorigni in oigdi do gach coimaitech duna cethri comaichthib uilid uimi*' [= *AL* v 14.32-33].
[19] See B G Scott, *Early Irish Ironworking* (Belfast, nd [1990?]) pp 184f.
[20] *CIH* i 268.6-11 [= *AL* iii 190.25-192.8].
[21] Lines 221-23 in D A Binchy's edition of *Críth Gablach* (Dublin, 1941). For a translation, see MacNeill, 'Status or franchise', p 292.

The 'Patrick's *ól*' of the blacksmith is the same size as the 'mead *ól*' of the silversmith.[22]

However, the glosses to *Uraicecht Becc* do acknowledge that some craftsmen could combine expertise in several crafts. A man who was a master of both blacksmithing and metal-working could, on this basis, double his honour-price; from the four cows paid to the *aire déso* to eight cows.[23] Nevertheless, this total is still short of the honour-price of the next grade of lord, the *aire tuíseo*, who had an honour-price of nine cows.[24]

Legal standards for manufactured metal items
We have already seen that legal commentary indicates that there were particular volumes prescribed for certain cups and cauldrons, one of these measures being the 'Patrick's *ól*'. The basic '*ól*' was a vessel containing 144 eggshell-measures of liquid. The 'Patrick's *ól*' was twelve times larger than this, and the 'Fenian *ol*' was a large vat twice as big again. (We know from the text *Críth Gablach* that every prosperous commoner was expected to own a range of vessels of various sizes: 'a cauldron with its spit and supports, a vat in which a measure of ale can be brewed, a cauldron for ordinary use, small vessels, ... a washing trough and a vessel for head bathing, a tub .... [and] a copper cauldron in which there is room for a boar'.[25])

The terms 'true *ól*', 'Patrick's *ól*', and 'Fenian *ól*' appear to have been used of iron vessels. However, the first two of these had their counterparts in terms of volume among the silver vessels made by the metal-wright.

Table 1: Relationship between iron and silver vessels

Volume	Blacksmith	Metal-wright
144 eggshells	true *ól*	cup
x 12	Patrick's *ól*	mead *ól*
x 2	Fenian *ól*	

What is particularly significant here is that the law recognised certain standard capacities for vessels sold under certain legal descriptions. The corollary to this is that an action for damages (or for fraud) could be brought if the vessel sold did not match the legal standard under which it was marketed.

---

[22] The translation is taken from my discussion of this passage in Neil McLeod, 'The *ól*: standard drinks in medieval Irish law', *Australian Celtic Journal* 5 (1996-97) 5-8, p 6.
[23] *CIH* v 1616.1-2 [= *AL* v 104.18-20].
[24] *CIH* v 1600.33 [= *AL* v 44.18].
[25] See D A Binchy, *Críth Gablach*, lines 174-77, 197.

There were also legal standards governing the fitness of vessels for the use for which they were purchased. If a vessel leaked, or a metal tool was defective, the contract of purchase could be rescinded. The supplier was deemed to have breached an implied condition that their goods would be, to use the modern parlance, of 'merchantable quality'. The commentary to the text on contracts, *Di Astud Chor*, mentions a couple of the common defects in metal items for which rescission could be obtained: 'For articles of iron: rustiness and being without sharpness. For articles of copper: being breached or cracked.'[26]

The same commentary indicates that there were legal standards of purity in the case of precious metals. Among the defects in items made of precious metals it lists: 'Concealed deficiencies in gold: bronze or silver through it. A concealed deficiency in silver: bronze through it.' A further law-text, *Córus Iubaile*, provides that a purchaser has a period of three years in which to bring a legal action if a newly manufactured item of gold or silver does not meet its description. (In the case of second-hand items this 'limitation period' was only forty days.)[27]

Valuation of metal
We have some interesting legal material on the relative value of metals. For example, there is a fascinating account in the legal manuscripts (as yet untranslated) of a large payment of compensation awarded to the legendary King Conchobar Mac Nessa.[28] This compensation appears to have been awarded as a result of an incident which occurred in the lead up to the *Táin Bó Cuailgne*. The payment is described as having been levied upon Fergus mac Roích,[29] apparently after he exacted revenge on two sons of Traiglethan, following the murder of the sons of Uisliu.[30] Fergus despatched his victims while they were on the green (*faithche*) of Emain Macha, and thus under King Conchobar's protection.[31]

The compensation is said to have included a payment of ten brooches of gold, each worth ten ounces of (unworked) silver, and ten brooches of

---

[26] Neil McLeod, *Early Irish Contract Law* (Sydney, nd [1992]), p 304.
[27] *ibid*, p 48.
[28] This commentary is to be found at *CIH* v 1572.26f.
[29] *CIH* v 1572.24: '*Ictha eneclann Concobuir .i. is uad rohicad in eiric, o Fergus*'; '[These amounts] were paid as the honour-price of Conchobar, ie it is by him the *éric* was paid, by Fergus'.
[30] See the episode in 'The Exile of the Sons of Uisliu' translated by Jeffrey Ganz in *Early Irish Myths and Sagas* (Penguin Books, 1981) p 263.
[31] Cf *CIH* v 1573.15-16: '*dias urrad romarbad ann sin for comairc[i] Concubair*'; 'It was a pair of local freemen who were killed in that case while under the protection of Conchobar.' Note also the (somewhat different) version at *CIH* iv 1295.31f which states that part of the payment was due for the defilement of Emain Macha ('*a n-eillned na h-emna*': *CIH* iv 1295.35).

silver, each worth two ounces of (unworked) silver.[32] This suggests that, at the time this commentary was written, gold was worth only five times more than silver. If that is the case it may point to a relative abundance of gold in Ireland. For example, it appears that the roughly contemporary laws of Norway (c thirteenth century) valued gold at eight times the value of silver.[33]

The compensation paid to King Conchobar involved finished brooches. There is other evidence that suggests that the normal rate of exchange between unworked red-gold and silver in Ireland was as low as 1:4. A small piece of commentary imported into one version of *Uraicecht Becc*[34] states that the restitution fine for illegally appropriating an otter was eight times that paid for a salmon. The restitution fine for the otter is said to be '*screpal deargoir no ceithre screpail airigid*', 'a scruple [weight] of red-gold or four scruples of silver'. This gives a ratio of only 1:4 as between red-gold and silver.

However, Thomas Charles-Edwards[35] states that the normal rate of exchange between gold and silver in Western Europe c AD 700 appears to have been 1:12. He also claims that there is a passage in the Irish laws in which an ounce of red-gold is equated with 12 cows.[36] Since the (milk) cow is valued in the laws at one ounce of silver,[37] this too would give a gold:silver ratio of 1:12. However, Charles-Edwards has omitted the first word of the phrase in question. This is printed in *CIH* i 149.1 as '*ni.*' with a suspension stroke over the *i*.[38] However, an inspection of the microfilm of this manuscript reveals that this word consists rather of three instances of the letter *i* (with hair strokes clearly visible above each, so that there is no possibility of an '*n*'). The word is simply '*.iii.*', 'three'. (The initial dot occurs at the end of the previous line; in *CIH* it is treated as if it were a fullstop at the end of the final word in that line.) What we have, then, is '*.iii. uinge dergor ar da buaibh decc*', 'three ounces of red-gold for twelve

---

[32] *CIH* v 1572.33-35.
[33] See Laurence Larson, *The Earliest Norwegian Laws* (New York, 1935) p 421.
[34] *CIH* vi 2266.39-42. This passage is noted by Fergus Kelly, *Early Irish Farming* (Dublin, 1997) p 594.
[35] Thomas Charles-Edwards, *Early Irish and Welsh Kinship* (Oxford, 1993) p 482, citing P Grierson, 'The Monetary Reforms of 'Abd al-Malik: their Metrological Basis and their Financial Repercussions', *Journal of Economic and social history of the orient*, 3 (1960) p 263, reprinted in Grierson, *Dark Age Numismatics* (London, 1979).
[36] See also Kelly, *Early Irish Farming*, p 594.
[37] See Neil McLeod, 'Interpreting Early Irish Law: Status and Currency (Part II)', *Zeitschrift für celtische Philologie* 42 (1987) 41-115, p 90.
[38] Apart from a missing dot at the beginning, this would be the standard abbreviation for *ni ansae*, 'it is not difficult' - a phrase often used to introduce answers to questions. But there is no question in this passage.

cows'. This in fact confirms a ratio of red-gold to cows, and of red-gold to silver, of 1:4.

A surviving fragment of the lost *Bretha Creidini* supplies some more information on the relative value of metals. This fragment consists of a short quotation from the Old Irish text, and a small piece of commentary. It notes that miners use the term *dírna* ('*denarius*') to refer to a measure of ore equal to two ounces. This is contrasted to the use of the term *dírna* by metal-wrights, who use it to refer to six ounces of refined metal.

The commentary to *Bretha Creidini* then gives the relative values of a number of metals. Red copper is said to be of the same value as tin. White-copper is twice as valuable as red copper or tin, and four times the value of lead. Silver is twenty-four times more valuable than white-copper. This commentary uses the standard system of valuation based on the ounce of refined silver. The ounce of silver was divided into 24 scruples. A scruple was divided further into three silver pennies. As the commentary explains, a silver penny weighed the same as eight grains of wheat.[39]

As no complete translation of this fragment of *Bretha Creidini* is yet in print, I provide one below.[40]

> *Dinnra clasaighe .i. tommhus bís [a]con lucht claides in clais: di uingi is ed ata inn .i. boingidh mein in uma. Dinnra cerda do dergumha: .ui. uinghi ann & screpal a logh. Ma finnumha, is da screpall a logh. Pinginn is fiu in uingi finnumha, & lethpinginn is fiu an uingi derguma. & comtrom uingi airgid i[s] sí an uingi uma. & comlogh in derguma & in sdan. & ocht ngrainni cruithnechta comtrom na pinginni airgid. & .iiii. dirnna do luaidhi ar dinnra finnuma, ar is do luaidhe donither in tath.*
>
> The miner's *denarius*, ie a measure which is in use among the folk who excavate the trench: it weighs two ounces. [The miner,] ie he extracts the copper ore.
>
> The metal-wright's *denarius* of red-copper: it weighs six ounces and its value is a scruple. If it be white-copper, it is two scruples in value [= six pennies]. An ounce of white-copper is worth a penny, and an ounce of red-copper is worth a half-penny.

---

[39] On silver as currency, see further McLeod, 'Interpreting Early Irish Law: Status and Currency' p 89; and Kelly, *Early Irish Farming* pp 593-98.

[40] This passage is noted by Liam Breatnach ('On the original extent of the *Senchas Már*', *Ériu* 47 (1996) 1-43, p 33) and discussed by Fergus Kelly in *Early Irish Farming*, p 586. I do not understand why Kelly believes that 'it is difficult to reconcile all the equivalences which are given' in this commentary. They seem consistent to me.

And the ounce of silver is of the same weight as the ounce of copper. And red-copper is equal in value to tin. And eight grains of wheat are equal in weight to the penny of silver. And four *denarii* of lead [are equal in value] to the *denarius* of white-copper, for it is of lead that the soldering is made.

Iron was, of course, of considerably less value than gold or silver, or even copper. According to a commentary to *Uraicecht Becc*,[41] six ounces of smelted iron was worth only one-twelfth of an ounce of unworked silver.

From these passages of commentary we can construct the following table of values and equivalences for refined metals.

Table 2: Relative values of metals

1 ounce of gold	=	4 ounces of silver
1 ounce of white-copper	=	1/24 of an ounce of silver (= 1 penny)
1 ounce of red-copper	=	1/48 of an ounce of silver (= 1 half-penny)
1 ounce of tin	=	1/48 of an ounce of silver (= 1 half-penny)
1 ounce of iron	=	1/72 of an ounce of silver
1 ounce of lead	=	1/96 of an ounce of silver

Fees

A passage of commentary in *Uraicecht Becc* deals with the status of lawyers. The lowest class of lawyer was the *glasaigne* ('fettering-' or 'ensuring-advocate').[42] The *glasaigne* supervised the procedures that ensured legal rights were enforced or brought to court. The basic grade of *glasaigne* supervised the legal process known as distraint. But an upper grade of the *glasaigne* specialised in the law relating to the professions.

> (CIH 1614.12-13) *In glasaigni is ferr .i. eolus aicgi i mbrethaib creithine & luctine & dian [c]echt & goibnend ...*
> The best ensuring-advocate, namely the one who has expertise in [the law to be found in] *Bretha Creidini* and *Bretha Luchtaini*, and *Bretha Déin Chécht* and *Bretha Goibnenn* ...

This commentary goes on to confirm that all four of these texts focussed on the level of fees chargeable by the professions they regulated. Most interestingly, it is anticipated that the members of each profession might themselves be well-versed in the laws relating to that profession.

---

[41] The commentary is to be found at *CIH* v 1593.37f [= *AL* v 16.28f].

[42] See Liam Breatnach, 'Lawyers in Early Ireland' in D Hogan and W N Osborough (eds), *Brehons, Serjeants & Attorneys* (Dublin, 1990) 1-13, p 11 note 42. [Cf *AL* v 100.25f.]

(*CIH* 1614.14-18) *Acht masa eolaig*[43] *na daine-sin fein ina n-eladnaib, .i. credhini agus luchtine agus cach arcena, nó a loigidecht a n-elaedan in tan bit ig mesemnugud fora n-oigdib, is iat fodein do breth doib brethi uir gach ní dlegaid, agus is iat-sum do beth 'na fhiadnaissi arna rucad imarcraid.*

If those [professional] people are themselves experts in [the Judgements concerning] their professions, ie [the Judgements] of Creidine and of Luchtaine and the others, or in the fees chargeable in their profession when they are valuing their works, it is they themselves [who are] to give a decision on every thing to which they are entitled, and it is these [advocates] who are to act [merely] as witnesses, so that too much is not charged.

It was only if the wright was not sufficiently knowledgeable to do this that the *glasaigne* stepped in to perform the calculation.

(*CIH* 1614.18-19) *Munab eolaig iad immurgu fodein ina n-eladnaib agus i loigiacht a n-eladan, is iad-sum do breth brethi doib, agus oili deg do breth doib.*

However, if those [professionals] are not experts in [the Judgements concerning] their professions and the fees chargeable in their professions, it is these [advocates] who are to give a decision on them, and a twelfth [of the fee they pronounce] is to be awarded to them.

The fact that the *glasaigne* stood to cream off one-twelfth of the professional's fee would of itself be an incentive to the professional to master the law governing the setting of those fees. This may well explain why two ancient legal texts dealing with doctors, *Bretha Crólige* and *Bretha Déin Chécht*, were preserved in a fifteenth-century collection of medical works. D A Binchy (who edited both texts) thought that this was rather 'curious' because he assumed that the scribe who assembled the collection 'must have been unlearned in the law'.[44] But if professionals had to know the law in order to set their fees (and so avoid having to hire a *glasaigne* to do it for them), then they may have been more familiar with the legal texts governing their profession than Binchy was inclined to give them credit for.

The commentary to *Uraicecht Becc*[45] gives us some important information on the way that blacksmiths set their fees. From the six ounces of iron, the blacksmith produced a vessel worth three ounces of unworked silver. The blacksmith's fee for doing this was one ounce of silver, a third

---

[43] *CIH* mistakenly prints 'col*aig*'.
[44] D A Binchy, *Bretha Crólige, Ériu* 12 (1938) 1-77, p 1.
[45] *CIH* v 1593.37f [= *AL* v 16.28f].

of the value of the finished item. (It should be noted that the customer had also to supply or, more probably, pay for the six ounces of iron used.)

From another passage of commentary[46] we learn something of the basis on which metal-wrights set their fees. The metal-wright received one-twelfth of the finished value of a gold ring which he made, and one-ninth of the value of a larger piece such as a gold headband. This important scrap of information is supplied as an illustrative aside in a passage of commentary otherwise dedicated to the valuation of pigs. It is likely that much more is available for the careful researcher to retrieve from the mass of surviving legal materials.[47]

---

[46] *CIH* i 175.33f [= *AL* ii 414.20f]. This commentary is found in *Cáin Lánamna*, the text regulating marriage.

[47] The potential to extract riches from these materials has been well illustrated for us by Brian Scott's masterful use of a legal commentary to *Bretha Étgid* to recover intricate details about the blacksmith's trade. See B G Scott, 'An Early Irish Law Tract on the blacksmith's forge', *The Journal of Irish Archaeology* 1 (1983) 59-62, and B G Scott, *Early Irish Ironworking*, pp 191f.

The blood-feud in medieval Ireland

Neil McLeod

In 1452, Owen O'Neill,[1] over-king of much of Ulster, led a large raid against the English settlers in the Fews (in the south of modern Co Armagh). O'Neill's forces were swollen by those of his ally Thomas Maguire,[2] the king of Fir Manach (roughly equivalent to modern Co Fermanagh). This raid started off well. O'Neill's party carried off plenty of booty and turned for home in high spirits. But then something unexpected happened. One of Owen's sons (Owen junior), together with a party of Maguires, had been pursuing booty in the region of Cloch-an-bodaigh.[3] They unexpectedly encountered a strong force which gave chase. Owen O'Neill's own forces came to the aid of his son. But the pursuers wrought havoc, slaying (among many others) Sorley MacDonald,[4] the leader of O'Neill's crack Scottish mercenaries. According to the *Annals of Ulster*, 'O'Neill went to his stronghold that night in great wrath'.[5]

Had the pursuing force been made up entirely of English settlers, O'Neill might only have been shocked and humiliated by the unexpected rout. But the ranks of the pursuers included warriors from Oriel (roughly equivalent to modern Co Monaghan), whose king, Hugh MacMahon,[6] had been installed by O'Neill himself.[7] O'Neill was furious with MacMahon for the treacherous part his people had played in this reversal. And yet that fury did not translate into a vengeful invasion of Oriel. Instead, the matter was settled by the payment of legal compensation. MacMahon paid an *éric* fine for the killing of MacDonald, and made another payment for his dishonouring of O'Neill.[8]

---

[1] Properly, Eoghan Ua Neill. I have used English versions for the names here only because I know that large numbers of unfamiliar names can be confusing. To those who are familiar with them (and to the protagonists themselves), I apologise.
[2] Tomás Óg Mag Uidhir.
[3] Given what followed, it is possible that Cloch-an-bodaigh was in or near Oriel (Ir Oirghialla), the territory of the MacMahons. Some suspicion must fall on the Maguire forces in all of this. The state of antagonism between the Maguires and the MacMahons is illustrated by further clashes in that same year (1452) and again in 1457. See W Hennessy and B MacCarthy (eds), *Annals of Ulster [AU]* (Dublin, 1887-1901) Vol iii pp 177 (slaying of the sons of Philip Maguire) and 189 (war).
[4] Somhairle Mór Mac Domhnaill.
[5] *AU* iii p 177.
[6] Aedh Mag Mathghamhna.
[7] For O'Neill's role in securing the kingship for Hugh see *AU* iii p 157 note 1.
[8] *AU* iii p 177.

How was it that this incident was settled in this way? Why didn't it escalate into open warfare? From MacMahon's point of view the factors working towards a peaceful settlement are rather obvious. The political and military reality was that O'Neill was in a position to mount a superior force. It is true that O'Neill's raiding party had been routed when taken by surprise in foreign terrain. But if it came to full scale war, Hugh MacMahon was in real danger of suffering a terrible defeat. O'Neill had installed MacMahon as king of Oriel; and what O'Neill had given he might well take away. Furthermore, there were advantages for Oriel in remaining a secure member of the powerful O'Neill over-lordship. There was safety in numbers, and Oriel's neighbours were hostile to it. It is not hard to see why Hugh MacMahon was prepared to make reparations.

What then of O'Neill? Why did he accept a legal settlement for this politically damaging and personally insulting behaviour? Again, there are a number of factors that may have come into play. His over-lordship of Oriel had distinct advantages for him as well; it meant tribute, political support, and military aid, all of which were important to him. If he decimated Oriel in revenge, he would dramatically reduce its value to him.

Furthermore, O'Neill's great aim was to subjugate the powerful kingdom of Tir Conaill (roughly equivalent to modern Co Donegal) and thereby achieve the uncontested over-kingship of all of Ulster. To this end he was bent on building alliances, not destroying them. He could ill-afford an escalating confrontation with Oriel. Inevitably, any action against Oriel would distract and weaken his own forces.

And yet the most important factor of all appears to have been the role played by Owen O'Neill's son, Henry.[9] It was Henry who brokered the settlement between his father and MacMahon.[10] Earlier in the year Henry had shown his brilliance as a tactician by engineering a power struggle within Tir Conaill and backing the forces of revolt against its king, Naughton O'Donnell.[11] O'Donnell had been slain and the kingdom spilt in two. Henry had himself taken a share of the spoils, regaining the border kingdom of Cenél Moein and a castle on the river Finn.[12] All of Henry's good work in the west (and his newly won possessions there) was put at risk by the trouble brewing on the eastern front.

The advantages of reaching a compromise with MacMahon may have seemed more obvious to Henry than they did to his father. After all, Henry had not himself received any personal slight, nor himself felt the

---

[9] Enri Ua Neill.
[10] *AU* iii p 177.
[11] Nechtain Ua Domhnaill.
[12] These had been won for Henry by his father in 1442, but appear to have fallen back into O'Donnell's hands in the interim.

humiliation of the rout of the raiding party. Henry had nothing to gain from a revenge attack, and a lot to lose.

It may have been difficult for Owen O'Neill to have settled his grievance with Hugh MacMahon had Henry not intervened. To have struck an agreement directly with Hugh might have made Owen look weak; it risked giving the impression that Hugh was on equal bargaining terms with him. The loss of face that Owen had suffered in the rout would have been exacerbated rather than assuaged. However, an entirely different complexion was given to the settlement when it was secured by Henry's intervention. Owen was able to maintain the role of the justifiably wrathful lord, well able to crush the upstart Oriel, but instead listening wisely to the counsel of a very able and well-loved son. Now the legal compromise appeared magisterial, and there was no question of Hugh having wrested it from him.

Those 'in great wrath' often find it difficult to refrain from lashing out, especially when they have the means to do so against a vulnerable opponent. When they do restrain themselves, it is usually because the interest they have in exacting revenge is outweighed by other interests. Those competing interests are to be found in the bonds of unity that link them to the object of their wrath (here, the bonds of over-lordship) and, much more importantly, in the bonds of unity that link them to a wider complex of social relationships (here, the interests of Owen's own kinsmen and allies in maintaining the pressure on Tir Conaill). These rather obvious truths also lie at the heart of the widely distributed legal institution known as 'the blood-feud'.

The blood-feud

In the Brehon law of Ireland, the word used for the blood-feud is *digal*, 'vengeance'. Put at its simplest, the blood-feud entails the right of an entire kin-group to avenge attacks against any of its members. And the legitimate object of that vengeance is the entire kin-group of the attacker.

In the Old Irish period (c AD 700), the relevant kin-grouping was the *derbfhine*. The *derbfhine* was a four-generation group of adult males, consisting of a common ancestor (usually dead) and his sons, grandsons and great-grandsons. In the time of the Middle Irish commentaries (c AD 1100 and following) the relevant kin-grouping may have shrunk to that of the *gelfhine*.[13] The *gelfhine* was a three-generation group of adult males consisting of a common ancestor and his sons and grandsons.[14]

The law-text *Córus Fine* ('the lawful order of the kin') contains considerable information on the rules regulating the blood-feud in medieval

---

[13] See for example D A Binchy (ed) *Corpus Iuris Hibernici [CIH]* (Dublin, 1978) Vol ii 733.37-38.

[14] See Neil McLeod, 'Kinship', *Ériu* 51 (2000) 1-22.

Ireland. The original Old Irish portion of this text (written around AD 700) states that 'there are four forgivable slayings of a man'. One of these is 'avenging [the murder] of a man of the *derbfhine*'.[15]

However, the blood-feud can be bought off: vengeance is avoided if the kin of the victim is paid the appropriate legal compensation. The major part of that compensation is known as the *corpdire*, 'body-fine'. The body-fine was a fixed payment equal to six *cumala*. The *cumal* was an amount equal in value to three milking cows.

According to *Córus Fine*, the body-fine for a slain man is divided among his *derbfhine* as follows. Two *cumala* go to his father, and two more to his sons. The fifth *cumal* is paid to his brothers, and the sixth to the other members of the *derbfhine*.[16] The important point to realise here is that the members of the kin-group stood to gain financially if the matter was settled.

This right to share in the compensation for murder came with strings attached. There was a corresponding duty to take revenge if the compensation was not forthcoming. And there was a flip-side to this as well. If a member of your own kin-group committed murder, you were a legitimate target for revenge. And if this revenge was bought off by compensation, then *in some cases* you had to pay your share of that financial liability.

However, the kin-group's liability to *pay* compensation should not be overstated. In most cases the kin-group was protected from direct financial loss: the main liability for payment rested with the offender himself. The upshot of this is that the kin-group of a murderer had a lot to lose if they didn't settle (they became legitimate targets for revenge), and little to lose if they did settle (the financial burden was borne by the offender).

There is a real danger that modern readers will miss the point of the blood-feud entirely. They will do this if they think of the blood-feud as a private vendetta waged between rival gangs, each bound by blood-relationship, from which the participants can extricate themselves by the payment of legal compensation. Firstly, the 'default setting' in the blood-feud is *not* vengeance. Rather, the blood-feud is, paradoxically enough, itself the mechanism which ensures that vengeance is avoided. Secondly, the blood-feud is *not* a state of private vendetta at all. It is a legal institution, and its operations are governed by law. If a kin-group purports to exact vengeance outside the legal rules governing the feud, then that vengeance is itself unlawful and punishable as out-and-out murder.

---

[15] I give the text and translation of the full passage below (under the heading 'Adoption').

[16] The Old Irish passage in question is transcribed at *CIH* ii 742.4-9.

The rules which govern the blood-feud channel the fury of the kin, and they channel it towards peaceful resolution. We need to look more closely at those rules to see how the institution worked in practice.

Sanctuary and protection
My focus in this paper is on murder, but let's consider first the procedure in the case of negligent injury. For even here there is a danger that the anger of the victim's kin will spill over into violence.

The procedure in cases of negligent injury is set out in *Críth Gablach*, a law-text of the early eighth century. According to *Críth Gablach*, the negligent party immediately and publicly appointed a surety to guarantee that he would pay the costs arising from his negligence.[17]

However, the law appreciates that this guarantee might not be enough to satisfy the victim's family in the heat of the moment. The next step then, according to *Críth Gablach*, is that the surety 'leads him from the scene of bloodshed into a noble sanctuary for his protection. He protects him against the onslaught of a host.'

Notice that the guilty party immediately seeks to involve a neutral third party. This third party takes him to a place of protection, and himself guarantees the payment of lawful amends.

The 'noble sanctuary' to which the surety took the negligent injurer may well have been the surety's own homestead. Every common freeman could offer such protection within his homestead (though only to persons of his own social grade or lower). If the person under protection was attacked there, it was an offence against the protector himself.[18] This right of protection was akin to the protection a freeman gave to his own dependants and to guests who were staying in his home. Again, any attack on them was an attack on him.

Such attacks had to be paid for with an amount equal to the protector's full honour-price if they occurred within his homestead. The normal homestead was the 'ring-fort', a group of buildings surrounded by a circular embankment. There was also a precinct outside the ring-fort within which attacks yielded half of the protector's honour-price. In the case of common freemen, this precinct was measured by the distance the freeman

---

[17] The Old Irish passage is found in D A Binchy (ed), *Crith Gablach* (Dublin, 1941) p 3 lines 52-62. There is a translation by Eoin MacNeill in 'Ancient Irish Law: the law of status or franchise', *Proceedings of the Royal Irish Academy* 36 C (1923) 265-316, p 285. [An inferior translation may be found in R Atkinson, W N Hancock, T O'Mahoney, and A G Richey (eds), *Ancient Laws of Ireland [AL]* (Dublin, 1865-1901) Vol iv p 303.]

[18] See Fergus Kelly, *A Guide to Early Irish Law* (Dublin, 1988) pp 140f.

could cast a spear from the gate of his ring-fort; a very literal measure of the protection he could give.[19]

In the case of nobles, the inner precinct extended beyond the central ring-fort to include the green (*faithche*) surrounding it.[20] The outer precinct was also of much larger extent, measured by multiple spear-casts (the number of spear-casts increasing for each successive grade of noble).[21]

The legal institution of 'sanctuary' was not designed to allow the guilty to escape justice. Rather it was designed to allow accused persons who were prepared to 'offer law' to escape unlawful vengeance. (We saw in *Críth Gablach* that the flight to the sanctuary was preceded by a promise to submit to law.)

The person who had reached the sanctuary of a protector's homestead had a limited time period within which to agree to settle the matter legally. The amount of time allowed varied with the status of the person acting as his protector.[22] Once that time period had elapsed, the sanctuary (*comairce*) had no legal validity if an offer of law (*taircsiu*) had not been made. In the absence of such an offer, the fugitive from justice could be slain in the sanctuary without giving rise to any lawful claim from his protector. Indeed, anyone who sheltered a fugitive in order to help him escape justice had themselves committed an offence. (As an accessory after the fact they were guilty of the same offence the fugitive had committed.[23] They also lost their honour-price.[24])

The purpose of sanctuary, then, was to provide a cooling-off period. It allowed time for the rage of the victim's kin to subside a little, and it provided a breathing space within which cooler heads might intervene and prevail.

For those closely related to the victim, honour might well demand that the perpetrator be slain. It might be very hard indeed to accept payment meekly from the killer who had brutally robbed them of a loved one. However, once a neutral party (the protector) is interposed, the rage of the victim's kin can be deflected without a loss of honour. They can accept guarantees of payment without appearing to have yielded to the offender himself. The protector, then, is an intermediary, and it is often the protector who communicates the offer of law.[25]

---

[19] See Binchy, *Críth Gablach* lines 217-220 = MacNeill, 'Status or franchise', p 292 [and *AL* iv 313].

[20] *CIH* vi 2111.17-27.

[21] *CIH* iv 1431.37-1432.2 = *AL* iv 227.

[22] For example, the period was three days where the protector was a prosperous farmer (*bóaire*), fifteen days where he was the noble ranking second to the king (*aire forgill*): *CIH* vi 2067.38-2068.6.

[23] *CIH* v 1557.31-32; iv 1367.11-12.

[24] *CIH* i 15.5; 15.7-8 = *AL* v 175.18f.

[25] *CIH* vi 2149.6-7.

Furthermore, an attack on the accused while he is under lawful protection is not just an attack on the honour of the protector. It renders the original law-suit against the accused killer void. Worse still, the protected killer (or his kin) can now sue for the unlawful revenge attack made upon him.[26]

Why were the legal rules governing the blood-feud obeyed?
We have seen that there were rules governing the institution of the blood-feud. To break those rules was to break the law. However, this begs the question, were those rules obeyed? After all, there was no equivalent to the modern police force, employed to prosecute law-breakers. Why mightn't independent kins take vengeance where they could?

The problem with that last question is its premise: that kin groups were independent units. Certainly, at first blush, it is easy to mistake them for autonomous units. After all, the members of a kin-group were all linked by blood. The kin-group was 'agnatic', ie children joined the kin of their father, not the kin of their mother. Land was passed down through that agnatic kin-group. While each member of the kin owned their own individual parcel of that land while they lived, it was nevertheless ultimately 'kin-land' (*fintiu*). An individual kinsman was not able to sell his land without the consent of his kin, and such consent would not be easy to obtain. If a man died without sons his land was divided among the other members of the kin-group. The kin-group had a 'contingent' or 'reversionary' ownership in all of the kin-land. It is therefore easy, though erroneous, to think of the agnatic kin-group as a self-contained and self-perpetuating unit.

Certainly kinship was central to medieval Irish society, and no more so than in the law governing the inheritance of land. But if a 'society' were made up of truly independent kin-groups it would not be a 'society' at all. It would degenerate into a conglomeration of petty clans, constantly at war with each other. Indeed, at the 'national' level there is evidence of just that kind of disunity. Ireland consisted of numerous petty kingdoms, a good number of which were either independent or loosely grouped together in small, and often short-term, alliances or over-kingships. Where such kingdoms were not bound by a mutuality of political interests, they fought and plundered each other.

However, *within* each kingdom, the bonds for unification were much stronger than they were at a 'national' level. And where you have a community of inter-related interests you will find law. The role of the law is to prevent competition among the various interest groups that make up a society from spilling over into violence. Law keeps the myriad tensions in

---

[26] *CIH* iv 1367.18-24.

society in balance. (This balancing act need not involve any guarantee of equality or fairness: the primary role of law is to preserve the social structures on which a society is based.)

In any society people will have competing interests in the way scarce material resources are distributed. People will form alliances with those who share a mutual interest in that matter. In any society there will also be competition for sexual partners. Again, alliances will be formed, quite possibly with a somewhat different group of persons. At times of crisis, or at peak periods of agricultural work, still other alliances will be formed with neighbours, based on further sets of mutual interests. Those with competing interests in some areas will have a mutuality of interests in other areas: for example, in the protection of the kingdom from external predators. It is in this way that a society is held together; by a web of intersecting mutual interests.[27] An important aspect of the operation of law is the way it regulates those alliances of mutual interest.

In Ireland, one of the most important alliances of mutual interest was the agnatic kin-group. But there were others of almost equal importance. Among these was the institution of clientship.

Clientship
Nobles acquired clients by distributing grants in the form of cattle. In return for these cattle, the client owed his lord annual renders of food and service.[28] Whole kin-groups might be in clientship to a single lord.[29] If his clients were caught up in a blood-feud, the lord had a vested interest in protecting them from reprisal attacks. The loss of a client meant the loss of a profitable unit of production.[30] The loss of a client also reduced the lord's status in the assembly of the freemen. And the failure of a lord to protect his clients from violence would not have formed the best advertisement for a lord seeking to expand his client base.

A lord also had an interest in encouraging his clients to accept compensation rather than seeking vengeance. If compensation was paid, the lord himself stood to gain a portion of it.[31]

---

[27] See Max Gluckman, *Custom and Conflict in Africa* (Oxford, 1956), especially chapter one, 'The Peace in the Feud'. Gluckman's analysis of Nuer society is the classic account of the functioning of the feud.
[28] See Kelly, *A Guide to Early Irish Law*, p 29.
[29] Cf Thomas Charles-Edwards, 'Kinship, Status and the Origins of the Hide', *Past and Present* 56 (1972) 3-33, p 18.
[30] The heirs of the dead client continued the service undertaken by their father: cf Thomas Charles-Edwards, *Early Christian Ireland* (Cambridge, 2000) p 74. However, the fact remained that the client-base of the lord had been reduced, especially if those heirs were already his clients.
[31] See Neil McLeod, 'Interpreting Early Irish Law: Status and Currency: Part II', *Zeitschrift für celtische Philologie* 42 (1987) 41-115, pp 110f.

The lord was a powerful individual, and the more powerful he was the more likely his interests were to span a number of different kin-groups. This would make conflicts between those kin-groups much less likely to degenerate into violence. A man would think twice about revenging an attack on a kinsman if it meant violating the interests of his own lord, and his lord would be keen to see the matter settled peacefully.

The maternal kin
Kinship is much less straightforward than it appears at first sight. In the important matter of inheritance, the relevant kin-group was certainly agnatic (ie calculated strictly through the male line). But kin-groups served important functions in addition to regulating the inheritance of land. In those other roles, the calculation of kinship was not so strictly agnatic. Bonds of kinship traced through female relatives also played a significant part.

Consider, for example, the definition of 'kin-slaying' (*fingal*) in early Irish law. This can be ascertained from an Old Irish Penitential which sets out the penance for that offence. This penitential shows that a person committed kin-slaying when they killed another member of their own agnatic *derbfhine*, or any relative within the same degrees of relationship among their mother's kin.[32]

Likewise, the obligations of the blood-feud extended beyond the agnatic kin-group. The 'four forgivable slayings of a man' listed in *Córus Fine* include 'the avenging [of the murder] of a son of one's kinswomen'. The sons of your kinswomen did not belong to your own kin-group; they belonged to the kin-groups of their own fathers. But the obligations of the blood-feud still applied. You had a role to play in avenging their deaths.

It needs to be borne in mind that the wives and mothers of each set of sons in a kin-group would come from a range of different kins, and that the daughters of each man of the kin-group could marry into (and bear sons for) yet another set of kins. Within the agnatic kin-group then, each individual would have links to quite an array of other such kin-groups.

Given the sparse population of early Irish kingdoms, it is not at all unlikely that many kin-groups would have some link via marriage with most of their neighbours. So if a member of one kin-group killed a member of another kin-group, it is not at all unlikely that some members of the victim's kin-group would feel uncomfortable about pursuing the blood-feud. For some of them revenge would involve killing one of their own in-laws. Those placed in that awkward position would have been inclined to urge the other members of their kin-group to accept legal compensation.

---

[32] See Neil McLeod, 'Kinship', *Ériu* 51 (2001) 1-22, pp 18-20.

Fosterage

There was another important form of kinship in Ireland. This was kinship through fosterage. Fosterage was a common institution. It involved parents sending their children to be fostered by another family. Often this would be done for a fee.[33] Almost always it would have been done with an eye to promoting or maintaining political or social links between the kin-groups involved. The familial bonds between a foster-child on the one hand, and his foster parents and foster-siblings on the other, were as strong as that which existed within his natural family.

Among the 'four forgivable slayings of a man' listed in *Córus Fine* we find 'avenging [the murder] of a foster-son of the kin'.

If a blood-feud involved two kin-groups linked by fosterage, it would be the more likely that it would be settled by compensation. There was a financial reason for this as well. If the matter was settled by compensation, the foster-father and foster-brothers of the victim were entitled to a separate payment for the loss of the foster-child.[34]

Adoption

Adoption was a further method of establishing familial links. When a man and his wife grew old, they looked to their sons to maintain them. But sometimes they had no sons, or what sons they had had predeceased them. Occasionally their sons were alive but refused to look after them. In such circumstances the reluctant sons might be disowned. In any of these cases, this left the elderly couple with adequate resources for their retirement, but a declining ability to manage them profitably. In such cases the elderly man could, with the consent of his kin-group, adopt a son from outside the kin.[35] This landless young man would then move into a small hut[36] on the property and maintain the elderly couple. In return he became a legal member of the old man's kin-group and was entitled on the couple's death to inherit land up to the value of seven *cumala*,[37] ie the land appropriate to a small farmer (*ócaire*).[38]

If a member of his adoptive kin-group was killed by a kin-group linked to his own natural relations, it is likely that the adopted kinsman (and

---

[33] See Kelly, *A Guide to Early Irish Law*, pp 86-90.
[34] *CIH* ii 438.5-439.18 = Rudolf Thurneysen, *Irisches Recht* Abhandlungen der preussischen Akademie der Wissenschaften 1931 Phil-Hist Klasse Nr 2 (Berlin, 1931), pp 19-20 (*Dire* §§20-21).
[35] See Kelly, *A Guide to Early Irish Law*, pp 103, 105. In *Early Irish Farming* (Dublin, 1997) pp 362, 367, Kelly makes the dubious assumption that the imported maintainer was a 'fosterson' rather than an 'adopted son'.
[36] Binchy, *Crith Gablach*, lines 98-102, gives a description of this hut.
[37] Kelly, *A Guide to Early Irish Law*, p 103 (citing, in footnote 24, *CIH* ii 534.26-28 = *AL* iii 52.17-20).
[38] See Binchy, *Crith Gablach*, line 91.

even his new relatives) would be reluctant to pursue vengeance against them.

If the adopted kinsman was himself killed, he too could be avenged by his new kin. Such revenge is also listed among the 'forgivable slayings of a man' in *Córus Fine*. Here is the passage in full.

> Acht cummae ataat cethair gonai duini deithbiri nad élnet coimge láime: dígal fir derbfhine, & dígal daltai inna fine, & dígal fir fosisetar fine, & dígal maic ban.[39]
>
> But on the other hand there are four forgivable slayings of a man which do not violate the duty to restrain one's hand: the avenging of a man of the derbfhine, and the avenging of a foster-son of the kin, and the avenging of a man whom the kin adopts, and the avenging of a son of one's kinswomen.

In any dispute between two kin-groups there was a complex interplay of competing bonds and interests. It would be difficult for one kin-group to attack another without severely compromising the interests of some of its own members. The blood-feud, in extending the locus of the dispute to the whole kin-group of the attacker and the whole kin-group of the victim, virtually assured that cool heads would prevail and that the matter would be settled by compensation according to law.

But there is more.

'Forgivable' vengeance

The four cases of vengeance listed in our quote from *Córus Fine* are described as 'forgivable slayings' (*gonai deithbiri*). While revenge killings are less heinous because of the mitigating circumstances, the phrase is not primarily intended to indicate that they are 'forgivable' by society as a whole. The vengeful killing is still an offence at law, unless the kin responsible for the original killing have positively refused to offer compensation.

We have said that a killer under protection had a set time within which to make an offer of law. If revenge was taken against his kin before that time had elapsed, that vengeance was 'forgivable' in the eyes of the avenger's kin. But the original offender's kin would hardly forgive it. They now had a claim for compensation against the avenger's kin.

---

[39] This passage is found at *CIH* ii 733.35-38 and 734.20-22, and iv 1321.23-25 (see also *CIH* i 158.13-14 and vi 2014.3 and 2014.18 = *AL* iv 252.17f). I have normalised the forms of words to those of classical Old Irish. Cf the translation given by Thomas Charles-Edwards in *Early Irish and Welsh Kinship* (Oxford, 1993) p 505. Charles-Edwards appears to agree with *AL* on the translation of *coimge láime* (he has 'the integrity of the hand'). For the correct translation ('safeguarding [the kin from deeds] of the hand') cf Charles Plummer, 'Notes on Some Passages in the Brehon Laws', *Ériu* 9 (1921-23) 31-42, p 38.

However, because of the mitigating circumstances (the provocation caused by the original killing), the compensation due for the 'forgivable' reprisal-killing was only two-thirds of that which applied to an unprovoked homicide.[40] (The kin of the original killer could not claim their compensation unless they ensured that the original killer paid over the compensation due for his own offence.)

If the 'forgivable vengeance' was taken after the kin of the original killer had in fact offered compensation, but before it was actually paid over, the fine for the revenge attack was not reduced.[41]

If vengeance was taken after the original killer had paid the compensation due for his crime, then it was not (in a legal sense, at least) vengeance at all. At law, the perpetrator had committed a fresh 'unforgivable murder', and he faced the consequences of that deed.

Liability for 'unforgivable' murder

If the kin forgave only the four classes of 'slaying' (*guin*) listed in *Córus Fine*, it follows that all other intentional homicides were 'unforgivable'. Even the killer's own kin-group would condemn him. And, as a consequence, there was a real danger that the kin would refuse to support the offender in the blood-feud. They might simply turn him over to his victim's relatives.

The duties of kinship were manifold. One of these duties was the duty to protect your fellow kinsmen. This included the duty to avenge unlawful attacks made on them. But there was another aspect of this duty: this was the duty to protect your kinsmen from legal liability. A kinsman had a duty not to lay his kinsmen open to financial liability as a result of foolish contracts. He had a duty not to lay them open to legal liability by defaming someone. And he had a duty not to lay his kinsmen open to liability because of his criminal acts.[42] Each one of these 'unforgivable' acts had the potential to incur compensatory fines so large that they might deplete the kin-land (*fintiu*). This in turn would diminish the contingent inheritance rights of every member of the kin-group.

A man who attacked an innocent victim not only committed a crime against the kin of the victim, he had breached his duty to his own kin. He laid them open to physical attack, and he introduced a source of deep antagonism between them and some at least of the persons with whom they had important links of marriage or clientship or fosterage or adoption. And

---

[40] *CIH* i 273.6-8 = *AL* iii 216.14-16; *CIH* ii 730.22-23.
[41] *CIH* i 273.8-10 = *AL* iii 216.17-20.
[42] These three duties are described as the 'duty to restrain one's hand and mouth and tongue' (*coimge láime & béoil & tengad*). They comprise three of the five 'duties of restraint' discussed in detail in the commentary to *Córus Fine* at *CIH* i 156.21f and ii 731.31f.

even if the matter was settled swiftly, he had placed the kin-land in jeopardy.

The standard *éric* fine for murder was seven *cumala* (six *cumala* by way of body-fine, one *cumal* by way of restitution).[43] It may not be entirely coincidental that the minimum land-holding necessary for independent status was land worth seven *cumala*, enough to pay for a life. However, it needs to be borne in mind that a man could not alienate his share of the kin-land without his kin's consent. He could not extricate himself from murder by paying over his land unless his kin agreed. And they might not agree. The offender had broken his duty to the kin; by handing over his land they would diminish the kin-land itself; and the landless man would become a burden upon them. If there was a danger that he would re-offend in the future, bringing further difficulty and loss to the kin, they might decide to abandon him and hand him over to the victim's kin-group. If they did hand him over, they kept his share of the kin-land.[44] If he had no sons, they shared it among themselves.

The temptation to hand the offender over was very real. Indeed, it appears that handing him over was the legal norm. The commentary to *Córus Fine* sets out the following schedule of resources that go to pay for the intentional killing of an innocent victim.

1. The cattle and other moveable possessions of the killer.
2. The killer himself.

It is only if these are insufficient that the resources of the kin-group are called upon; and even then the liability does not pass to the kin-group as a whole but only to his closest relatives.[45] Note that even the killer's share of the kin-land cannot be used by him to save himself from punishment. The kin could step in to save him if it felt so inclined, and allow him to buy himself off with it;[46] but they need not do so and the 'default setting' appears to be that they won't.

If he did not have sufficient chattels to pay for his crime, the killer was handed over to the victim's kin. This released his kin-group from the danger of the blood-feud: they had effectively severed their ties of kinship with him. The kin of the victim were now in a position to prosecute the

---

[43] It was the body-fine which was shared among the kin-group. The restitution payment (*aithgein*) was given to the victim's nearest living relatives (usually his sons): *CIH* ii 742.24-25. In addition to these payments there were other payments due to the foster-kin and the maternal kin, and a range of honour-price payments of various sizes to members of the victim's extended agnatic kin. These are all discussed in the *Díre* text ed and trans Rudolf Thurneysen in *Irisches Recht* (cited above).
[44] *CIH* vi 2012.34-37.
[45] *CIH* i 156.1-3, ii 730.11-13, vi 2012.34-35.
[46] *CIH* vi 2012.35-37.

blood-feud by killing the offender himself. The favoured methods for doing this appear to have been the pit and the gallows.

However, as is well known (but too often ignored), the brutal killing of an offender has a brutalising effect on society itself. Institutionalised violence has a tendency to weaken the ability of other legal institutions to promote a non-violent accommodation of society's competing interests. Effective legal systems avoid violent solutions where they can. So it was with Brehon law. Even though the kin had abandoned the killer, they had not quite abandoned him to the mercy of his victim's kin-group.

If his kin wouldn't save the offender, perhaps someone else would. Before he could be executed, the killer had to be exhibited to every person who would have been likely to release him.[47] Perhaps his lord, or some other dignitary, would be willing to pay for his crimes and take him on as a servant. (According to *Crith Gablach*, a king's body-guard includes 'a man he frees from bloodshed, a man he frees from the gallows, a man he frees from captivity'.[48])

Liability for 'forgivable' negligence

Where death was due to negligence, the killer might stand a better chance of his kinsmen choosing to bail him out. His offence was not a deliberate breach of his duty to them and so it, too, was *deithbire*, 'forgivable, excusable'.[49] His kinsmen might consider him to be less likely to re-offend than a dangerous hot-head (or cold-blooded murderer). They would be more inclined to allow at least his share of the kin-land to go in payment for his offence. And indeed the law requires them to do just that. The commentary to *Córus Fine* gives the following schedule of resources that go to pay for negligent homicide.
  1. The cattle and other moveable possessions of the negligent killer.
  2. His share of the kin-land.
  3. The killer himself.

It was only if his land is insufficient to pay for his offence that his own life was put on the line.[50] The compensation due for negligent killing was half that payable for deliberate homicide,[51] and so it is quite likely that the kinsman's own land would cover his offence.[52]

---

[47] *CIH* ii 732.6-10.
[48] Binchy, *Crith Gablach* lines 578f.
[49] *CIH* ii 730.29-30, vi 2013.11-12. But the liability for payment was not shared equally among the kin-group.
[50] *CIH* ii 730.13-15, vi 2012.38-40.
[51] See Neil McLeod, *Bloodshed and Compensation in Ancient Ireland* (Perth, 1999) p 10.
[52] If he had no land, and was still dependent on his father, then his liabilities would have been met by his father.

Liability for 'forgivable' vengeance

If the kinsman has killed only in revenge, he is in quite a different position (provided the original killer had not already paid compensation for his crime). In cases of 'forgivable vengeance', the perpetrator has merely carried out his duty as a member of the kin-group. In such cases the financial liability for his act does not fall on him alone: the primary liability rests with the entire kin-group on whose behalf he was acting. *Each member of the kin-group has to contribute equally* to the compensation for the revenge killing.[53]

It follows that there might be an even greater temptation in such cases for a kin to abandon the killer to his fate, however immoral such a course of action might be. The individual wealth of each member of the kin-group is now *directly* affected. Handing the avenger over might appear to some of them to be a rather convenient expedient. In the face of such temptations, *Córus Fine* reminds kin-groups that they are not entitled to act in that way in a case of 'forgivable vengeance'.

> *Mad díberg deithbire,*
> *Cia gelltar gólai,*
> *Luigiu sealb sétaib,*
> *Sruithiu dóen díbad,*
> *Ferr fer orbu.*[54]
> In a case of forgivable vengeance,
> Though it be pledged to [avoid] the pit,
> Real estate is less valuable than treasured ones,
> A person is more important than an inheritance,
> A man is better than land.

In other words, where a kinsman has done his duty by avenging an attack against his relatives, the kin should be willing to pay the compensation due for his homicide, even though that means pledging the kin-land to save him from death in the pit.

---

[53] *CIH* ii 730.21-22.

[54] This alliterative poem is found at *CIH* iv 1144.30-32, iv 1318.12-14 (= *AL* iv 268.6-9) and vi 2012.28-32 (see also i 156.1 and ii 730.11). I have normalised the forms of words to those of classical Old Irish. As to the second word of the poem (*díberg*), this is written simply as *dibh* in two manuscript sources (= *CIH* i 156.1 and vi 2012.28) but as *dib-* in the other three. *CIH* follows *AL* in expanding these readings as *díbad* (possibly on the strength of the occurrence of that word in the fourth line of the poem). However, Binchy followed this expansion with a question mark on two of those occasions. I treat this word as *díberg*. *Díberg* generally means 'violence, pillage'. It represents *intentional* carnage. According to *Córus Fine*, among intentional killings only those carried out under the rules of the blood-feud are 'forgivable' (*deithbire*). So for clarity I have translated *díberg* here as 'vengeance'.

The fact that the kin-group shared the cost of compensating for revenge was a fundamental aspect of the blood-feud. It meant that vengeance remained a real threat. Those inclined to take revenge faced no overwhelming financial restraint.

This real threat of revenge was an incentive to an offender's kin to settle the matter promptly, precisely so that such a revenge killing could be avoided. The power of the blood-feud lay not in its realisation, but in its avoidance. The rules of the blood-feud were constructed in such a way that, in most cases, compensation would be forthcoming (even if that included handing the offender over).

The killer's kin had a lot to lose if they refused to settle the matter (even apart from the rupture caused to the links of fosterage and clientship and marriage discussed above). They faced the prospect of revenge being exacted against themselves. And that prospect was very real: the whole of the victim's kin-group would have been enraged at them. Not only had one of their kinsmen been killed, but insult would have been added to injury through a refusal to pay compensation for killing. The more aggressive members of the victim's kin-group knew that they could exact revenge without having to bear more than a small portion of any fines that arose from it. Even that small payment was likely to be largely offset by their own share of the compensation due for the original killing.

From the point of view of the victim's kin, the temptation to exact revenge disappeared once compensation was proffered. If that compensation was refused, not only would they lose out financially, any revenge that was taken would now be treated as a fresh offence. The perpetrators of such unlawful 'revenge' would have to face the sobering prospect of bearing the financial consequences alone.

Revenge across territorial borders

Within a single kingdom, the bonds of agnatic kinship, maternal kinship, kinship by marriage, kinship by adoption, and kinship by fosterage joined with the political and economic ties of clientship to produce a web of intersecting interests. These were badly disrupted by murder; but a revenge killing threatened to rupture them further. As we have seen, this web of intersecting relationships meant that there would normally be a large number of people whose main interests lay in urging the peaceful settlement of the dispute. At the same time, it was in the interests of the killer's kin to provide that settlement as swiftly as possible.

However, the forces for peace were much less powerful in the case of a murder which spanned the borders of independent kingdoms. That is, where a visitor to another kingdom was killed in that kingdom, or where the killer had committed his crime during a raid across the border. Bonds between kingdoms were weak; the Irish annals catalogue the constant raiding of kingdoms by their neighbours. (When the leader of Muinter-Peodachain, a sub-kingdom in Co Fermanagh,[55] died in 1445, he was eulogised in the Annals of Ulster as a man known for his 'hospitality and prowess and for defending his territory against its neighbours'.[56])

Within each kingdom, the peaceful resolution of a murderous dispute restored unity to society. But when the killer came from outside, the exaction of revenge could serve as a unifying force if viewed from the point of view of the victim's own kingdom. Where the feuding kingdoms had not developed sufficient bonds of unity between them, there were few mechanisms for restraint — apart from the difficulty of prosecuting the feud in a kingdom which had no interests in allowing the feud to be prosecuted.

The law provided a particular institution for the prosecution of the inter-kingdom blood-feud. This was the lordly office of the *aire échta*, the 'Lord of Slaughter'. The *aire échta* commanded a small group[57] of commando-style warriors who were available to prosecute a feud across the borders of their kingdom. The difficulty of operating in a hostile territory is reflected in the observation in one commentary that it is the *aire échta* who goes about his business both in the daylight and under the cover of darkness.[58]

We have a mythical account of the actions of a particular *aire échta*, Aengus Gaí Buaibthech (Angus of the Dread Spear). This is found in the introduction to a text on injuries, *Bretha Étgid*.[59] Here it is recounted that Aengus was an *aire échta* living within the kingdom of Tara, in the east of Ireland. He was employed to prosecute a blood-feud in the west of Ireland, against the Luigni (in Co Sligo). So Aengus went to the kingdom of the Luigni. Once there he forced his way into a house in order to find food.[60] The woman who lived there rebuked him with some startling news. She told him that while he was here defending the honour of someone else's kin, his own kin was under attack. Cellach, the son of the king of Tara, had taken advantage of his absence to abduct the daughter of one Aengus's own kinsman. The woman suggested that Aengus might be more profitably employed at home than in Sligo. And he agreed. He returned to Tara post haste, slew Cellach, and blinded the king, Cormac mac Airt, in the process. Cormac duly retired and wrote *Bretha Étgid*.

---

[55] See E Hogan, *Onomasticon Goidelicum* (Dublin, 1910, repr 2000) p 549.
[56] *AU* iii pp 155-57.
[57] A 'group of five' according to *Críth Gablach* (lines 358-59 of Binchy's edition); a group of thirty according to the commentary at *CIH* vi 2141.5f.
[58] *CIH* vi 2141.5-6.
[59] *CIH* i 250.1-16 = *AL* iii 82-84. The story belongs to the origin legend of the Déisi. See James MacKillop, *Dictionary of Celtic Mythology* (Oxford, 1998) p 119 and T F O'Rahilly, *Early Irish History and Mythology* (Dublin, 1946) p 63.
[60] This was second nature to an *aire échta*. Even while on duty at home he was entitled to help himself to an animal from each herd and flock to sustain him: *CIH* vi 2141.7.

However, the situation in the island as a whole was not entirely chaotic. It can be compared with the modern global situation under international law. There were many alliances between kingdoms, even though these tended to shift over time. At times, particularly powerful kings extended their influence over many of their neighbours, installing their own nominees in those sub-kingships and exacting support and tribute from them. Alliances of a more equal nature were also struck where that was to the political and military advantage of the kingdoms involved. Within such over-kingdoms and alliances there do exist influential forces for cohesion. And legal institutions are usually at hand to promote them.

The Church was possibly the most important source of cohesion between kingdoms. While secular alliances were volatile and fragile, religious federations were more stable and enduring. The Church's interests in promoting peace between kingdoms were obvious: religious centres were prime targets in inter-territorial raids.

In medieval Ireland, the chief procedural mechanism for resolving disputes across borders appears to have been the treaty (*cairde*). Neighbouring kingdoms could institute a protocol (*béscnae*) for the payment of compensation for the killing of each other's citizens.[61] Once such measures had been agreed to, the functions of the *aire échta* were curtailed.[62] The *aire échta* who was involved in a killing which violated the terms of a treaty was guilty of common murder.[63]

One commentary which discusses the operation of inter-territorial protocols focuses mainly on the killing of a foster-son who has been fostered from beyond the border.[64] This suggests that fosterage may well have been particularly important in the creation of links between kingdoms.

The growth in the forces of cohesion can be seen in the decline of the status of the *aire échta* over time. In the Old Irish status texts *Críth Gablach* and *Uraicecht Becc* the *aire échta* has an honour-price of 10 *séts* (equal to five ounces of silver). This is the honour-price of the lowest lordly grade.[65] But in *Bretha Crólige*, another Old Irish text dealing specifically with deadly injuries, the *aire échta* is demoted to the status of the common *bóaire*.[66] By the time of the Middle Irish commentaries, this demotion had taken hold. In those commentaries we find an 'upper *aire échta*' ranked with the common *bóaire*, and a 'lower *aire échta*' ranked with the small farmer (*ócaire*).[67]

---

[61] Cf. *CIH* i 272.28f = *AL* iii 214.12f.
[62] See Kelly, *A Guide to Early Irish Law*, p 127.
[63] Cf *CIH* vi 2140.9f.
[64] *CIH* i 118.35f.
[65] See Neil McLeod, 'Status and Currency II', pp 81, 90.
[66] See *ibid*, pp 48f.
[67] *CIH* iv 1230.36-37, vi 2141.5f.

The story of Aengus Gaí Buaibthech may itself reflect the suppression of the role of the *aire échta*. To the modern reader, the advice of the woman of the Luigni is reminiscent of the propaganda found in leaflets dropped upon the enemy in time of war. ('While you are fighting here so far from home, your wives and daughters are falling prey to your allies on R and R'.) The message seems to be that a man is better off protecting his own kin than in a far-off territory avenging someone else's. (Of course, from the point of view of Cellach, it also stresses the real threat posed by the blood-feud in the case of offences committed in one's *own* kingdom.)

Dynastic disputes
The peaceful functioning of the blood-feud relies on an intersecting web of mutual interests. These make violence an intolerable option for those in a position to put a stop to it.

In the absence of such bonds, violence is more likely. Those bonds are likely to be absent during dynastic disputes. Nobles attempting to secure the kingship, or the over-lordship of other kingdoms, will construct allegiances which are designed to be clearly differentiated from each other. Each will marshall groups of clients and supporters for themselves, and against their opponents.

Dynastic rivals will also be, by definition, among the most powerful members of their kingdoms. They will not be subject to the normal restraints exerted by peers, let alone those from superiors. The only people superior to them are likely to be the ones they are plotting against. Everywhere in Irish history the failure of social institutions to restrain dynastic disputes is evident. Dynastic murders often form part of a long and escalating cycle of violence and revenge. This cycle is ended only by the clear supremacy of one of the dynastic branches; and that state of affairs is often obtained only by the annihilation of its rivals. (Before long, of course, the successful branch expands, and splits into new rival factions.)

Let us return, by way of illustration, to the kingdom of the Luigni in Co Sligo. This time our example is historical rather than mythological. In the late eighth century, separate branches of the Uí Briúin jostled for the over-kingship of Connacht. One of these branches was led by Muirgius mac Tommaltaig. Muirgius eventually defeated his rivals and became over-king of Connacht. During the dynastic battles that led up to this final victory, the Luigni appear to have sided with Muirgius's rivals.[68] Muirgius, perhaps partly as an expression of his dissatisfaction at that, slew the son of a Luigni warrior. This murder produced a series of escalating revenge

---

[68] See Gearóid Mac Niocaill, *Ireland Before the Vikings* (Dublin, 1972) 135-37, p 137. For another account of Muirgius's reign, see Francis J Byrne, *Irish Kings and High-Kings*, (2nd ed, Dublin, 2001) pp 251-53.

killings which are recorded in the Annals of Ulster for the year AD 809 (properly AD 810).

First, the father of the slain man sought revenge. He appears to have raided Muirgius's territory in the manner characteristic of an *aire échta*, accompanied by a band of Luigni warriors. In this attack he took revenge by 'plying his sword on the throat' of Muirgius's own son, Tadc.[69] Tadc was a legitimate target under the blood-feud. However, the raiding party went further than this, for they also killed Tadc's brother Flaithnia for good measure.

This escalation of the vendetta was met by a further, and massive, reprisal by Muirgius, who carried out 'a devastation of the Luigni'.[70]

Here we have an example of a situation where the legal restraints operating within the blood-feud proved ineffectual. The initial killing entailed a threat of reprisal. But that threat was insufficient to make Muirgius consider paying compensation. It was not that the threat was too small, it was rather that Muirgius was too big. There was no one able to act as an intermediary and counsel in favour of compensation. Even had there been such a person, Muirgius would not have heard of such a thing: he was probably itching for an excuse to show the Luigni who was boss. Muirgius had a tendency to indulge in acts of massive retribution. This may help account for his obituary in the Annals of Ulster. In the entry given for AD 814 (properly AD 815), he is described as 'a fiery red king without compassion'.[71]

Conclusion

In medieval Ireland, the threat of violence was real and ever present. But within kingdoms, an intersecting web of mutual interests meant that the threat of violence could be harnessed as a force for peace. This was less the case as between kingdoms, and the forces for peace were especially weak across dynastic schisms. These exceptions aside, the rules governing the blood-feud provide an illustration of the way in which law functions as an organic aspect of society.

---

[69] Seán Mac Airt and Gearóid Mac Niocaill (ed), *The Annals of Ulster* (Dublin, 1983) p 267.
[70] Mac Airt and Mac Niocaill, p 271.
[71] *ibid.*

Heroic epic as propaganda: the manipulation of honour in *Táin Bó Cúalnge*

David N Wilson

In this paper I shall discuss the way in which Irish epic tales may have been manipulated for political purposes[1]. As an example, I shall use some episodes from a tale in the Ulster Cycle: the 'Táin Bó Cúalnge', otherwise known as 'The Cattle Raid of the Cooley'. As there are several recensions of this tale, I shall generally use the recension from the twelfth-century Book of Leinster, which is the latest, and considered by many to have the most literary merit.[2]

The tales recorded by the Ulster Cycle present a picture of a legendary, pre-Christian, tribal society: a society dominated by warriors who delighted in fighting and cattle raiding. The stories are set in the distant heroic past: divinities appear, the people of the otherworld participate, the heroes are of gigantic stature, and there are giant beasts. The stories are also partly creation myths since they tell of events that formed the land and gave names to its features.

The Ulster Cycle is preserved in manuscripts which date from the twelfth century. At first reading, the stories give the impression that they have been preserved unaltered from pre-Christian oral traditions. Yet this is not the case. In the first place, it is clear that the stories have been modified to make them acceptable to the church. Celtic gods are rarely mentioned: they become miraculous heroes or members of the spirit-world. Celtic religious practices are not mentioned at all. In the second place, the stories may have been manipulated to accommodate elements of royalist propaganda. This would have been done for the benefit of the Uí Néill, the most powerful dynasty at the time and the appropriators of the Ulaid traditions.

Scholars have discussed some of these propaganda themes[3]. The themes include the legitimacy conferred on a king by the holding of a

---

[1] Ann Trindade, Neil McLeod and Lyn Olson kindly provided useful comments on an earlier version of this paper. Any continuing infelicities are entirely my own.

[2] The two major complete recensions are Cecile O'Rahilly (ed and trans), *Táin Bó Cúalnge from the Book of Leinster* (Dublin, 1967) and Cecile O'Rahilly (ed and trans), *Táin Bó Cúalnge Recension 1* (Dublin, 1976). Both books have detailed introductions which provide accounts of the recensions' history.

[3] Joan Radner argues that the Ulster Epic tales have been reworked by Uí Néill historians to achieve several propaganda aims. The tales present the Ulaid as heroic but doomed, with the Uí Néill having legitimately inherited their power. Radner considers that the Ulaid were doomed because of defective kingship and the

sacred site, and the portrayal of the earlier society as socially, politically and religiously dysfunctional, with the implication that the new kings had remedied this dysfunction.

I think that there is another propaganda theme to be found in these tales. This theme involves the manipulation of the warrior honour code to support the political pretensions of the Uí Néill kings and their clients.

The ancient Irish were very concerned with issues of personal honour and status[4]. The warrior code originated in small-scale tribal, social patterns, and was reinforced by continual inter-tribal conflicts and the ruthless competition for leadership positions.[5] Maintaining the loyalty of networks of clients and their dependent warriors was the most important activity for any Irish king. Codes of honour are persistent cultural constructs[6]. The early medieval Irish society was still a tribal warrior

---

malignant influences of the old gods, attributes which were corrected by the advent of Christian and, supposedly, good Uí Néill kings. Joan N Radner, '"Fury Destroys the World" Historical Strategy in Ireland's Ulster Epic', *Mankind Quarterly* XXIII/1 (1982) 41-60. H M and N K Chadwick have pointed out that Heroic Literature is aristocratic in outlook: 'As Virtues it recognizes loyalty, prowess, and fulfilment of one's word', quoted in Eleanor Knott and Gerard Murphy, *Early Irish Literature* (London, 1967) p 114.

[4] Honour was an important principle in early Irish law and the concept of honour-price was central. Honour-price was largely dependent upon a person's social status and wealth, but could be reduced if the person's behaviour did not meet the standard required for the position. See F Kelly, *A Guide to Early Irish Law* (Dublin, 1988) p19. For a discussion of the interaction of honour price, welath and rank, see Nerys Patterson, *Cattle Lords and Clansmen: The Social Structure of Early Ireland* (London, 1994) pp 181-206.

[5] Honour codes in general, and warrior codes in particular, served the dual purpose of preserving and enhancing a warrior's personal honour and of acting as a mechanism of social control. The values of honour are concerned with reciprocity, the paying back of the good and the bad. See William Ian Miller, *Humiliation, and other Essays on Honour, Social Discomfort, and Violence* (Ithaca and London, 1993) p113. It was the warrior's concern to be seen to act with appropriate reciprocity that required them to avenge personal slights and to refuse to back down from a fight. Over time, these honour codes became highly formalised, with many exceptions and rules. For example, warriors might only fight with equals, as to fight with subordinate persons might be demeaning. For example, Cú Chulainn's claim that 'I do not wound charioteers or messengers or folk unarmed'; *Táin Bó Cúalnge from the Book of Leinster*, lines 1732-1736, translated at p 186. See also Dean A Miller, *The Epic Hero* (Baltimore, 2000) p 332.

[6] On the persistence of honour codes I would mention the continuation of military codes of honour, and the honour code of the Mafia. A Mafioso is not a member of a gang but a person who adopts a code of behaviour; Mafiosi refer to themselves as 'men of honour'. See Henner Hess, *Mafia & Mafiosi; Origin, Power and Myth* (Bathurst, 1970).

middling warriors. He is treated with scorn and ridicule, and is subject to deceit and treachery. He has to fight friends, relations of friends, his foster father, and a beloved foster brother. He sustains terrible wounds. Cú Chulainn demonstrates how the ideal warrior should deal with all of these situations whilst enhancing his honour. For the Uí Néill warriors, each episode was a lesson. They would have keenly appreciated and judged Cú Chulainn's actions with respect to the finer points of warrior behaviour and honour. They would also have understood the situations in which people were struggling to resolve a complex network of often conflicting personal obligations.

The first episode is when the Men of Ireland had arrived to raid the Ulaid, and Cú Chulainn defended the Ulaid territory by forcing the enemy to engage with him, one at a time, in single combat. After many of her warriors had been killed by Cú Chulainn, Queen Medb asked Fergus to fight him. Fergus replied, 'It would not be fitting for me ... to encounter a young and beardless lad, my own fosterling'[9].

Fosterage was a common institution in medieval Ireland and fostering parents held their foster-children in the same regard as their biological children. Fergus tried to make Medb aware that her demand placed him and Cú Chulainn in a potentially tragic situation. However, Medb insisted and Fergus was unable to refuse. The next morning Fergus met Cú Chulainn. Fergus said that he could not bear weapons against him, his own foster-son. He proposed that Cú Chulainn should be seen to flee from him. Cú Chulainn replied that he was loath to do this. Fergus then proposed a deal. If Cú Chulainn would flee from him now, he, Fergus would flee from Cú Chulainn later 'when you shall be covered with wounds and blood and pieced with stabs in the battle of the Táin, and when I alone shall flee, then the Men of Ireland will flee'.[10]

The point here is that Fergus was proposing to betray the Men of Ireland at a crucial point in the forthcoming battle. Cú Chulainn accepted the deal. Then, as agreed, he fled in rout from Fergus and the Men of Ireland. The tale says that Cú Chulainn did this because he was eager to do whatever was for the Ulaid's benefit.

How are we to understand Cú Chulainn actions? Whilst Fergus could not bring himself to fight his foster-son, Cú Chulainn seemed to need further inducement to break off the fight. He is shown as being more loyal to king and country than to familial sentiment.[11] In his arrangement with

---

[9] *Táin Bó Cúalnge from the Book of Leinster*, lines 2479-81, translated at p 207.
[10] *Táin Bó Cúalnge from the Book of Leinster*, lines 2497-99, translated at p 208.
[11] This theme is repeated in the tale 'The Death of Aife's Only Son', which is a rather crude set-piece tragedy whose main message was that Cú Chulainn placed loyalty to homeland and warrior duty over familial sentiment. J Gantz (ed and trans), 'The Death of Aife's Only Son' in *Early Irish Myths and Sagas* (London, 1981).

society[7]. The warrior honour code, with its emphasis on personal honour, resulted in unruly behaviour that caused enormous difficulties for kings, such as the Uí Néill, who wished to form coherent territorial domains from many different tribal groups. In this they where probably influenced by British and European examples of larger and more powerful territorial domains than had ever existed in Ireland.

Now the Táin Bó Cúalnge (henceforth 'Táin') tells how Medb, the Queen of Connacht, organised 'the Men of Ireland' into a raid upon the Ulaid, to capture their great magical bull, the Brown Bull of Cúalnge. The most important character is Cú Chulainn, a superhuman warrior and the champion of the Ulaid. Most of the story concerns the actions of Cú Chulainn in defending the territory of the Ulaid from the raiders. In contrast to Cú Chulainn as the ideal warrior, Medb is presented as an archetype of the bad leader. Two other important characters in the Táin are Fergus, the previous king of the Ulaid who had been forced from the kingship into exile, and Conchobor, his stepson, who had seized the Kingship of the Ulaid from Fergus. After he was exiled Fergus joined Medb in Connacht and became her lover and the leader of her raiders. Cú Chulainn was a nephew of Conchobor and foster son of Fergus. Thus the story has been set up for a conflict of personal and military obligations. This was a common theme in epic tales. In 'Choice and Consequence in Irish Heroic Literature', O'Leary comments:

> Clearly the redactors of the prose tales were fascinated by the narrative, thematic, and ethical possibilities suggested by situations in which a man (or woman) is confronted with balanced and conflicting claims or obligations and compelled, in the absence of entirely satisfactory precedents, to make a personal choice either consonant with the heroic value system, or even transcending it.[8]

To show how my proposed propaganda theme operated within the Táin, I shall consider two episodes. In order to understand the significance of these two scenes, it is important to remember that the Táin contains many accounts of Cú Chulainn in single-handed combat. In each of these episodes, Cú Chulainn finely matches his demeanour and actions to the opponent and the situation. He faces powerful warriors, and weak and

---

[7] Whilst it could be argued that the honour code portrayed within the texts was an ideal or a literary trope, like some representations of medieval chivalry, I would argue that the ideal behaviours portrayed were intended to have, and did have, a socially ameliorating effect, by setting up a model of how people should behave. Whilst the Irish heroic epics contained much that was fanciful, I do not believe that these epics were a fantasy of manners for the original audience.

[8] P O'Leary, 'Choice and Consequence in Irish Heroic Literature' in *Cambrian Medieval Studies* 27 (Summer 1994) p 49.

Fergus, Cú Chulainn was prepared suffer the dishonour of running away from a fight in order to resolve his personal predicament, and to ensure the victory of the Ulaid.[12] Fergus, however, has resolved his predicament by betraying his Queen and his companions. Cú Chulainn seems to have driven a hard bargain with Fergus.

The second episode comes in the final battle between the Men of Ireland and the Ulaid. When the battle was under way, Medb told Fergus to go and join the fight. Fergus asked upon whom he should ply his sword and Medb answered 'On the hosts that surround you on all sides. ... Let none receive mercy or quarter from you today except a true friend.'[13]

Fergus fought through the ranks of the Ulaid until he came upon their king, Conchobor. They were evenly matched and traded tremendous blows. Fergus, who hadn't recognised him, asked who it was who was able to withstand him. Conchobor responded with the insulting taunt that he was the younger, more noble and better man and that Fergus was dependent upon a woman. Greatly angered, Fergus prepared to give Conchobor a mighty blow:

> With that, Fergus raised his sword for a vengeful two-handed stroke at Conchobor. As the point touched the ground, Cormac Connlogas [Conchobor's son who was in exile with Fergus] flung his arms around him and caught his two hands at the wrists.
> 'Harshly, harshly, friend Fergus,' Cormac said. 'That would be mean and shameful, and spoil friendships. These wicked blows will cheapen your enmity and break your pacts.
> 'Then where am I to strike?' Fergus cried.
> 'Turn your hand aside. Strike out anywhere. Strike crosswise at those three hills. But remember that Ulster's honour was never thrown away, and never will be unless you do it today. Leave us, Conchobor,' said Cormac to his father. 'This man will pour his rage on Ulstermen no more.'
> Now the sword, the sword of Fergus, was the Sword of Leite from the elf-mounds. When one wished to strike with it, it was as big as a rainbow in the air. Then Fergus turned his hand level above the heads of the hosts and cuts off the tops

---

[12] As evidence, from within the story, that this behaviour would be seen as dishonourable, we have the scene where Fergus is verbally attacking Dubthach Dóeltenga. Fergus provides an interesting catalogue of dishonourable activities for a warrior. It starts with 'If this is Dubthach Dóeltenga, he draws back in the rear of the host. He has done nothing good since he slaughtered the women-folk.' [lines 2406-9, translated at p205] If drawing back from the fight was dishonourable, running away must have been far more so.

[13] *Táin Bó Cúalnge from the Book of Leinster*, line 4722-23, translated at p205.

of the three hills which are still there in the marshy plain as evidence.[14]

In this example it seems that Fergus again betrayed his obligation to Medb to fight the Ulaid. Medb's instructions were 'Let none receive mercy or quarter from you except a true friend'. Yet Fergus spared the enemy leader Conchobor, who could hardly be considered a true friend. Under the terms of the honour code, Fergus had a personal duty of honour to take revenge, given that Conchobor had forced him into exile and had made other grievous assaults to his honour. How then could killing such a man be 'wicked' or 'cheapen his enmity'?

Cormac's pleas to Fergus were pleas to the emotions rather than to any concepts of honour and obligation. Yet the audience of the story did not have time to consider the unreasonableness of Cormac's pleas to Fergus and the assault on the principles of traditional warrior honour that they implied, because the story moved on quickly to the dramatic and magical scene of Fergus cutting off the tops of the hills. Had Fergus lowered his sword a bit, he could have taken off the heads of the hosts of the Ulaid, and won the battle for the Men of Ireland.

Meanwhile, Cú Chulainn, who had been stricken with wounds from his many combats, had been prevented by the Ulaid from joining the battle. Yet, on hearing Fergus' great blows against the shield of Conchobor and the blows against the hills, Cú Chulainn leapt up, breaking his bonds and causing his many wounds to gush blood. He joined the battle and wrought carnage on the Men of Ireland until he came to Fergus. He announced himself to Fergus and reminded him:

'you promised that you would flee before me when I should be wounded, bloody and pierced with stabs in the battle of the Táin, for I fled before you in your own battle of the Táin.' Fergus heard that, and he turned and took three mighty, heroic strides, and when he turned all the men of Ireland turned and were routed westward over the hill.[15]

Note how Fergus's betrayal of the Men of Ireland is described. It is said that 'he turned and took three mighty, heroic strides'. What Fergus actually did was to run away before the foe. This is surely an heroic spin on his act of betrayal and his retreat. But again the story moves on quickly, and there is no time for the audience to consider this lapse from honour. In the next scene Medb undergoes a particular humiliation. As Medb and Fergus were fleeing the rout, Medb's menstruation came upon her and she had to stop to

---

[14] Thomas Kinsella, *The Tain, Translated from the Irish Epic Tain Bo Cuailnge* (London, 1970) p 248. I have used Kinsella's translation for this passage as O'Rahilly's translations of both the Book of Leinster and the Recension 1 versions of this passage are confusing and some lines make little sense.

[15] *Táin Bó Cúalnge from the Book of Leinster*, lines 4809-14, translated at p 269.

relieve herself. They were captured by Cú Chulainn as she did so. Fergus then verbally attacked Medb, blaming her for the defeat. Fergus asked 'what could you expect from a campaign led by a woman'! A surprising attack, and one that the modern reader finds particularly unfair. But the story has set up Medb to take the blame, thus allowing Fergus to be a greater Ulaid hero.

The actions of Fergus in his abandonment of his fight with Conchobor and his betrayal of the Men of Ireland, and of Cú Chulainn in running away from Fergus, were actions that ran counter to the warrior honour code as it is presented in the Ulster Cycle. Yet these unconventional actions saved the day for the Ulaid. Fergus, when forced to decide, placed home-land sentiment over his personal honour and his obligations to Medb and the Men of Ireland. Cú Chulainn was prepared to accept the shame of fleeing from his opponent in order to secure the deal that betrayed the Men of Ireland. Nevertheless, I think that these episodes have been artfully constructed to distract the audience from evaluating their lapses from the ideals of honourable warrior behaviour.

At this point we can see how this theme of royalist propaganda operated. The lessons that the hearers were to take from the story were that a warrior's greatest loyalty was to his homeland (and, by implication, to its legitimate authority: its king) and that loyalty to the homeland took precedence over personal honour and other contractual obligations. Furthermore, this loyalty was still owed, even though, as in Fergus's case, the homeland and its King had ruined, insulted or exiled him. Fergus is a tragic figure of compromised honour. In one tale he is accused, somewhat unfairly, of selling his honour for beer[16]. But in this story, I think that the intention was that Fergus's actions to save the Ulaid should redeem him in the eyes of the audience.

On the whole this propaganda theme has been unsuccessful. The Irish have never given their unconditional loyalty to a leader who could control the whole country. Nor have Celtic fighters ever been convinced that running away from a fight was a good thing to do, no matter what the strategic advantage may have been.

---

[16] J Gantz (ed and trans), 'Exile of the Sons of Uisliu' in *Early Irish Myths and Sagas* (London, 1981) p 266.

The ambivalent image of Irish Christianity in Gerald of Wales

Constant J Mews

The writing of Gerald of Wales (1146-1223) about Ireland defies easy classification. His most recent biographer, Robert Bartlett, observes that towards Ireland he is a hostile outsider.[1] The long years of study he spent in Paris, initially between 1165 and 1172, and then again between 1176 and 1179, did not prepare him in any way for his experiences in Ireland, invaded by Anglo-Norman settlers in 1169. When he travelled to Ireland, initially in the company of his elder brother, Philip de Barri, lord of Manorbier, in 1183, and then again in 1184-85 in the court of prince John, he shared the values and excitement of a settler elite, for whom Ireland was a land of opportunity. Gerald's first major composition, the *Topography of Ireland*, written between 1185 and 1188, is often remembered as being unsympathetic to the Irish, and grossly unreliable in the anecdotes that he tells.[2] Gerald himself was forced to defend the work from criticism that many of his stories were too extravagant.[3] Yet the *Topography* is also a remarkable achievement of geographic and ethnographic observation. The large number of surviving manuscripts, the different recensions of which still need to be studied, attests to its great popularity.[4] His testimony on Ireland seems frustrating to many, both because many of his anecdotes seem implausible, and because he seems to be so much the representative of an alien culture.

---

[1] Robert Bartlett, *Gerald of Wales 1146-1223* (Oxford, 1982) p 31. See the similar comments of Michael Richter, *Giraldus Cambrensis: the Growth of the Welsh Nation* (2nd ed, Aberystwyth, 1976) p 36. I am indebted to discussion with Lyn Olson on many points in this paper.

[2] For a review of critical comments on Gerald's *Topography of Ireland*, see James F Dimock, *Giraldi Cambrensis Opera* (Rolls Series 5, London, 1867) pp lxxv-lxxxii; Dimock edits the *Topography* on pp 1-204. J J O'Meara edits the earliest recension of the Latin text in 'Giraldus Cambrensis in Topographiae Hibernie. Text of the First Recension', *Proceedings of the Royal Irish Academy* 52 C 4 (1948-50) 113-78, and translates it in Giraldus Cambrensis, *The History and Topography of Ireland* (rev ed, Mountrath, Portlaoise, 1982). Unless otherwise indicated, my references to the *Topography* are to the Dimock edition, followed by references to the O'Meara edition and translation.

[3] Giraldus Cambrensis, *Expugnatio Hibernica. The Conquest of Ireland* (ed A B Scott and F X Martin, Dublin, 1978) p 4.

[4] Surviving manuscripts and recensions are listed by Bartlett, *Gerald of Wales*, pp 212f.

One of the major difficulties that I sense with scholarly discussion of the *Topography* is that it has tended to focus too much on the issue of its reliability, and not enough on the craft that Gerald has put into its literary construction or the originality of his reflection. There can be no doubt about the vigour of his prejudices about the Irish. 'They are a wild and inhospitable people. They live on beasts only, and live like beasts. They have not progressed at all from the primitive habits of pastoral living.'[5] His comments are often richly revealing of the economic and social values of his own class. He cannot understand why the Irish did not mine

> the different types of minerals with which the hidden veins of the earth are full ... precisely because of the same laziness ... For given only to leisure, and devoted only to laziness, they think that the greatest pleasure is not to work, and the greatest wealth is to enjoy liberty ... Their natural qualities are excellent. But almost everything acquired is deplorable.[6]

If one quotes only from the third part of the *Topography*, it would seem that he has nothing but contempt for everything Irish:

> While man usually progresses from the woods to the fields, and from the fields to the settlements and communities of citizens, this people despises work on the land, has little use for the money-making of towns, contemns the rights and privileges of citizenship, and desires neither to abandon, nor lose respect for, the life which it has been accustomed to lead in the woods and countryside. They use the fields generally as pasture, but pasture in poor condition. Little is cultivated, and even less is sown.[7]

Gerald displays the horror of an ecclesiastical administrator in the way that he describes the organization and practice of religion:

> They do not yet pay tithes or first fruits or contract marriages. They do not avoid incest. They do not attend God's church with due reverence. Moreover, and this is surely a detestable thing and contrary not only to the Faith but to any feeling of honour — men in many places in Ireland, I shall not say marry, but rather debauch, the wives of their dead brothers. They abuse them in having such evil and incestuous relations with them. In this (wishing to imitate the ancients more eagerly in vice than in virtue) they follow the apparent teaching, and not the true doctrine of the Old Testament.[8]

---

[5] *Topographia*, III.x, p 151; ed O'Meara, p 162; trans O'Meara, 3.93, p 101.
[6] *ibid*, III.x, p 152; ed O'Meara, p 162; trans O'Meara, p 102.
[7] *ibid*, III.x, pp 151f; ed O'Meara, p 162; trans O'Meara, pp 101f.
[8] *ibid*, III.xviii, pp 164f; ed O'Meara, p 166; trans O'Meara, 3.96, p 106.

In these passages, Gerald shows himself to be quintessentially unsympathetic to a pastoral society, in which levirate marriage was still practiced to protect the kin group, and economic submission to the Church was far from widely achieved. He has a keen eye for behaviour that he finds abhorrent.

Yet Gerald's writing is not simply critical or abusive about the Irish. He singles out the Irish clergy as commendable for their observance, reserving his particular disapproval for prelates who neglect their pastoral duties.[9] Above all, he is fascinated by the natural prosperity of Ireland and the great example which has been set by the great Irish saints of the past. Perhaps the most widely quoted anecdote in the *Topography* comes from its central section, which climaxes in an account of various miracles associated with St Brigit of Kildare. Demonstrating his capacity for acute observation, he describes an ancient manuscript very similar to the Book of Kells, preserved at Kildare.

> Of all the miracles of Kildare nothing seems to me more miraculous than a marvellous book which, they say, was written at the dictation of an angel. This book contains the four gospels according to the concordance of St. Jerome, with almost as many drawings as it has pages and all resplendent in varying colours. Here you can look on the face of the divine majesty wonderfully drawn, here the mystical forms of the evangelists, now with six, now four, now two wings. Here you will see the eagle, there the calf, here a human face, there that of a lion, and there is an almost infinite number of other drawings. If you look at these without attention and in the ordinary way they may appear like smudges rather than careful compositions. And you will see nothing subtle where there is nothing but subtlety. But if you take care to look very closely at the very point of vision and penetrate the secret of the art, you will see such delicacies and subtleties, such art and artistry, so interlaced and closely wrought, so interlocked and bound together and still so fresh in their colourings you will not hesitate to declare that these must have been done by angelic rather than human carefulness.[10]

---

[9] *ibid*, III.xxvi-xxviii; ed O'Meara, p 168; trans O'Meara, 3.103-4, p 112.

[10] *ibid*, III.xxxviii, p 123; ed O'Meara, pp 151f; trans O'Meara, 2.71, p 84: '*De libro miraculose conscripto. Inter uniuersa kyldarei miracula nichil mihi miraculosius occurrit, quam liber ille mirandus tempore uirginis ut aiunt angelo dictante conscriptus. Continet hic liber .iiii.or euangeliorum iuxta ieronimum concordantiam, ubi quot pagine fere tot figure diuerse, uariisque coloribus distinctissime. Hic maiestatis uultum, uideas diuinitus inpressum, hinc misticas euangelistarum formas,*

In a later recension of the *Topography*, Gerald adds an extra line: 'The more often and the more carefully I look on these things, the more I am astonished anew.' The addition implies that he frequently returned to look again at the manuscript, which clearly held great significance for him.[11]

How can we reconcile Gerald's evident hostility to the primitivism of Irish culture with his evident fascination for the manuscript of Kildare, and indeed with the stories that he heard about St Brigit? In particular, what is the significance of Gerald's fascination with observing the world, whether it is the social behaviour or the customs of the Irish, their artistic achievements, or the natural world? Gerald is much more than simply a hostile outsider. He is both the representative of a colonizing elite, and an attentive observer, fascinated by the otherness of the culture that he encounters.

Gerald's originality in devising the *Topography* must be measured against the intellectual training and literary models that he encountered during his studies in France. In Paris, he initially devoted himself to the liberal arts. When he returned to Paris between 1172 and 1175, he studied theology and canon law, essential to promotion as an ecclesiastical administrator.[12] Yet Gerald also had an enduring fascination with philosophical and literary questions, above all about the natural world and about history. Two of his earliest writings, produced sometime in his twenties, included a *Chronographia* (now lost) and a *Cosmographia*, in which he reflected 'on the teachings of the philosophers rather than of the theologians'.[13] The latter work is a poem of 260 lines, *De mundi creatione*,

---

nunc senas . nunc quaternas, nunc binas alas habentes, hinc aquilam, inde uitulum, hinc hominis faciem, inde leonis, aliasque figuras fere infinitas, quas si superficialiter et usuali more, minus acute conspexeris litura potius uidebitur quam ligatura. Nec ullam prorsus attendes Subtilitatem. ubi nichil tamen preter subtilitatem, sin autem ad perspicatius intuendum oculorum aciem inuitaueris et longe penitus ad artis archana transpenetraueris, tam delicatas et subtiles . tam artas et artitas . tam nodosas et uinculatim colligatas, tamque recentibus adhuc coloribus illustratas notatare portis intricaturis: ut uere hec omnia potius angelica quam humana diligentia iam asseueraueris esse composita.' The passage is frequently quoted by art historians; see Francoise Henry, *The Book of Kells. Reproductions from the Manuscript in Trinity College Dublin* (London, 1974) pp 165f; Peter Brown, *The Book of Kells. Forty-Eight Pages and Details in Colour from the Manuscript in Trinity College, Dublin* (London, 1980) p 83; Bernard Meehan, *The Book of Kells. An Illustrated Introduction to the Manuscript in Trinity College Dublin* (London, 1994) p 89.

[11] *Topographia* III.xxxviii, p 124: '*Haec et equidem quanto frequentius et diligentius intueor semper quasi nouis obstupeo.*'

[12] *Epistola ad capitulum Herefordense de libris a se scriptis* in *Giraldi Cambrensis Opera* (ed James Brewer, Rolls Series 1, London, 1861) p 141.

[13] *Epistola*, in *Opera* 1: 414, 421; the poem is included within the *Symbolum electorum*, *Opera* 1, 341-9.

inspired by the *Cosmographia* of Bernard Sylvester. This great composition, a combination of prose and verse, publicly recited before Pope Eugenius III in 1147, deals with the structure of the universe, but through the abstract Platonic categories of *Nous* and *Natura*, rather than through any Aristotelian knowledge of the natural world.[14] In its first part, *Megacosmos*, Nature addresses *Nous* or Mind, while in the second, *Microcosmus*, *Nous* addresses Nature. Intellectually Bernard is heir to a Platonic tradition, previously developed by Thierry of Chartres and William of Conches, which privileged intellectual awareness of eternal forms over transient sense perception. As Bartlett has observed, Gerald's treatise is no mere plagiarised summary of the work of Bernard.[15] Gerald incorporates much information about the seasons, about the ages of man, the elements and humours into a broader philosophical reflection on the created world. Its scientific knowledge is drawn from books. While he endeavours to integrate scientific information into a broadly Platonic mould, the poem is very much written within a conventional academic mould, integrating information drawn more from books, like Bede and Isidore, than observation. He also follows Bernard Sylvester in being concerned only with the natural world, not with human society. Another early composition to which he refers in the *Topography* is a poem *De philosophicis flosculis*, which apparently dealt with explanations of the tides and the influence of the moon.[16]

Writing the *Topography of Ireland* enabled Gerald to combine into a single treatise his interests in the natural world, the miraculous, and the foibles of human history, all tightly focussed into discussion of a single place. In writing about Ireland, Gerald could draw some inspiration from Bede, who had provided a precedent for writing about the saints of Ireland, and in the twelfth century provided stimulus for a revival of respect for Celtic saints.[17] Gerald wanted to do much more than simply write history, however. By invoking the term *Topographia*, rare in medieval literary tradition, but used by Augustine to refer to descriptions of place, he sought to create a new synthesis of learning.[18] Gerald's Greek title reflects his

---

[14] Bernardus Sylvestris, *Cosmographia* (ed Peter Dronke, Leiden, 1978) translated by Winthrop Wetherbee, *The Cosmographia of Bernardus Silvestris* (New York and London, 1973).
[15] Bartlett, *Gerald of Wales* pp 128-32.
[16] *Topography* II.iii, p 79; ed O'Meara, p 136; trans O'Meara, 2.26, p 60.
[17] See Ian Bradley, *Celtic Christianity: Making Myths and Chasing Dreams* (New York, 1999) pp 25-32, 39-76.
[18] The only occurrence of the term in patristic literature is Augustine, *Quaestionum in heptateuchum libri septem* 2.177, ed J Fraipoint, *Corpus Christianorum Series Latina [CCSL]* 33 (Turnhout, 1958) p 153: '*libri multa dicuntur, quae faciant difficultatem intellegendi, sicut solet omnis topographia, id est loci alicuius descriptio in omni historia facere*'.

desire to resurrect an ancient tradition. Having imitated the more established genres of *Chronographia* and *Cosmographia*, he uses the notion of *Topographia* to combine his scientific, spiritual and historical interests. Its three sections or distinctions relate to nature, the apparent rupture of the natural through the miraculous, and then the falling away from nature in human society. Rather than constructing a Platonically inspired theoretical synthesis like the *Cosmographia* of Bernard Sylvester, Gerald focuses on place, in this case on Ireland, to combine his interests in nature, the divine and human culture. His binding theme is the primacy he gives to observation:

> I have put down nothing in this book the truth of which I have not found out either by the testimony of my own eyes, or that of reliable men found worthy of credence and coming from the districts in which the events took place.[19]

Elsewhere, he claims that in the first two parts of the *Topography* he relies only on his own enquiry, not on any Irish text. Only in its third part does he acknowledge that he has drawn on some ancient chronicles.[20] As it happens, Gerald certainly relies on Cassiodorus and Bede for some of his information. What matters for Gerald, however, is that he emphasises the value of visual observation as a guiding principle to his writing, whether applied to nature, visual culture or ethnography, unlike the *History of the kings of Britain*, by Geoffrey of Monmouth, bishop of St Asaph (c 1100-1154). Whereas Geoffrey's account of the ancient Britons had acquired a reputation for being consciously mythical, Gerald wanted his *Topography* to be much more of a synthesis of scientific learning, purportedly based on his own observation and careful research.

Something of the complexity of the *Topography* is evident from the account that he gives in his autobiography of his public reading of the work at Oxford, perhaps around 1188. He relates its tripartite structure to three different groups in society:

> On the first [day] he received and entertained in his lodging all the poor of the whole city, whom he had called together for the purpose; on the next day he entertained all the doctors of the different faculties, and their pupils of greatest fame and renown; and on the third day the rest of the scholars with the knights, the citizens and others of the borough. This was indeed a costly and noble undertaking, by which were renewed in some fashion the authentic and

---

[19] *ibid*, II Praef, p 75; ed O'Meara, p 135; trans O'Meara, 2.33, p 57.
[20] *ibid*, Introitus in recitationem, p 8.

ancient times of the poets; nor can either the present age nor any past age in England show such a day.[21] The account tells us about the audience Gerald wanted to reach, rather than who actually came to the reading. He saw its first part, about Ireland's natural prosperity, as relevant to the poor, its second part, about Ireland's miracles and saints, as of interest to teachers and students, and its third section, rich in hostile stereotypes, as appealing to a lay audience. Most importantly, Gerald saw the *Topography* as a work of literature. It is much more than simply a collection of anecdotes. The *Topography* is a carefully crafted treatise that effectively develops a theme about the abundance of *natura*, the great wonders of the saints, and the falling away from those wonderful achievements by much of the contemporary Church in Ireland.

The opening, about the natural wealth of Ireland, perhaps deliberately parallels what Geoffrey of Monmouth has to say about the natural wealth of Britain in his more consciously mythical masterpiece, *History of the kings of Britain*.[22] Gerald is eager to present his account as much more credible than that of Geoffrey. While Gerald certainly did not travel outside that part of Ireland that came under Anglo-Norman control, he describes the island, which he claims is watered by nine principal rivers, as effectively a kind of Garden of Eden, richly endowed with fish and in particular with many different kinds of bird life. His account reflects not just personal observation, nor text, but perceptions that he gained from those 'credible witnesses' whom he chose to trust. While he explicitly acknowledges some information about young birds, gleaned from Cassiodorus, he may also have relied, directly or indirectly, on other sources. In many ways, Gerald's fascination with different animals and birds parallels similar scientific concerns reflected in two seventh-century Irish texts, the *De ordine creaturarum* and the *De mirabilibus sacrae scripturae*.[23] Marina Smyth has eloquently analysed how richly informed these seventh-century treatises are in description of the natural world. They are distinguished by their concern to explain the processes of the natural world in a historical rather than an allegorical manner, as above and beyond the work of the seven days of creation.[24] The *De ordine* reports that there are 153 different types of birds,

---

[21] *De rebus* 2.16, in *Opera* 1, 72-3 and *Epistolae*, in *Opera* 1, 410; see Michael Richter, 'Gerald of Wales: a public reading in Oxford in 1188 or 1189', *Neophilologus: An International Journal of Modern and Mediaeval Language and Literature* 62 (1978) 455-8.
[22] Geoffrey of Monmouth, *The Historia regum Britannie of Geoffrey of Monmouth* 1 (ed Neil Wright, Cambridge, 1985) p 2.
[23] *De mirabilibus sanctae scripturae*, PL 35, 2149-200, and *Liber de ordine creaturarum. Un anonimo Irleandés del Siglo II: Estudio y Edición Critica* (ed Manual C Diaz y Diaz, Santiago de Compostela, 1972) also printed in PL 83, 913-54.
[24] Marina Smyth, 'The Earliest Written Evidence for an Irish View of the World' in Doris Edel (ed), *Cultural Identity and Cultural Integration. Ireland and Europe in*

and explains how each is suited to their habitat: this is a naturalism far beyond anything found in Bede or Isidore. Above all, these treatises expand richly on the mystical significance of birds in Scripture, a relic of creation from before the time of the Fall and the Flood. The author of the *de ordine creaturarum* makes only a single criticism of pagan Irish teaching: a Druid belief that their ancestors used to fly around as birds. The notion of humans being transformed into birds is a rich theme in early Irish vernacular literature. The first section of Gerald's *Topography* effectively provides valuable insight into the continuing vitality of these Irish traditions into the twelfth century. Aristotelian texts of natural science had not yet begun to be translated or diffused in the Latin West. Gerald does make some allegorical remarks about different birds — such as about the eagle which contemplates the sun, in the manner of holy men contemplating heaven (remarks which delighted the archbishop of Canterbury when he recited his text), or about swans singing at the moment of death, like the saints — but they are combined with practical observation.

Underpinning the first section of the *Topography* is the theme that there are no natural poisons in Ireland, unlike the East, where 'the well of poisons brims over'. Gerald recognises the reality of change from a state of natural perfection: 'This indeed was the true course of nature; but as the world began to grow old, and as it were, began to slip into the decrepitude of old age, and to come to the end, the nature of almost all things became corrupted and changed for the worse.' Yet even though it is hard to see even in summer 'three consecutive days of really fine weather', there is no fundamental unhealthiness in the natural environment.[25] Gerald consciously breaks with an ancient tradition of looking to the east as the seat of Paradise, of Eden, as well as the seat of the Holy Land, the proverbial land of milk and honey:

> For just as the marvels of the East have through the work of certain authors come to the light of public notice, so the marvels of the West which, so far, have remained hidden away and almost unknown, may eventually find in me one to make them known even in these later days.[26]

The irony of this is that Gerald wrote this treatise at the same time as Jerusalem was slipping out of Christian control, and that in 1188 he would engage in a preaching tour in Wales, to promote a new Crusade to the East.

Gerald builds on an observation of Bede about the natural health of the Irish soil and its freedom from snakes, and acknowledges 'the pleasant conjecture that Saint Patrick and other saints of the land purged the island of

---

the *Early Middle Ages* (Dublin, 1995) 23-44; *idem, Understanding the Universe in Seventh-Century Ireland* (Woodbridge, 1996).
[25] *Topographia* I.xxxiii, p 67; ed O'Meara, p 133; trans O'Meara, 1.26, p 53.
[26] *ibid*, I.xl, p 79; ed O'Meara, p 134; trans O'Meara, 1.32, p 56.

all harmful animals'. He thinks it more likely that the country had been free from such creatures before the Christian period.[27] Gerald identifies dangerous reptiles as present outside Ireland, on remote islands, or even in the Isle of Man, closer to Britain, but not Ireland.[28] Gerald tells us that he has read, in the ancient writings of the saints of the land, that snakes were imported into the country in bronze containers, but still died when they arrived. He argues that it is the soil of the land, rather than St Patrick, which keeps the reptiles away. The story of the expulsion of snakes, not preserved in Muirchu's *Life of Patrick*, but first recorded only in the late twelfth century, builds on a strong tradition in the Patrick legend of emphasising his conflict with the ancient Druids.[29] Although Muirchu acknowledged the authority of the *Life of Brigit* by Cogitosus, his presentation of Patrick's confrontation with the Druids as like Moses countering the priests of Pharaoh is radically different from that given by Cogitosus of Brigit, in which the heroine is presented as a fount of fertility, able to befriend wild boars, wolves, and wild ducks. Where Cogitosus emphasises continuities in the attributes of Brigit with the pagan goddess of the same name, Muirchu presents Patrick as imposing his authority on a hostile world, and Armagh, rather than Kildare, as claiming supremacy in the church of Ireland.[30] The stories about Brigit that Gerald records suggest that he was much closer in sympathy to the traditions of Kildare than those of Armagh. His interest in showing saints as having affinity with wild birds and animals is closer to the stories told about Brigit, than about Patrick. Bede speaks of Columba, but never mentions Brigit or Patrick in his *Ecclesiastical History*. At a time of the growing influence of Patrick and Armagh, Gerald wanted to make sure that Brigit of Kildare was not forgotten. Gerald's reserve towards the memory of Patrick may also be evident in the fact that only in a late recension does he identify as St Patrick's Purgatory the island in the lake in Ulster (Lough Derg) where there is a very beautiful church on one side, and a place of great ugliness that effectively enables penitents to avoid the pains of hell.[31] This is the first time in the *Topography* that the demonic is invoked, but effectively to indicate here that a pilgrim can escape the powers of hell.

---

[27] *ibid*, I.xxviii, p 62; ed O'Meara, p 130; trans O'Meara, 1.21, p 50.

[28] Bede, *Ecclesiastical History of the English People* i.1 (ed Bertram Colgrave and R A B Mynors (Oxford, 1969) pp 18-20.

[29] For a translation of Muirchu's Life of St Patrick, see Liam de Paor, *Saint Patrick's World* (Dublin, 1993) 175-98; for Jocelyn's life, see *Four Latin Lives of Saint Patrick* (ed L Bieler, Scriptores Latini Hiberniae 8, Dublin, 1971); Bartlett, *Gerald of Wales*, pp 139f.

[30] See Richard Sharpe, 'St Patrick and the see of Armagh', *Cambridge Medieval Celtic Studies* 4 (1982) 33-59; Cormac Bourke, *Patrick. The Archaeology of a Saint* (Belfast, 1993) pp 12f.

[31] *Topography* I.v, pp 82f; ed O'Meara, pp 139f; trans O'Meara 2.38, p 61.

Only very gradually in the second part does Gerald introduce stories about humans. Significantly, they begin with a story not about Christian saints but about the builders of megaliths. Perhaps consciously wanting to outdo a story told by Geoffrey of Monmouth about Merlin's involvement in bringing Stonehenge to England, Gerald explains that Stonehenge, or 'the Giant's Dance', had been transported to Ireland by giants from Africa, but that it had been brought by the king of the Britons (with the help of Merlin) to Britain, where it served as a memorial for Britons slain by Saxons.[32]

> It is amazing how so many great stones were ever brought together or erected in one place, and with what skill upon such great and high stones others no less great were placed. These latter seem to be hanging, as it were, and suspended in space, so as to rest rather on the skill of the craftsmen than on the base of stones beneath.[33]

These comments about the skill of the original craftsmen of Stonehenge are the first of a series of remarks in the *Topography* about the skill of native craftsman, whether they are scribes (as in the case of the Book of Kildare) or musicians, for which Gerald thought the Irish enjoyed great competence.

This leads into a set of anecdotes which consciously question conventional antitheses between the natural and the human world. He tells the story told to him about a priest who encountered two wolves, who then turn out to be humans sent into exile. As Caroline Bynum has recently argued, Gerald's anecdote is much more about identity than metamorphosis, because the wolves' skin is peeled back to reveal a human form. It is really about an encounter with liminality.[34] A priest who befriends that which is normally wild and dangerous, and discovers that in reality these wolves are two humans, unjustly ostracised from their society. It is a story about the goodness of a priest, who wanted to share his story at a synod of bishops. Gerald is fascinated that a story about such an encounter at the very margins of civilisation could be reported even to the Pope. In a later recension, he adds a prophecy given by the wolf to the priest, that the invasion is a punishment for the sin of his people.[35] The scriptural anecdote lying behind the exemplum is the story of Balaam's ass (*Numbers* 22-24), in which the ass utters oracles to Balaam, and thus to Balak, king of the Moabites.

This leads into a succession of stories about relationships between humans and beasts, as well as humans and birds, which serve to teach a

---

[32] *Historia Regum Britannie*, ed Wright, pp 90-92.
[33] *Topography* II.xviii, p 100; ed O'Meara, p 143; trans O'Meara, 2.51, p 69.
[34] *ibid*, I.xix, pp 101-107; ed O'Meara, pp 143-5; trans O'Meara, 2.52, pp 69-72. See Caroline Walker Bynum, 'Metamorphosis, or Gerald and the Werewolf' in *Metamorphosis and Identity* (New York, 2001) 77-111, previously published in *Speculum* 73 (1998) 987-1013.
[35] *ibid*, II.xix, p 103.

lesson about the location of true order in the natural world. Rather than reading these as tall stories, we should appreciate them as moral tales about how right relationships need to prevail in creation: stories that may well transmit local folk traditions that he had heard. He tells a story about a willow tree of St Kevin revered throughout Ireland for a certain fruit (white and oblong in shape) that had therapeutic properties.[36] St Kevin also kept ravens at bay while allowing a blackbird to nest on his hand. There is a great deal in the *Topography* that he has clearly learned by talking with locals. Gerald is fascinated by the stories he has heard about the saints of Ireland keeping the land free from harmful creatures, like fleas and rats, although he may not be sure about their veracity.[37]

Many of the stories that Gerald tells relate to Leinster. If anyone killed the birds of St Colman on the lake of Leinster, misfortune would befall him. Gerald tells the story of one of these birds being killed by an archer, in the retinue of Robert FitzStephen, then travelling with Diairmait Mac Murchada, king of Leinster.[38] When he (presumably the archer) realised that a sacred bird had been put into a cooking pot, he lamented that disaster would occur, as demonstrated by the subsequent death of that archer. There was a political angle to his story, effectively a warning to Anglo-Norman soldiers to treat sacred places and sacred birds with caution. Diairmait, king of Leinster, had initiated the invasion of Ireland by seeking to ally himself with Henry II, and linking himself to Robert FitzStephen, half brother to Gerald's uncles, William FitzGerald, Maurice FitzGerald and David FitzGerald, bishop of St David's (1148-76). In the *Expugnatio Hibernica* Gerald tells the story of how Robert FitzStephen took control of Leinster, with the help of his own relatives, a military encounter which involved treacherous behaviour by the bishops of Wexford and Kildare.[39] Gerald's own family were given extensive lands in the region, which provided a base for his own travels in Ireland. Relating the traditions of the saints of the region was an important way for Gerald to explain to his audience how settlers in Ireland needed to respect its sacred traditions if they were to claim authority in the region.

Some of the most important stories in the *Topography* relate to Kildare, where another relation of Gerald, Meiler FitzHenry, held significant estates, later transferred to another line of his family.[40] The

---

[36] *Topography* II.xxviii, pp 113f; ed O'Meara, pp 147f; trans O'Meara, 2.61, p 77.
[37] *ibid*, II.xxxi-xxxii, pp 119f; ed O'Meara, p 149; trans O'Meara 2.64-5, pp 80f.
[38] *ibid*, II.xxix, p 117; ed O'Meara, pp 148f; trans O'Meara, 2.62, p 80.
[39] *Expugnatio Hibernica* 1.1-12, ed Scott and Martin, pp 20-54; see B Eager, 'The Cambro-Normans and the Lordship of Leinster' in J. Bradley (ed), *Settlement and Society in Medieval Ireland* (Kilkenny, 1988) 193-205.
[40] *ibid*, 2.4, 2.23, pp 142, 194, 325 note 251. Gerald, son of Maurice FitzGerald, became Earl of Kildare; see the family tree given by Bartlett, *Gerald of Wales*, p 26.

emphasis that Gerald gives to stories about Kildare (Cell-Dara) and St Brigit reflect his own sense of the importance of this ancient monastery and its patron, closely identified with the kingdom of Leinster as a whole.[41] Gerald begins his report of the miracles of Kildare by describing the inextinguishable fire protected by nuns and holy women. He is clearly aware that reverence for Brigit embodies a sense of Christian continuity with pagan tradition, very different from the emphasis of stories about Patrick that emphasise his hostility to Druid teaching. Unlike the stories about Patrick, stories about Brigit relate to fertility and the crafts, precisely those attributes traditionally associated with a pagan divinity also known as Brigit. The lives of Brigit from the seventh century kept alive a sense at Kildare that its monastic community once claimed to exercise authority over all Ireland.[42] The stories told by Gerald, not identical to those told by Cogitosus, are nonetheless fully of a piece with that seventh-century *Life*. They effectively confirm the ongoing vitality of reverence for Brigit in the twelfth century, and warn his readers — even members of his own family, settled in the region — to respect the traditions of the land which they now occupy. His story about the falcon who had until recently always lived on the tower of the church of Kildare, but had been killed by a rustic, provides another moral lesson about respect for good order. He interprets its fidelity to the church tower as an example of the honour due to churchmen.

Gerald's account of the manuscript written at Kildare, apparently with coloured drawings on every page, provides a climax to his account of miracles achieved by the saints.[43] While art historians tend to quote his description because of its evident similarity to the Book of Kells, they tend to ignore the significance of what he has to say about how the manuscript was written through the prayers of Brigit. Just as the monks of Kells preserved their gospel manuscript as a sign of their link to Columba, so the monks and nuns of Kildare preserved their own manuscript, as a link back to the time of Brigit.[44] Gerald was particularly interested in the page

---

[41] On Kildare itself, see James F Kenney, *The Sources for the Early History of Ireland: Ecclesiastical* (Dublin, 1979) pp 357f.

[42] *ibid*, 2.20, ed Scott and Martin, p 188. The *Life of Brigit* by Cogitosus is translated by Liam de Paor, *St Patrick's World*, 207-24. On the various lives and the political claims of Kildare that they articulate, see Richard Sharpe, 'Vitae S. Brigitae: The Oldest Texts', *Peritia* 1 (1982) 81-106; Kim McCone, 'Brigit in the Seventh Century: A Saint with Three Lives?', *Peritia* 1 (1982) 107-45. For a sensitive review of the Brigit tradition, see Joseph Falaky Nagy, *Conversing with Angels and Ancients. Literary Myths of Medieval Ireland* (Ithaca, 1997) pp 231-38; Lisa M Bitel, 'Body of a saint, story of a goddess: origins of the Brigidine tradition', *Textual Practice* 16:2 (2002) 209-28.

[43] *Topography* III.xxxviii, p 123; ed O'Meara, pp 151f; trans O'Meara, 2.71, p 84.

[44] George Henderson, *From Durrow to Kells. The Insular Gospel-books 650-800* (London, 1987) pp 195-98.

providing mystical representations of the evangelists as the eagle (John), the calf (Luke), the man (Matthew) and the lion (Mark). The idea of identifying the four evangelists with the four winged animals around the throne, each with different faces (*Revelation* 4:7) goes back to Jerome, and was much appreciated by early Irish scribes: Jerome saw Matthew as presented by a man, because his Gospel begins with Christ's ancestry. Mark, the most abrupt of evangelists, is a lion, because he begins with a voice crying in the wilderness. Luke is a calf because his Gospel begins with Zachary's sacrifice of a calf in the temple (prefiguring that of Christ). John is an eagle who speaks of the Word of God. These four creatures, bird, man, wild beast, and domestic animal, symbolize four levels of creation, as well as different stages in the life of Christ.[45] Gregory the Great similarly repeated the idea that these different creatures represented different stages in the life of Christ. Gerald singles out this page, I suggest, not just because of its beauty, but because it connects to his broader theme that birds and animals had in themselves a sacred significance. Even in the first part of the *Topography* he has highlighted how the eagle is a symbol of contemplating the divine, the task of all true monks. By describing this page of the illuminated manuscript, he effectively brings to a climax a theme already hinted at in the first part of the *Topography*, about Ireland as richly endowed with natural creatures that reflect the full wonder of God.

Gerald also uses his description of the Book of Kildare, written 'more by angelic than human carefulness' (*potius angelica quam humana diligentia*), to reinforce his theme about human artistry and divine inspiration. Designs which might seem at first sight to lack skill demonstrate their artistry on closer inspection, the same point as he makes later in the *Topography* in relation to music.[46] Gerald describes how the scribe was shown a drawing by an angel, but panicked because he felt insufficiently skilled to copy it. The angel then told the monk to speak to Brigit 'so that she may pour forth prayers for you to the Lord, that he may open both your bodily and mental eyes so as to see the more keenly and understand the more subtly, and may direct your hands to draw correctly.' Just as the pagan Brigit had been goddess of craftsmen, so St Brigit now provided inspiration to the scribe. The monk did as he was told, and 'with the angel indicating the designs, Brigit praying, and the scribe imitating, that book was composed.'[47] The magnificent interlace of human and animal, bird and fish forms that can be seen on almost every page of the Book of Kells illustrates the theme, so often found in Irish religious poetry

---

[45] Jerome, *Commentarii in Ezechielem* 1.1.6-8a (ed F Glorie, CCSL 75, Turnhout, 1964), pp 11-14; Gregory the Great, *Hom. In Ezechielem* 1.4 (ed M Adriaen, CCSL 142, Turnhout, 1971) p 47.
[46] See note 10 above, and III.xi, p 154; ed O'Meara, p 164; trans O'Meara, 3.94, p 104.
[47] *Topography* III.xxxix, p 124; ed O'Meara, p 152; trans O'Meara, 2.72, p 85.

of the early medieval period, that the whole of creation itself spoke of the Word of God. Whether or not the inspiration for all the Kells animal decorations are Pictish, as has been argued by Isabel Henderson, there is no doubt that the books of both Kells and Kildare reflect a deeper synthesis of natural and textual worlds than found in the more classically formed Lindisfarne Gospels.[48] Not only do the mystical images of the evangelists connect with what he has said earlier about birds and animals, but his account of the artistry of the scribe deliberately recalls what he has to say about the makers of the megaliths, and in the third section about the skill of the Celts in making music. The story about St Brigit provides a climax to what Gerald has to say about the potential of human craft.

Only in the third book does Gerald move to discuss Irish history. Having cast doubt on the claim about Patrick having cast out snakes from Ireland, he effectively acknowledges the major political claim of Armagh to establish supremacy over Ireland by reporting how in the year that prince John first came to Ireland (1185), the new ruler of Ulster, John de Courci, 'discovered' the bodies of Columba and Brigit, on either side of Patrick's body in the city of Down in Ulster.[49] This so-called 'discovery' was in fact very convenient for the new ruler of Ulster, John de Courcy, who took charge of the reburial of these saints. The 'discovery' helped connect the patron saints of Kildare and Kells to the cult of Patrick and thus to validate the authority of Armagh.[50] It helped dissolve rival claims between the northern and southern parts of Ireland. Given the historic rivalries between Kildare and Armagh, evident even in the seventh-century lives of both Brigit and Patrick, it is all the more interesting that Gerald is aware of the political pressure to recognize the authority of Patrick. Armagh had already gained great success over Kildare in being made the most senior of the four new archbishoprics of Ireland, created in 1152 at the Council of Kells, by John Paparo. Kildare became subordinate to Dublin.[51] This program of reform and Romanisation was consolidated at the second synod of Cashel in 1172. In his account of the conquest of Ireland (written 1188-89), Gerald expresses his admiration for John de Courcy because of his reverence for a certain book of Irish prophecies in which St Columba purportedly predicted the troubles that would befall the Irish.[52] Gerald's stories about St Brigit demonstrate a similar pattern of using Irish saints to demonstrate that

---

[48] Isabel Henderson, 'Pictish art and the Book of Kells' in D Whitelock *et al* (eds), *Ireland in Early Mediaeval Europe* (Cambridge, 1982) 79-105.
[49] *Topographia* III.xviii, p 163; ed O'Meara, p 165; trans O'Meara, 3.97, p 105; *Expugnatio Hibernica* 2.35, p 234.
[50] On John de Courcy, *Expugnatio Hibernica* 2.18, pp 178-80.
[51] On the significance of the Synod of Kells, see Aubrey Gwynn, *The Irish Church in the 11th and 12th Centuries* (Dublin, 1992) pp 218-33, 265-70.
[52] *Expugnatio Hibernica* 2.17, pp 176-78.

churchmen arrived from England could legitimately connect to Ireland's sacred past. The fact that Gerald was cautious about the miracles of St Patrick and never mentions miracles of Columba in the *Topography* reinforces the suggestion that he was actively promoting the importance of Brigit and Kildare in Leinster, the region where his own family had important connections.

Gerald subsequently relates how an archer of earl Richard crossed the hedge and blew on Brigit's fire, only to suffer subsequently a fatal thirst; another male transgressor was made permanently lame.[53] These are warnings directed to soldiers. Gerald had a strong sense of the need to respect sacred places, and was critical of soldiers who did not respect them. He tells a similar story about a mill of saint Fechin in a town in Meath, where women could not enter. An archer dragged a woman into this mill and raped her, only to be stricken with hell-fire in his member, to die the same night.[54] His message is directed as much against the barbarism of the invading armies in Ireland, as against the behaviour of the local population. There are spaces in society confined to one or other sex, or to men of the Church. Disrespect for these boundaries will inevitably incur disaster.

Gerald's complaints about the barbarism of the Irish, found in the third part of the *Topography*, are part of a broader contrast between the behaviour of the saints and of godly people, as opposed to those whose behaviour has fallen away from perfection. Through his studies in France, Gerald would have been familiar with an old literary tradition identifying *Britones* as on the margins of civilization, in being wild and temperamental by nature.[55] His presentation of the Irish as similarly uncontrolled and lacking discipline fits into a common stereotype. Where he differs from earlier writers, however, is in the detail that he gives to describing their way of life. The significance of this part of the *Topography* is not just that it provides a justification and legitimation for the Anglo-Norman conquest, but that it includes unexpected insights within passages about the barbarity of much of Irish civilization. Thus after a long description of how the Irish are not devoted to industry, he provides a detailed account of their expertise in making music, and makes an observation about how the ear is often deaf to subtle artistry, very similar to his comment about the artistry of the Book of Kildare:

> Hence it happens that the very things that afford unspeakable delight to the minds of those who have a fine perception and

---

[53] *Topography* II.xlviii, p 121; ed O'Meara, p 154; trans O'Meara, 3.77, p 88.
[54] *ibid*, II.lii, p 134; ed O'Meara, p155; trans O'Meara, 2.81, p 90.
[55] Pierre Riché, 'Les Bretons victimes des lieux communs dans le haut moyen âge' in G Le Menn and J-Y Le Moing (eds), *Bretagne et pays celtiques. Langues, histoire, civilisation. Mélanges offerts a la mémoire de Léon Fleuriot* (Saint-Brieux-Rennes, 1992) 111-15. I am indebted to Lyn Olson for this reference.

> can penetrate carefully to the secrets of the art, bore, rather than delight, those who have no such perception — who look without seeing and hear without being able to understand. When the audience is unsympathetic they succeed only in causing boredom with what appears to be but confused and disordered noise.[56]

Gerald uses Irish music to repeat his broader argument about the importance of sensitive observation, that we must avoid coming to swift judgements, when the fault may lie more in our perception than in what is outside of ourselves.

Gerald's remarks about the Irish clergy are similarly nuanced. His hostility is reserved not to the clergy, 'on the whole to be commended for the observance' but to the prelates, whom he reproves for not living up to their task:

> If the prelates from the time of Patrick through all those years had done a man's job as they should have done, in preaching and instructing, chastising and correcting, they would have extirpated at any rate to a certain extent those abominations of the people already mentioned, and would have impressed upon them some semblance of honour and religious feeling.[57]

Gerald certainly supports the cause of reform, but he does not indulge in blanket condemnations of the Irish Church, such as would have been widespread among Anglo-Norman ecclesiastical authorities. He recounts the story of how the archbishop of Cashel reproved a cleric of the church of Rome, called Gerard, who was 'blaming the prelates especially for the terrible enormities of the country, using the very strong argument that no one had ever in that kingdom won the crown of martyrdom in defence of the church of God'. Gerald implicitly acknowledges the archbishop's criticism of the hard-line Roman cleric, in arguing that the Irish have always paid honour and reverence to Churchmen. This sly and prophetic comment articulates Gerald's awareness that there was no easy definition of Irish Christianity.

Gerald's *Topography* provided justification for the major reforms taking place in Ireland, imposing a firm structure of ecclesiastical order on the Irish Church, and in legitimising the subjection of the country to the English crown. Yet within that framework he was also urging both ecclesiastical and secular authorities in Ireland to respect its holy places and traditions, as rich as any to be found in the rest of the British Isles. He is much more than simply a hostile outsider. Like Bede, Gerald is always complex in his judgements. The experience of travelling in Ireland exposed

---

[56] *Topography* III.xi, p 154; ed O'Meara, p 164; trans O'Meara, 3.94, p 104.
[57] *ibid*, III.xxxviii, p 173; ed O'Meara, p 169; trans O'Meara, 3.105, pp 112f.

Gerald not just to a new landscape, but to an ancient Christian culture with traditions very different from his own. When studying in Paris, he had drawn on a philosophical model of the natural world presented by Bernard Sylvester to help construct a vision of the universe. The idea of writing about Ireland provided Gerald with a much more satisfying and tightly drawn way of describing his respect for nature, his fascination with the marvellous, and his distaste for behaviour that he considered barbarous. His intention was much more than simply to entertain.[58] He sought to nuance those hasty judgements, based on a quick glance at an ancient manuscript or an inattentive hearing of Irish music, by arguing that one had to pay attention to the details of art or music to appreciate the subtlety involved. Similarly, settlers and soldiers needed to respect the holy places of the culture which they sought to suppress through force of arms. Gerald introduces a similar nuance in the *Expugnatio Hibernica*, in which he not only celebrates the achievements of his own family, the Geraldines, but is also ruthlessly critical of aggressive Normans, concerned only to exploit their position. He used the opportunity of writing his account of Prophetic History (*Vaticinalis Historia*) as a vehicle to warn that while force was needed against the Irish, care should be taken to treat them with respect.[59] He was fascinated by the prophecies of Merlin of Celidon and Merlin Ambrosius because he saw these figures as effectively engaging in the task which was his own, to warn others by proclaiming truth.[60] Gerald's experience in Ireland provided him with inspiration for carving out a career as a writer, very different from anything that he could have expected when he was a student in Paris.

---

[58] F X Martin argues that 'In the *Topography* he had set out to entertain'; *Expugnatio Hibernica*, p 272.
[59] *Expugnatio Hibernica*, 2.36, p 250.
[60] *ibid*, 3, p 254.

Culhane of Brunswick on early medieval Ireland

Val Noone

In the middle of the twentieth century, Thomas Culhane of Brunswick, Victoria, published high-level popularisations of scholarly work on Irish history and literature in the Melbourne Catholic magazine, *The Advocate*. Born in 1891 in County Limerick, Culhane had been educated at Mungret College Limerick, All Hallows Seminary Dublin and Queen's University Belfast before migrating to Australia in 1927 with his wife, Kathleen Naughton. Although he held a master's degree, Culhane did not find work as a scholar or teacher but rather worked first on his wife's uncle's farm at Elmore, then in the public service at the munitions works at Maribyrnong, and later in the office of Standard Motors, a motor vehicle manufacturer. He nonetheless corresponded with scholars in Ireland, subscribed to scholarly journals, and found time to write regular substantial 1500-word pieces.[1] In this paper I will discuss his articles on early medieval Ireland in *The Advocate* under five headings: Irish manuscripts; early Irish and church history; Irish music and poetry; the Normans; and European scholars of Ireland.[2]

Irish manuscripts

In 1940 Culhane wrote a survey of ancient Irish manuscripts.[3] Starting from a reference to press publicity about a lost manuscript known as the Book of Clonenagh which is said to have come to Australia in the mid-1800s, he quoted Rudolf Thurneysen and Connell MacGeoghegan's translation of the *Annals of Clonmacnoise*, surveyed Norman and Tudor conquests, and drew attention to the writings of the Four Masters. The

---

[1] Ita Collard, 'Tom Culhane: Gaelic scholar down under', *Táin* 14 (Aug-Sept 2001) 32-33; Thomas J Byrne, Tom Donovan, Bernard Stack (eds), *Home Thoughts from Abroad: the Australian Letters of Thomas F Culhane* (Glin Historical Society, 1998); Thomas J O'Donoghue, 'Tribute to Thomas F Culhane', *Ballyguiltenane Rural Journal* (c 1980-1981); Padraig O Cearbhaill, 'Reminiscence', *Ballyguiltenane Rural Journal* (c 1980-1981); Val Noone, '"A recognised authority on Irish Studies": Thomas Culhane's writings in the *Melbourne Advocate*' in Louis de Paor (ed), *Papers of the Twelfth Irish Australian Conference, Galway 2002* (forthcoming).
[2] The articles filled one tabloid page, closely typeset, occasionally running onto a second page, and were at the front of a section called 'Advocate Magazine'. I wish to thank Ita Collard for giving me photocopies of these articles. Also I wish to thank Mary Doyle, Nóirín Keane, Kit Aherne and Mairéad MacGrath for their assistance with this research project, and Ann Trindade and Greg Byrnes for their comments on an earlier draft of this paper.
[3] 'In search of a lost ancient manuscript', *The Advocate* (2 May 1940) p 15.

accompanying picture of Nicholas O'Donnell had a caption drawing attention to O'Donnell's gift of Irish manuscripts to the Newman College library in Melbourne. In this piece, Culhane wrote of a still little-known aspect of the transmission of Irish culture in Australia.

In 1953, Culhane returned to the issue of manuscripts in an article on the Irish Manuscripts Commission.[4] He praised the work of collecting and preserving historical Irish records carried out under Professor Eoin MacNeill. He remarked that 'a complete set of the published works of the Commission has been presented by the Irish Government to the Central Catholic Library, Melbourne'. This article included an example of Culhane's claims to scholarship:

> [MacNeill's] mastery of the whole field of documentary evidence was complete. Nothing escaped him. What MacNeill conceived was a picture of every phase of Gaelic civilisation from its most primitive origins to its last submergences or survivals. He embraced the whole of that subject with an incomparable knowledge and sympathy which does not blind him but rather gives him vision and intuition.

Surveying the commission's publications to date, Culhane said that
> the earliest and in some respects the most important of these was a facsimile reproduction of the oldest of the Brehon law tracts, known as the *Senchus Mor*. Because of the intense interest taken in Ireland's ancient legal systems by students of comparative law, [the commission will publish more on this] ... They are among the most enduring things which ancient Ireland has given to posterity ... Thus is it that the Brehon laws preserve in a semi-fossilized condition many primitive Aryan institutions which are but dimly reflected in the oldest legal survivals of cognate systems.

With reference to this last point, Culhane compared the Irish publications with *Monumenta Germaniae Historica* and cited the work of Gardiner on seventeenth-century England, as well as Giesebrecht and Janssen on medieval Europe.

The earlier dearth of Irish scholarship, Culhane said, 'was in accordance with nineteenth century British policy that little stimulus should be given to the study of any branch of historical inquiry which might arouse undesirable national aspirations'. Anticipating later views, Culhane drew attention to ways of working around the loss of records in the 1922 bombardment of the Four Courts. He sought to inspire in his readers a love of scholarship and Irish history.

---

[4] 'Historic work of Irish manuscripts commission', *The Advocate* (8 October 1953) p 9.

Greg Byrnes has read the manuscripts in the State Library of Victoria which Culhane referred to and found there some annotations by Culhane on two of them. Byrnes records that in 1936 Culhane copied some verse into an 1823 O'Curry manuscript and signed his name. On a small 1822 anthology of poetry
> [Culhane] wrote much more freely, commenting on the poet Séamas Mac Gearailt who was born in the same place as Culhane and expressing the hope that he would be able to return there to die. He also prayed for the original scribe, trusting that he was watching him from heaven and not angry at Culhane for writing on his manuscript.[5]

When confronting an Irish manuscript in an Australian library, the Gaelic scholar living in Brunswick felt strong and inspired but lonely.

Early Church and Irish history

Culhane wrote a good deal about Irish and church history, and these topics intersected with everything else that he wrote. In this section let us note his views on Origen, St Patrick, St Columbanus (he called him Columban), Pelagius and the matter of early Irish scholars.

In 1954, the seventeenth centenary of the death of Origen (185-254), a theologian of Alexandria in Egypt, was the occasion for Culhane to expound some of the views of that thinker.[6] He noted that Church authorities have suspected the orthodoxy of Origen but sided with those who revere him as wise and innovative. A striking feature of this article is Culhane's praise of a French theologian and commentator on Origen, Henri de Lubac. De Lubac was at that time under suspicion of heresy by Roman authorities. Culhane wrote:
> Origen has today zealous friends and fair-minded critics whose erudition and industry are beyond all praise. The most illustrious of all these is Henri de Lubac SJ, a scholar of amazing boldness and wisdom, the author of *Surnaturel*, a truly extraordinary work, which has led to much theological controversy in recent years.

When I was a student in the diocesan theological college in the 1950s and early 1960s, *Surnaturel* was one of the books locked away for which one needed special permission to borrow and read. The 1950 papal encyclical, *Humani Generis*, had included warnings about views on nature and grace, which were generally taken as an attack on de Lubac's work. Culhane

---

[5] Greg Byrnes, 'Irish manuscripts in Australia: a partial shelf list', in Richard Davis et al (eds), *Irish-Australian Studies: Papers delivered at the Eighth Irish-Australian Conference, Hobart July 1995* (Sydney, 1996) 242-246.

[6] 'Origen: great apologist of the Early Church', *The Advocate* (25 November 1954) p 17.

suggests that 'it seems that it has been reserved for our time to recognize the value of [Origen's] genius."

When he came to writing about St Patrick, Culhane showed an interest in critical scholarship.[7] The heading of his article referred to St Patrick as 'one of history's most disputed figures', and his introduction says:

> St Patrick is said to have left the strongest and most permanent impression of his personality upon a people, with the single and eminent exception of Moses, yet he continues to be a subject of controversy. It is even argued that St Patrick, as we know him, was in fact two people, one of whom was Palladius.

In Ireland the previous year, the well-known Thomas Davis lectures on Irish radio had been on St Patrick.[8] It is thus possible that in this case Culhane was relaying for his Australian readers material he had recently read. Further research might determine to what extent he was commenting on the material and adapting it in the light of his own researches.[9]

In line with a sympathy for Origen and an openness on the disputes about Patrick, Culhane had a good word for Pelagius, a theologian of the late fourth and early fifth centuries.[10] The introduction to his article said:

> Since the German Celticist H Zimmer wrote his provocative work on Pelagius almost sixty years ago much research has been done into the origin and nationality of this remarkable man, who in his lifetime was famous as few writers have ever been. He was read from end to end of the civilised world and for centuries after his death his name had only to be mentioned to evoke the most tremendous contention and controversy. In our own days one aspect of his teaching concerning the lot of infants who die without baptism has been the subject of much discussion between theologians.

On infant baptism, Culhane seemed to say in cautious and scholarly prose that Pelagius was right and that that was now being recognised.

In 1958, a year before he wrote the above piece on Patrick, Culhane commented on the role of St Columban (c 543-615) as 'a man of heroic

---

[7] 'St Patrick: one of history's most disputed figures', *The Advocate* (12 March 1959) p 11.

[8] I wish to thank Seamus Doyle of Mt Eliza, Victoria, for information about the 1958 Thomas Davis lectures. These were published as John Ryan SJ (ed), *St Patrick*.

[9] Culhane also had access to the publications of the Dublin Institute for Advanced Studies, and was therefore probably familiar with T F O'Rahilly, *The Two Patricks* (Dublin, 1942, repr 1957), in which the conflation of Palladius and Patrick was argued.

[10] 'It took Saint Augustine to silence Pelagius', *The Advocate* (17 March 1960).

stature and one of the makers of our European tradition'.[11] In his view, the Rev G S Walker, a minister of the Presbyterian Church, was 'a welcome recruit to the large band of scholars who interest themselves in the activities of St Columban'. Culhane praised the Dublin Institute for Advanced Studies which had published a complete works of Columban with an English translation.[12]

In 1964, commemorating the annual feast of St Patrick, Culhane argued that Western civilisation owed a special debt to Irish scholarship.[13] Indeed, this was a major theme of his writing, whatever the explicit topic. On this occasion, his writing anticipated the argument of Thomas Cahill in his *How the Irish Saved Civilisation*. Culhane followed Heinrich Zimmer's hypothesis that the classical Greek and Latin texts were brought to Ireland by Gallic scholars fleeing war and destruction,[14] and argued that Irish missionaries and scholars made a great and unique contribution to European learning and civilisation. 'They furnished the impulse that helped to erect a new Western Europe upon the debris of the Roman Empire', he said.

The introduction to this article suggested that Culhane had a considerable local reputation. The editor wrote:

> An important recent book, *Ireland: Harbinger of the Middle Ages*, by an illustrious scholar, Professor Ludwig Bieler, was reviewed on this page on 9 January last by Dr Eoin MacWhite, who arrived in Australia as chargé d'affaires at the Irish Embassy, Canberra, and is himself a distinguished scholar and member of the Irish academy. Professor Bieler is responsible for the publication of Hiberno-Latin texts in a new series known as *Scriptores Latini Hiberniae*. The significance of these texts is stressed here by Mr Thomas F Culhane of Melbourne, a recognised authority on Irish Studies.

Thus, a local news magazine expected, or hoped for, a high level of interest from readers who would know Culhane as 'a recognised authority on Irish Studies'.

Culhane revealed, again, a breadth of reading. He showed respect for Christopher Dawson's work and was enthusiastic about the work of an Hiberno-Latin studies centre in Dublin (which, at that time, under Ludwig Bieler's direction, was microfilming continental manuscripts). Praising Wattenbach, Culhane went on to draw attention to the work of Bruno Krusch 'who has lorded over the whole field of Columban enquiry for many

---

[11] 'St Columban, a maker of our European tradition', *The Advocate* (31 July 1958) p 11.
[12] G S M Walker, *Sancti Columbani opera* (Dublin, 1957).
[13] 'Civilisation's debt to Irish scholarship', *The Advocate* (12 March 1964) p 9.
[14] Zimmer's hypothesis had found little favour with other scholars; see Eoin MacNeill, *Phases of Irish History* (1919, repr Kennikat, 1970) pp 164ff.

years'. Moreover, Culhane remarked on Ireland's 'everlasting debt of gratitude to Ludwig Traube' for his contributions to Irish palaeography:

> Traube combined qualities which have perhaps never been united before in any one man. Hence his work is unique. He is best remembered for the magnificent work he has done in throwing light on every phase of Irish activity in medieval times. His work in this sphere is a revelation of critical and interpretative insight.

These lines convey Culhane's sense of having an overview of European sources on Irish history, Ireland's relationship with Europe, and Hiberno-Latin texts.

I finished reading this essay by Culhane recalling asides by seminary lecturers to matters such as these but feeling regret that as a student of theology and Church history in the Melbourne diocesan seminary at the very time that he was writing these scholarly pieces, I and my cohort did not have the opportunity to hear him lecture on these key aspects of our inheritance.

Of Irish music and poetry

In 1957 Culhane wrote about a then recently published anthology, *Early Irish Lyrics*[15] by Professor Gerard Murphy, 'one of the most brilliant of the younger generation of Irish students'.[16] In Culhane's view, this book revealed

> the infinite variety, the plenitude and power of learning during Ireland's golden age and contains the first poem to Our Lady in any European language outside the classical world.

In this connection, Culhane quoted Kuno Meyer's views of seventy years earlier:

> the anonymous and neglected poems once properly collected, edited and translated will strongly appeal to all lovers of poetry, for there is in them such delicate art, so true and deep a note, that, with the exception of the masterpieces of Welsh poetry, I know nothing to put beside them.

Meyer's work seems to have had a marked influence on all Culhane's writings.

On a later occasion, continuing his study in this area, Culhane reviewed Donal O'Sullivan's newly published work, *Songs of the Irish*.[17]

---

[15] Gerard Murphy, *Early Irish Lyrics* (Oxford, 1957). Murphy's work was republished by Four Courts Press in 1998.
[16] 'Fragments of a lost argosy of Celtic poetry', *The Advocate* (28 March 1957) p 11.
[17] 'Gaelic song goes back to the dawn of civilisation', *The Advocate* (9 March 1961) p 11.

For Culhane, Gaelic song went back to 'the dawn of civilisation' and was 'regarded, even by authorities with anti-Irish political prejudices, as the finest music that exists'. Culhane put the Irish composers alongside Mozart and Schubert to form 'a triad unsurpassed in the whole range of the art of sheer melody'.

Culhane also wrote about a commentary by Melbourne scholar Percy Jones on a tenth-century work on music by Irish philosopher Scottus Eriugena.[18] In the manuscript under discussion, Eriugena was commenting on *De Musica* by Martianus Capella. When Culhane wrote, the Reverend Percy Jones was director of St Patrick's Cathedral Choir, president of the diocesan committee for liturgy and sacred music, and assistant director of the Conservatorium of Music, University of Melbourne. In his biography of Jones, Donald Cave does not mention this work. Jones, who was born in Geelong, studied in Europe from 1930 and returned to Australia in 1939, aged 25. He had been ordained in 1937 and this thesis may be the work of 1937-39.

The work in question was a thesis which Jones submitted on the manuscript of Scottus Eriugena, discovered by Jones in the Bibliotheque Nationale, Paris. Culhane drew attention to Jones' contribution on the neglected topic of early Irish church music:

> Dr Jones makes a trenchant analysis of Grattan Flood's exaggerated claims that the Irish were the earliest to adopt neumatic notation for the chant of the Western Church, that they had an intimate acquaintance with the diatonic scale and he shows that Dr Flood's assertions are unscholarly, misleading and have no contemporary evidence to prove them.

Jones, and Culhane, here reject some earlier exaggerated claims for the leadership of the Irish in music.

On this occasion, as elsewhere, Culhane notes an anniversary. 1958, the year in which he was writing, was the eleventh centenary of Eriugena's translation of pseudo-Dionysius, once said to have been a disciple of Paul, whose work had unusual power in the medieval world:

> Eriugena as his name denotes was born in Ireland about 810 but the whole of his early life is shrouded in obscurity. Suddenly, at the very height of the Viking invasions, this meteoric figure appeared at the court of Charles the Bald in France, where he soon became master of the Palatine school.

Culhane went on to discuss Eriugena's intervention in debates about predestination.

---

[18] 'Dr Percy Jones' work on John Scottus Eriugena', *The Advocate* (12 June 1958) p 11. Culhane does not however give the bibliographical details of Jones' work. Donald Cave, *Percy Jones: Priest, Musician, Teacher* (Melbourne, 1988).

Writing of Eriugena gave Culhane the opportunity to return to his earlier argument about the role of Irish scholars in transmitting Greek culture. He has a section on the history of pseudo-Dionysius's influence in Europe, and claims that Eriugena was 'the greatest Hellenist of the early Middle Ages'. In Culhane's view, Traube and Dummler have shown that:

> all knowledge of Greek in Western Europe at that time had an Irish source. ... Early Irish tracts, like *Da Bron Flatha Nime* (The two Sorrows of the Kingdom of Heaven) and *Tenga Bith-nua* (The Ever-new Tongue) are based on Greek originals and show that a knowledge of that language was far from uncommon in the Irish schools.

Culhane turns to critics of Eriugena who thought him pantheist and neo-Platonist: 'but he rejects the most characteristic feature of neo-Platonism - namely, its monism - for he holds that the substance of God and created substances are not identical.' Culhane quotes R Lane Poole on Eriugena as

> the loneliest figure in the history of European thought ... in the vast solitude that separates Aquinas from the great thinkers of antiquity, he stands alone like some giant mountain peak in the midst of an arid desert.

The closing remark about Eriugena may have echoed some of Culhane's loneliness in Australia.

The Normans and the Pope

Over his nearly thirty years of scholarly journalism, Culhane touched on a number of other topics in Irish and European history. In 1963, he wrote about the bull, *Laudabiliter*, whereby Pope Adrian IV (1154-9) gave approval to Henry II's conquest of Ireland.[19] While damning Henry II and the 1169 Norman invaders, ('unbridled rapacity' and 'excessive debauchery' of 'unholy felons'), Culhane balanced 'the traditional acerbity of Irish scholarship' with a good word for the English Pope Adrian as one who had acted according to his lights. Culhane said that the Irish St Malachy influenced Adrian IV towards a negative view of the Irish. Culhane quoted Donal O'Neill of the fourteenth century on Adrian as anti-Christ, politely doing so in Latin rather than English: '*qui dici meruit potius Antichrist quam justis pontifex*' ('who deserves to be called an Antichrist rather than a good pope'). Answering the stated reason for *Laudabiliter*, namely to reform the monasteries, Culhane argued that the Irish monasteries reformed themselves, as shown by Henry II's synod of Cashel.

Culhane pointed to Bernard of Clairveaux's denunciation of the Irish as 'a barbarous people and as a nation of beasts rather than men'. Marriage,

---

[19] 'Pope Adrian IV and the Bull *Laudabiliter*', *The Advocate* (14 March 1963).

divorce and the Brehon laws are at the centre of this and other claims of the era. Culhane defended the Brehon law as natural law and suggested that Irish practices on marriage and divorce in the twelfth century were a result of there not being enough clergy to enforce Canon law. Culhane said, moreover, that after the Norse invasion Ireland experienced two centuries of great intellectual and artistic achievement as symbolised by the Cross of Cong.

Culhane located the *Laudabiliter* issue in the wider context of English aggression against the Scots and Pope John XXII's excommunication of Scottish and Irish followers of Edward Bruce. That pope, Culhane said, had a 'pathetic belief' in England's mystical claims to rule. Culhane quoted Jocelyn of Furness as saying that the Irish were the holiest of peoples, this against Giraldus Cambrensis who, he said, hated Ireland for its lack of martyrs. Culhane dryly remarked that the Normans 'speedily removed that stigma'. He announced that he would deal more fully with Constance and Reformation treatment of the bull on a later occasion, but we do not seem to have that piece. Writing to Maighread McGrath of Athea, Culhane said that this article was 'badly mauled and mangled by the editor whose knowledge of medieval history is nil. It is a portion of a two-hour lecture I gave at Melbourne University school of history'.[20]

Praise for selected European scholars
While contemporary scholars of early medieval Ireland such as Eoin MacNeill, Osborn Bergin, Alfred O'Rahilly, and Gerard Murphy gained Culhane's attention, he wrote also about earlier scholars whom he regarded as key figures in the transmission of Irish, or Christian, culture. We have already noted his interest in Origen, Pelagius and Scottus Eriugena. Here are his views on some seventeenth-century scholars, along with his exuberant comments on two nineteenth-century German scholars.

Of the seventeenth-century scholars, Culhane chose to write about Luke Wadding[21] and the Bollandists.[22] In 1957, again finding a centenary theme, Culhane praised the famous Franciscan scholar:

> The name of Father Luke Wadding has become legendary in the world of learning, so that this year, which marks the third centenary of his death, in 1657, is the occasion for articles about him in a variety of publications. He was a many-sided figure, a Franciscan, teacher, theologian, historian,

---

[20] *Home Thoughts*, p 76.
[21] 'Father Luke Wadding, famous Franciscan scholar', *The Advocate* (4 July 1957) p 11.
[22] 'The Bollandists: phenomenon in the history of learning', *The Advocate* (9 May 1968) p 17.

hagiographer, founder of three colleges, diplomatist and patriot.
And, in 1968, he turned to the Bollandists, a group of scholars which took its name from Jesuit John Bollandus who, in the footsteps of another Jesuit Herbert Rosweyde, produced an eighteen-volume series of lives of the saints. Culhane described them as 'a unique phenomenon in the history of learning and the world's most impressive achievement of co-operative scholarship'. Again the range of Culhane's knowledge of the literature about European Christianity is striking.

The two German scholars whom Culhane singled out were Johan Kaspar Zeuss (1806-1856) and Kuno Meyer (1858-1919). Culhane regarded Zeuss, from Bavaria, as the founder of Celtic philology.[23] Culhane's views of Zeuss's role are worth quoting for what they show about his world view:

> [early Irish literature] had a unique interest for the historians and students of primitive culture who at the beginning of the last century were taking such an extraordinary interest in the earliest phases of European civilisation. ... Long before the inception of the Celtic movement, students of Aryan philology had discovered that there was a very ancient and important literature in Irish, which was of the utmost value to those who were engaged in the study of early European civilisation and medieval literature and history. Nothing similar to it existed elsewhere in contemporary western Europe, for it is the earliest manifestation we have of the mind of a medieval people practically free from, and unmodified by, all external influences.

This last remark seems to ignore a key historical reality, namely that Christianity was initially 'external' to Celtic culture. While that and other points may need comment elsewhere, the scope of Culhane's interests is impressive as he went on to review the influence of half a dozen other scholars. In those years, Francis Shaw also wrote of the crucial role played by Zeuss.[24]

The second-last of Culhane's articles in *The Advocate* was about Kuno Meyer, a German scholar of early Irish culture.[25] In Culhane's opinion Meyer was outstanding for drawing the attention of scholars 'to the value of Irish culture in the evolution of European thought from the sixth

---

[23] 'Johann Kaspar Zeuss, founder of Celtic philology', *The Advocate* (8 November 1956) p 11.
[24] For example, Francis Shaw, 'Johann Kaspar Zeuss', *Studies* (Summer 1954) 194-206. I wish to thank Dáithí O Luasaigh for this reference.
[25] 'Dr Kuno Meyer: he called attention to Irish culture', *The Advocate* (14 March 1969) p 15.

century onwards'. Meyer's great achievement, Culhane said, was that of putting old Irish poetry on the European map. In the conclusion of this article, Culhane, however, said that one of the attractions of the old Celtic literature was the mystery it evoked:

> When he lifted the mists of centuries from the old Gaelic world, Meyer revealed to scholars the literature of a land that was already old two thousand years ago — a literature of magic, romance and high adventure. It attracted many admirers, charming some by the haunting strangeness of its atmosphere, for over it all there broods an atmosphere of age and wonder and that consciousness of antiquity and sense of the ages, which haunt so much of Gaelic literature and legend.

Combining pride in Irish cultural heritage with emphasis on the connection between Irish and continental European culture, this article made a fitting close to Culhane's work as a writer in *The Advocate*.

Culhane's views on Zeuss and Meyer have been echoed recently, and taken to a new level of argument, by Seán Ó Lúing in his volume of essays, *Celtic Studies in Europe*.[26] Ó Lúing agrees that Zeuss was indeed the father of Celtic philology and that Meyer had 'put Irish learning on the path of self-reliance' by leaving behind 'a body of disciples who staffed the newly founded national university'. Greg Byrnes has remarked that Flann O'Brien also celebrated (or mocked?) the role of the latter German scholar in the person of his Celtic character, Kún O'Meyer.[27]

Wide-ranging and lonely scholar

As the above survey shows, Thomas Culhane wrote about, with apparent competence, ancient Irish manuscripts, early Irish poetry and music, the Normans and the Pope, and European scholars of Celtic culture and language. The evidence presented here suggests that he had indeed earned the title given him by *The Advocate* editor in 1964, namely 'an authority on Irish studies'. If Culhane judged Plotinus and John Scottus Eriugena to be lonely scholars in their respective eras, we might comment that he was a lonely figure in Melbourne. His achievement in writing these articles for *The Advocate* in his spare time is remarkable.

---

[26] Seán Ó Lúing, *Celtic Studies in Europe and Other Essays* (Dublin, 2000). I wish to thank Pádraig O Fiannachta for drawing my attention to this work and Kit Ahern for giving me a copy of it.

[27] Greg Byrnes, letter to the author, 13 June 2003.

Future directions in early Irish studies

Ann Trindade

This paper attempts an overview of current directions in early Irish studies, selecting areas recently preoccupying scholars and identifying the contextual and methodological influences driving these debates. These reflections are based on the writer's own teaching and research over a number of years.[1] It is obviously impossible to claim expertise in all the areas touched upon, but in a symposium such as this, it is highly likely that all participants will quickly recognise common methodological or theoretical issues. From this will emerge a better appreciation of how such issues may develop in the future.

Many of these debates are not unfamiliar. They represent fresh perspectives on old questions. Such questions include the nature of the early Irish Church, the whole so-called 'Celtic' dimension, the interaction of 'conservation' and 'innovation' in the manuscript culture of early medieval Ireland, the nature of early Irish society — kingship, kinship, law and so forth — as well as the relationship between the material and textual evidence.

While in the past, as in other medieval fields, pre-Norman Ireland was a self-contained and often privileged area, protected from the turbulence associated with later Irish historiography, with its inevitable political overtones, this has not been the case for some time now. The revisionist debates centred on iconic items in the so-called nationalist narrative, all deriving from the often violent relations between Ireland and imperial England, have stretched back to the twelfth century and the coming of the Normans, starting with the fundamental question: was this an invasion, a settlement, or even an osmotic process which was inevitable and largely uncontested?[2] The tactful term 'intrusion' selected for the title of this conference recognises this prickly issue. In an argument with which Australians at least should be familiar, it has been suggested that the pre-Norman Irish were never in any sense a united people and thus to speak of conquest and resistance is at best anachronistic and at worst mendacious.

---

[1] Associate Professor Ann Trindade retired in early 2003, having taught medieval studies in both the Department of French and Italian Studies and the Department of History at the University of Melbourne for many years.

[2] F X Martin, 'No Hero in the House – Diarmait Mac Murchadha and the Coming of the Normans to Ireland' (The O'Donnell Lecture, Dublin, 1975). See also Martin, 'Diarmait Mac Murchadha and the Coming of the Normans' in T W Moody, F X Martin and F J Byrne (eds), *A New History of Ireland* (Oxford, 1976-1996) Vol 2 (ed A Cosgrove) 43-61.

This view has been fiercely resisted by others who see it as transparently political. Meanwhile the early Irish church, the dominant cultural influence in the period in question, has itself become a contested issue, not so much because of politicised denominational differences, but because of the rise of 'Celticism', the fascination with all things 'Celtic' extending from serious scholarly studies of the early Hallstatt grave finds to recurring revivals of interest in art styles, mythology and the rapid spin-off into 'Celtic spirituality'.[3]

This area, too, as I pointed out recently,[4] has attracted both self-styled neo-pagans and Christians of all denominations who look to an idealised primitive Christianity, which, as Ian Bradley[5] has aptly pointed out, just happens to present all those desirable attributes in which the modern denominations appear to be most deficient: respect for the environment, freedom from authoritarianism and stifling bureaucracy as well as a more libertarian attitude to sexual matters. Bradley, who has been teaching practical theology in Scottish Universities for a number of years, notes this response from the many students of all denominational backgrounds who enrol in his courses on early Celtic Christianity. In my own courses taught at the University of Melbourne over the last decade I have seen a similar process, not from practising Christian students, who, apart from those visiting from the US, tend to keep their heads below the parapet, but from those innocents for whom the word 'pagan' has a counter-cultural, almost Utopian resonance. Many were apt to become cross and disappointed to learn that the pre-Christian 'pagan' Celts, as far as we can access their cultural mentalities, were far from the 'life-affirming' 'woman-centred' 'environmentally conscious' folk that they were led to believe in.

Underlying many of these questions was the tension between the view which saw Ireland as different and separate and the opposing position which situated Ireland and its history within the European context, or, more narrowly, within the Imperial British context. In my view, this polarisation has also influenced at least a part of the debate about the Celts, and this can be seen very clearly in the writings of some modern contributors to the debate as well as a host of other more popular writers. But as with the Celts in general, 'separate and different' can be construed in two ways: separate and therefore privileged, and by implication, better, or separate, marginal

---

[3] To describe 'Celticism' as a growth industry is a massive understatement. See, for instance, T Brown, *Celticism* (Amsterdam, 1996); P Sims-Williams, 'Celtomania and Celtosceptism', *Cambrian Medieval Celtic Studies* 30 (1998) 1-35; and further references in Bradley, note 5 below.

[4] 'Celticism, Revisionism and the Early Irish Church' (unpublished seminar paper delivered at the departmental research seminar, Department of History, University of Melbourne, 2001).

[5] Ian Bradley, *Celtic Christianity: Making Myths and Chasing Dreams* (Edinburgh, 1999).

and thus inferior. It seems obvious enough that this type of dichotomy is a product of colonialism, since it crops up in different guises in many other contexts.

But recently, as often happens, there has emerged something of a 'third way' in early Irish studies. This approach, put on the agenda at an important conference in Bristol, I think, about five or six years ago – I was unable to attend and am not aware whether the proceedings of that conference are yet in published form – has rehabilitated the term 'British history' which for many people outside the specialist field still probably has an unwelcome imperialist ring to it. 'British' in this usage is primarily but not exclusively geographical. Early scholars had in fact suggested different terms to describe what in German might be called a *Kulturgebiet* (cultural area is not quite adequate). Myles Dillon spoke of the 'North Sea Province', for instance, to describe the island societies of early medieval Europe, in which the central heartland included both Celtic Britain and Germanic England – a symbiosis, if you like, reflected in the monastic culture of Jarrow, Lindisfarne, Kells and Iona – as well as Ireland, Alba (Scotland) and the outer fringes reaching to Scandinavia and its Norse outposts. Colmán Etchingham[6] of NUI Maynooth has been writing recently on related topics, while in the electronic journal *Chronicon*, produced by UCC, Donnchadh Ó Corráin[7] has published valuable work of a similar nature in relation particularly to the Viking period.

I do not propose to discuss these wider issues any further, though I shall return to some of the sub-topics later. Nor would it be appropriate to try to cover all the separate areas of early Irish studies in any detail. Although I firmly believe all those working in the area ought to keep an eye on the wider field, especially if one is engaged in teaching, it takes a lifetime of scholarship to be able to speak with authority on every aspect of this wider field, and the academic environment today, unfortunately, is such that no such slow maturing is possible. There have been and still are, in my view, Irish, North American and British scholars with such wide-ranging skills, though it would be invidious to name them in print. Most of them are scholars of mature years, who have held chairs in distinguished institutions and whose teaching and publication record spans many decades. Such expertise cannot be acquired quickly and with short cuts, and the creation of the 'job market' in academia means that few younger scholars can look forward to such opportunities.

I have no doubt that all these distinguished scholars would agree on the importance of a regular return to first principles. Setting aside for the

---

[6] Colmán Etchingham, *Viking raids on Irish church settlements in the ninth century: a reconsideration of the annals* (Maynooth, 1996).

[7] Donnchadh Ó Corráin, 'The Vikings in Scotland and Ireland in the ninth century', *Chronicon* 2 (1998) 3: 1-45, http://www.ucc/chronicon/ocorr2.htm

moment the whole question of what has been termed, rather clumsily, 'positionality',[8] the point of departure for the Irish medievalist must always be the evidence itself. For early Christian Ireland – I use the term traditionally favoured here – there are two sources of evidence, the material and the textual. The collection, classification and interpretation of these two types of source must continue: though the discovery of new manuscript material is rare, better editions and translations continue to be produced, while archaeology provides its own regular surprises. I recall Barry Raftery once telling a group of people at the annual Maynooth conference about his experiences as a young boy, accompanying his father on an inspection of a site at Lake Garrah, where the water level had recently been disturbed by the activity of the Office of Public Works. He was able to literally pick up material from the ground around him, full of wonder about the story these simple pieces of stone or more rarely wood might one day tell about the history of his nation. That sense of wonder and connectedness comes through in much of his writing; I am thinking for instance of the intriguingly titled chapter 'The Road to God Knows Where' in his much read and justly praised *Pagan Celtic Ireland*.[9] The same eager sense of discovery rewards the student who manages to complete, for the first time, his or her own reading of a difficult vernacular text: in my own case, it was that powerful literary tale *Togail Bruidne da Derga*,[10] over 30 years ago, with the dearly loved and respected Idris Foster as guide.

From these painstaking exercises in gathering, compiling and contextualising, others have built up piece by piece a picture of the societies represented, or undertaken the far more risky task of trying to correlate the material with the textual record. And here, of course, theory and method are very important. I would just cite two relatively recent works which I consider seminal and which I have used extensively in my own teaching. Harold Mytum[11] is an archaeologist who has examined the nature of the agricultural society in Ireland in the fifth to eighth centuries, drawing important conclusions from the material record about the patterns of settlement, about the nature and origin of the earliest Christian contacts, and about the social and religious hierarchies. One elegant diagram, much liked by my students, showed how vital cattle were to that society by demonstrating the use of every part of the herd, male and female and the material evidence on which his conclusions were based. It is easy to superimpose on this several other systems which emerge from the written

---

[8] I have heard this term used mainly by postgraduates in seminar presentations. I assume it is part of the post-modernist lexicon.
[9] Barry Raftery, *Pagan Celtic Ireland* (London, 1994).
[10] E Knott (ed), *Togail Bruidne da Derga* (Medieval and Modern Irish Series, Dublin, 1936).
[11] Harold Mytum, *The Origins of Early Christian Ireland* (Andover, 1992).

record. In the first instance, the Irish language itself preserves a large cattle-based element in both its everyday vocabulary and its topographical nomenclature. The honour system, which seems to have underpinned the social hierarchies of rank and order, is also predicated on cattle ownership and distribution. Literary scholars, in their turn, have showed how the use of animal imagery in tales of conflict and drama reflects the use of cattle as a marker of status and value.[12]

The other work, by the Welsh anthropologist, Nerys Patterson,[13] also looks at the honour system, the social hierarchies and the economic processes of the period in question. She has an excellent introductory chapter on the use of evidence, which complements the earlier surveys of historians like Kenney[14] and Kathleen Hughes.[15] Many of my students also found it instructive to look at the works of anthropologists working in a wider field, in particular Bruce Lincoln,[16] whose discussion of other cattle-rearing cultures provided significant parallels and incidentally reinforced the importance of the Indo-European dimension, a favoured theme in the works of earlier Celticists like Myles Dillon[17] and Gerard Murphy but recently under attack from various disparate quarters.

I have mentioned these two particular approaches as a limited sample of the interdisciplinary nature of early Irish studies and the importance of trying to keep abreast of developments in different areas, if only in a general way. But this, too, requires time. Yet not just in the early Irish area but in medieval studies in general, scholars working in universities are under increasing pressure not just to turn out the requisite number of pages ("Never Mind the Quality, Feel the Funding"), but to participate in time-consuming activities such as 'bench-marking', 'quality control', income generation, 'marketing your product', justifying your salary, not to mention endless form-filling. The notion that 'research' encompasses extending one's *own* skills in language and other ancillary areas in order to be both a better scholar and a better teacher is not encouraged in the current climate. Many of these skills are essential for the medievalist, even at undergraduate level. Yet if we were to insist on language skills, at anything less than a purely practical level, in our undergraduate courses, we would be quickly out of students, fingers would be wagged and jobs on the line. It is

---

[12] See, for instance, M Tymoczko, 'Animal Imagery in *Longes mac nUislenn*', *Studia Celtica* 20/21 (1985-6) 145-166.
[13] Nerys Patterson, *Cattle Lords and Clansmen* (Indiana and London, 1994).
[14] J Kenney, *The Sources for the Early History of Ireland* I: Ecclesiastical (Cornell, 1929) (no further volumes appeared).
[15] Kathleen Hughes, *Early Christian Ireland: Introduction to the Sources* (London, 1972).
[16] Bruce Lincoln, *Myth, Cosmos and Society* (Harvard, 1986).
[17] Myles Dillon, 'The Archaism of the Irish Tradition', *Proceedings of the British Academy* 37 (1940) and see also *Celts and Aryans* (Simla, 1975).

tempting, instead, for the ambitious young scholar to find a small area and subject it to some fashionable 'theorising', secure in the knowledge that very few people will read the end product (the rebarbative jargon inseparable from such exercises will make this inevitable) and you have your runs on the board as you approach the next hurdle, be it tenure, confirmation, promotion, study leave or the all important external grant round. Of course, as we are so often reminded through the pursed lips of those who know better, it is a whole new ball game now and we had better get used to it. But will this mean that the best research will be limited to those few institutions which have ample private funding, or do no undergraduate teaching, or to independent scholars with the means to pursue research without strings? I don't know, but if our Universities are to produce scholars comparable to the medievalists of the past, something is going to have to change.

The disappearance of serious language study from the curricula of Universities in many English-speaking countries has been a major disaster for the disciplines of ancient and medieval studies and (I would argue) for historians generally. For none of this interdisciplinary work would be much more than speculative unless it could take for granted the accuracy and authenticity of the findings of the philologists and codicologists who enabled the manuscript material to be made available to other types of specialist. As Tom Shippey, in his book *The Road to Middle Earth*[18] pointed out, the philologist, once a revered figure in academia, but now as remote to the average undergraduate as the last of the dinosaurs, was the key figure in the early days of medieval studies. Mainly German and male, first in the Romance and Germanic fields, later with Pokorny and Kuno Meyer and Windisch and others in Celtic, these scholars demonstrated that the same skills which had ensured for Classical studies pride of place in the academic canon in all European countries since the Renaissance, could do the same thing for the forgotten vernaculars of northern and western Europe. Their researches opened up a whole new field of study for their successors, through the establishment of reliable, accurate editions and translations of early texts.

It is no coincidence that many of the leading Celtic scholars of today are philologically trained scholars with expertise not only in the Celtic languages in all stages of their development but with widespread competence in other vernaculars old and new. This was as true in the case of incumbents of the Jesus Chair of Celtic in Oxford, as it was of the great names in early Irish learning. So it will always be important, in the future, to ensure that the study of the Irish language, in its earliest forms, and in the context, if possible of comparative Celtic philology, is supported in

---

[18] T M Shippey, *The road to Middle-earth* (London, Boston and Sydney, 1982). (There is a new, revised edition in print now, 2003).

institutions where medieval Irish studies are taught and researched. One result of Irish involvement in the European Union is that exchanges between Ireland and countries like the Netherlands, Germany and France, where Celtic studies have traditionally been well represented, have been immensely strengthened, resulting in co-authored publications, visiting appointments and fellowships and the like. All the languages of the EU are to be heard at international Celtic conferences, in recognition, increasingly, of a shared heritage, and this means that much of the secondary literature, particularly the older works such as Thurneysen's *Heldensage*,[19] which were not translated, will be available to new generations of scholars in all the participating countries. But if Australian universities continue to offer language study as a purely practical, skills-based activity, our younger generations will not be participants in these debates. If American and Canadian academies, equally affected by the 'tyranny of distance', have got the message, why haven't we?

The next direction which new developments may be expected to take is the urgent task of providing new narrative syntheses. Two multi-volume series have been regularly used for a number of years, the *New History of Ireland* series – the medieval period covered in Art Cosgrove's volume – and the smaller series called the *Gill History of Ireland*. In this series the two earliest volumes, *Ireland before the Vikings*[20] and *Ireland before the Normans*,[21] by Gearóid Mac Niocaill and Donnchadh Ó Corráin respectively, are still in my opinion an excellent source of information. More recently Dáibhí Ó Cróinín's *Early Medieval Ireland*[22] has been useful for students, but the inclusion at the beginning of the book of a so-called time line, while initially reassuring, seems to me to have been misleading. It is impossible to provide a tidy 'time line' of the 'landmarks in history' type for pre-Norman Ireland, simply because the sources themselves, mainly the annals, are notoriously unreliable and difficult to analyse and there is very little external corroboration. I encouraged my students to try to compose their own time-line and they found that between the more-or-less agreed date of the Patrician mission (432) and the rather better attested Treaty of Windsor (1175), it was difficult to come up with more than a dozen or so 'reliable' dates! And all too often, even the best philologist or codicologist will be able to say of a given manuscript only that it was produced 'somewhere' in the early twelfth century, while lost books of fundamental importance such as the *Cin Dromma Sneachta* can only be dated on the basis of reconstruction.

---

[19] R Thurneysen, *Die irische Helden- und Königsage bis zum 17. Jahrhundert* (Halle 1921).
[20] Gearóid Mac Niocaill, *Ireland before the Vikings* (Dublin, 1972).
[21] Donnchadh Ó Corráin, *Ireland before the Normans* (Dublin, 1972).
[22] Dáibhí Ó Cróinín, *Early Medieval Ireland* (London, 1995).

In view of all this, the latest contribution to the overall history of early Christian Ireland, by Thomas Charles-Edwards,[23] represents a welcome departure from the usual linear method. He starts with an imagined journey around seventh-century Ireland, through the pages of Tirechán's account of Patrick's missionary circuits, guiding the reader through the morass of territories, dynasties and persons, often confusingly and inconsistently rendered in the inter-related textual tradition, not ignoring the wider context of Irish relations with the rest of Christendom, complementing here the earlier work of Michael Richter[24] and other continental scholars. He then concentrates on the all-important institution of kingship, the social hierarchies and the honour system which sustained these. This section of the work is fully referenced from an impressive range of sources, reinforcing what I said earlier about the depth and range of scholarship needed to produce an overview. The other two subjects treated in detail in a number of discrete chapters are firstly the structure and organisation of the early Irish Church, to which I will return, and the rise and fall of the Uí Néill, certainly the dominant political feature in the latter part of the period, under whose auspices much of the textual production was first carried out.

Many of the sources used by Charles-Edwards are literary sources, and those unfamiliar with the Irish area often express surprise at the use by historians of overtly literary material, as opposed to traditional sources such as charters, chronicles, wills and the like. It is important to point out that the manuscript culture of early Ireland is unusual in that different types of text are closely meshed in together, resonate with echoes of other texts, and were probably produced by the same class of monastic *literati*.[25] In addition, of course, the traditional type of source used in the study of, say, medieval England, only became plentiful after the Norman incursion. Take any of the great manuscript books, such as the *Book of Leinster*[26] for instance: in that book we find devotional, genealogical, annalistic and gnomic material together with sagas, tracts on status and synthetic pseudo-histories. Mac Cana has argued, in his classic essay 'Conservation and Innovation',[27] that the early generation of monks who redacted, transcribed

---

[23] Thomas Charles-Edwards, *Early Christian Ireland* (Cambridge, 2000).
[24] M Richter, *Medieval Ireland* (London, 1988) especially ch 6 'Christian Ireland in the Seventh and Eighth Centuries'. See also *Ireland and her Neighbours in the Seventh Century* (Dublin 1999).
[25] See Erich Poppe, 'Reconstructing Medieval Irish Literary Theory: the Lesson of *Airec Menman Uraird maic Coise*', *Cambrian Medieval Celtic Studies* 37 (Summer 1999) 33-54. The extensive footnotes review all the significant contributions to date.
[26] R A Best, Osborn Bergin and M A O'Brien (eds), *The Book of Leinster [LL]* (3 vols, Dublin, 1954-1957).
[27] P Mac Cana, 'Conservation, Innovation in Early Celtic Literature', *Etudes Celtiques* 13 (1972) 61-119.

and perhaps composed these texts were probably well versed in the old tradition of the *filid*, or high status poets and men of letters. He argues, too, that these Irish *literati* held a different view of their own pre-Christian culture, and in transcribing and transmitting these traditional materials, in a new Christian context, their attitude was characterised by what he labelled a 'benign ecumenism'.

This view, which was shared by most other scholars in the field, was partly challenged in the 1950s by James Carney,[28] who stressed the innovative aspect of the Christian redactors, pointing to the influence of both Biblical and classical themes and motifs, and who coined the word 'nativist' to describe the views he was criticising. In 1990 Kim McCone, an Oxford-trained philologist, launched a rather intemperate attack on the so-called 'nativist' approach in his book *Pagan Past and Christian Present*.[29] McCone's critics have sometimes pointed out that in at least three of his chapters, some of the positions he took up were themselves implicitly nativist, while others demonstrated that his attack was predicated on an ill-formed understanding of the process of inculturation generally. At the 1991 Celtic Congress in Paris, James Mackey voiced some of these criticisms,[30] though in a scholarly and eirenic way. No revealed religion, he explained, could establish itself in a vacuum. Those that did, eschewing any contact with, or adaptation of, pre-existing beliefs or customs, were doomed to failure. (Perhaps the later unwillingness of the Irish people to accept the Protestant faith of the colonisers is in part due to this.) So for instance, the notion that some Christian saints, Brigit for example, were syncretistic figures, drawing on the pre-Christian cults of pagan divinities, seems perfectly acceptable and indeed normal. The theology expressed in the old hymn *Tantum Ergo* perfectly expresses this truth and many would argue that the capacity of the Catholic Church to absorb many so-called 'pagan' practices is a strength rather than a weakness.

McCone's attack on the so-called 'nativists' was expressed aggressively and often in an *ad hominem* way. The inevitable result was that sides were taken and a degree of rancour has remained: David Dumville's review of one of McCone's co-edited books is a good example.[31] But I think it is clear that the controversy itself has become a dead issue, with recent publications by John Carey[32] and others re-emphasising what Mac Cana himself had originally pointed out, namely the

---

[28] J Carney, *Studies in Early Irish History and Literature* (Dublin, 1955).

[29] Kim McCone, *Pagan Past and Christian Present* (Maynooth, 1990).

[30] Subsequently published as 'Christian Past and Primal Present', *Etudes Celtiques* 29 (1992) 285-297.

[31] I have summarised the debate briefly in *Australian Celtic Journal* 7 (2000-2001) 25-36, p 33 note 5.

[32] See, for instance, Carey's excellent introduction in *King of Mysteries* (Dublin, 1998).

syncretism of these early texts, even those heavily overlaid with Christian didacticism. This is clearly demonstrated in the emphasis that many of the narrative texts, particularly the sagas, place on the institution of kingship.[33] While many of these sagas, from all the principal cycles, as the modern classification has labelled them, are concerned with establishing legitimacy and pedigree, in keeping with the rising aspirations to dominance of particular dynasties or tribal groupings, they also repeat a fictionalised attempt to harmonise the old and the new in the person of a given king, whether that figure be semi-mythological like Conaire Már mac Etarscéla,[34] or historically attested like some of the kings in the eponymous cycle. Because the remote antecedents of tribal Irish kingship are archaic and sacral, the peculiarly Irish variant of the universal *hieros gamos*, or sacred marriage, stresses the marriage of the king to the territory he rules, often personified by the tutelary goddess, sometimes called the Sovereignty goddess.[35] Katherine Simms[36] has pointed out that until well into the colonial period, inauguration rituals for tribal chieftains and minor kings retained fossilised elements of what was in the remote past a form of symbolic marriage. Long after such archaic rituals or the belief systems on which they depended had lost their meaning in Christian Ireland, the literature continues to depict them.

In, for instance, a couple of sagas about 'bad' kings, the Violent Deaths of Diarmait mac Cerrbel,[37] and Muirchertach mac Erca[38], these kings who defied the Church are brought low through their connections with detribalised, often otherworld, women who represent the old, discredited order. In the case of *Aided Muirchertach*, which has the advantage (for the scholar) of being a clumsily told heavily didactic tale devoid of any distracting aesthetic merit, the king abandons his virtuous and legitimate consort, an O'Neill princess with significant clerical connections, for a mysterious pagan enchantress. She then persuades him to do all sorts of idiotic things, which bring about the destruction of his kingdom and his own demise. In this tale the wronged queen clearly represents a Church-

---

[33] The classic exposition is F J Byrne's *Irish Kings and High Kings* (London, 1973) (second edition published in 2001). A more recent but less satisfactory overview is Bart Jaski, *Early Irish Kingship and Succession* (Dublin, 2000). McCone (*Pagan Past*) also referred to the 'obsessive concern' with kingship of medieval Irish writers, and the 'pivotal role' such a concern reflected.

[34] See note 10 above.

[35] The literature here is extensive. This is one area in which serious scholarly studies compete with New Age popularising. Even within the former category there is some disagreement. Fuller references in Trindade, 'Death and Gender: Some Reflections on *Aided Medbe*', *Australian Celtic Journal* 7 (2000-2001), p 34 note 11.

[36] Katherine Simms, *From Kings to Warlords* (Boydell, 1987) especially ch 2.

[37] ed S H O'Grady, *Silva Gadelica* I (London, 1892) pp 72-82.

[38] ed L Nic Dhonnachadha (Dublin, 1964).

sanctioned remake of the old pagan sovereignty goddess, while the usurper is a false sovereignty figure, unable, despite her pathetic and ridiculous demonstrations of magic, to ensure the welfare of the land and its people, the traditional consequence of the sacred marriage between king and territory. On the other hand, this theme, which Mac Cana has also treated in his articles on King and Goddess,[39] also manifests itself in the repeated reference to the maternal ancestry of kings as derived either from the supernatural order – Conaire's mother and grandmother for instance, or the druid's daughter who gives birth to the great Christian king Cormac mac Airt[40] — or from the defeated indigenous people, the shadowy Erainn.

The apparent contradiction between these two uses of a traditional motif suggests ambivalence on the part of the clerical redactors towards the inherited culture. In the Muirchertach story and others like it, the message is a polarised and polemic one: sovereignty is now to be placed under the authority of the Church. In the pattern represented in the constructed ancestry of Cormac, the purpose seems to be to emphasise a dual legitimacy in both the old and the new traditions. This message is reinforced in the *Scela Cormaic* by the immediate and voluntary surrender of authority to the Christian king by Lugaid mac Con, the dispossessed representative of the old indigenous order. It is clear, then, that kingship in the sagas is about much more than individuals, real or imagined. It is about identity, legitimacy and the land. For this reason, there will continue to be a focus on early Irish kingship which may seem puzzling to medievalists working in other areas where an undue focus on kingship has been seen as little more than a '1066 and All That' approach.

Kinship is another important topic, which has been treated extensively by Thomas Charles-Edwards[41] and recently by Neil McLeod in *Ériu*.[42] Again, in these seemingly fanciful literary tales a cast of characters, semi-historical or purely fictional, play out agendas which the law tracts and other non-fictional texts describe in the abstract. So the mechanism of the archaic tale *Fingal Rónáin*,[43] a Middle Irish analogue to the classical tale of Phaedra and Hippolytus, is only apparent to the reader who understands how kinship works and why prohibitions infringed bring about disaster and the destruction of the social order. In this short and powerful tale, the woman who disrupts the harmony of the kingdom and sets father against son with tragic results is an outsider, from the North, an unsuitable consort

---

[39] 'Aspects of the theme of king and goddess in Irish literature', *Etudes Celtiques* 7 (1955-6) 76-114; 356-413; 8 (1958) 59-65.
[40] *Scéla Eogan agus Cormaic* in T Ó Cathasaigh, *The Heroic Biography of Cormac mac Airt* (Dublin, 1977).
[41] Thomas Charles-Edwards, *Early Irish and Welsh Kinship* (Oxford, 1993).
[42] Neil McLeod, 'Kinship', *Ériu* 51 (2000) 1-22.
[43] ed D Greene (Dublin, 1955).

for the widowed Ronán. Not only does she bring death and destruction to her husband's kingdom, culminating in the act of *fingal* or kin-slaying, which automatically de-legitimises a king's position, but she disrupts and disgraces her own family. The message is pushed home when the bereaved males re-bond in death while she dies isolated and disgraced. Cultural notions of gender roles not exclusive to early Ireland reinforce the moral of the tale and make it all the more effective.[44]

I will conclude with one well-known instance of the way in which kinship ties, described in the abstract in non-literary texts, explain how a literary text would have worked. This is the highly rhetorical set piece in the *Book of Leinster* version of the *Táin* known as the combat at the ford.[45] In this purplest of passages, the Ulster hero Cú Chulainn fights to the death with his foster brother Fer Diad, at the instigation of the evil queen Medb of Connacht. Perhaps, like much in this epic and in the Ulster cycle in general, this incident had its beginnings in oral tradition but this text is far removed from what Mac Cana[46] called the pared-down and elliptic style of those tales he considered to be summaries of traditional material (*Fingal Rónáin* for instance). As the two warriors are locked in a deathly embrace, slashing and gashing at each other, they utter doleful rhetorics which speak of their shared youth as fellow fosterlings of a warrior woman, of their undying love and sorrow at this last tragic encounter. The very texture of the language helps to heighten their plight, playing on the contrast in Irish between the two words for blood, *fuil* and *cró*, corresponding semantically to the Latin *sanguis* and *cruor*, meaning blood flowing as the life force and dead blood or gore.[47] There are many layers of meaning in this text, gendered ones among others, but the importance of the institution of fosterage and the strength of tribal loyalties are the most important. I conclude from this that many more perceptive readings of the sagas and

---

[44] This powerfully told tale has attracted considerable discussion. See further Trindade, 'Modalities of Gender and Power - the Medieval Irish *Fingal Rónáin* and the myth of Hippolytus', *Australian Celtic Journal* 4 (1994) 31-42.

[45] *Táin Bó Cúalnge from the Book of Leinster* (ed and trans C O'Rahilly, Irish Texts Society, Dublin, 1967).

[46] The best summary of Mac Cana's views on the development of early prose narratives is found in *The Learned Tales of Medieval Ireland* (Dublin, 1980). See also 'On the Early Development of Written Narrative Prose in Irish and Welsh', *Etudes Celtiques* 29 (1992) 51-68.

[47] I developed this point in an unpublished paper read to the International Conference of Medievalists in Leeds, July 1995. A useful secondary source is 'The inflexion of O Ir. *crú*', *Ériu* 39 (1988) 169-87. Terms denoting blood across the Indo-European spectrum cannot be traced to any original urform, suggesting that blood, like certain other properties, persons or animals, was, to the early Indo-European tribes, in some sense too sacred, dangerous or threatening to name directly. A most interesting discussion of this is found in Fritz Tschirch, *Spiegelungen Unternsuchungen vom Grenzrain Zwischen Germanistik und Theologie* (Berlin, 1966).

other fictional texts will continue to shed light on the society which produced them, not through direct representation of actual historical events, but through symbolism, didacticism and even through parody and humour. The historian, at least in the medieval period, cannot afford to dismiss literature but the literary scholar, equally, cannot afford to ignore context.

Before leaving the question of how to use those literary texts which F J Byrne has described, uncompromisingly, as valuable historical documentation,[48] a further step is yet to be taken. Perhaps one day scholars working in a multi-disciplinary context will be able to correlate the events and characters mentioned in saga literature or mythological texts, albeit in a highly fictionalised form, with the archaeological witness. For obvious reasons this is unlikely to yield instant results, and yet there are already tantalising hints here and there. For instance, the strange little story of how the Ulstermen became subject to the ancient curse known as the *couvade* – phantom pregnancy or labour pains – provides an aetiological explanation for the Irish name of Armagh – Ard Macha, the heights of Macha.[49] Furthermore, it would appear that long before the site became the focus of early Christianity in Ireland, it may have had a tutelary goddess with a horse connection. The same name links Armagh with the nearby site of Emhain Macha, regularly depicted in the Ulster cycle as the royal site of the Ulstermen under their king Conchobor. The archaeological teams working at Queen's University Belfast and elsewhere have been publishing a number of interesting articles particularly in their journal *Emania*. Evidence corroborating some of the events and practices described in the fictionalised setting has been found, including the discovery of early stables and a site entitled Haughey's fort; Haughey being a proper name derived from an Irish word for horse. Like many heroic societies depicted in epic across the Indo-European culture area, the warrior aristocracy of Ulster valued horses not just for their practical use but as a status symbol. The Celtic tradition is unlike some of the other cultural traditions, however, in assigning female gender to equine divinities. (Welsh Rhiannon and Gaulish Epona are two instances.[50]) Yet the ethos of the Ulster cycle is uncompromisingly masculine – except for this strange instance of gender-trading associated with the story of Macha and the debility of the Ulstermen. Was Ard Macha displaced in the pre-Christian period by a neighbouring site uncontaminated by female associations, a displacement reinforced in the Christian period when the cycle began to take shape? And did the Church then take back Ard Macha, when the 'defeat of the goddess' was safely in the past, as it never quite was, apparently, in Tara, to which a whiff of paganism still

---

[48] Byrne, *Irish Kings*, p 2.
[49] *Noínden Ulaid* in *LL* II, pp 467f.
[50] On Epona, see A Orr, 'Epona: Transformations of a Horse Goddess', *Australian Celtic Journal* 7 (2000-1) 49-61 and references therein.

clung for centuries after the conversion? Once again, these are fascinating issues which cannot be explored except slowly and cooperatively and in an interdisciplinary context.

Finally I'd like to consider the question of the nature and organisation of the early Irish church, which has been the subject of renewed attention in recent decades, though disagreement as to its earliest structure has been around for some time. As I indicated earlier, this topic too has not been free from political or denominational agendas. Scholars have long argued about whether the episcopal or the monastic model was paramount in the early centuries of Christianity in Ireland and this quickly became a point-scoring exercise for those who saw 'Celtic' Christianity as somehow opposed to 'Roman' Christianity and hence, if not proto-protestant, at least implicitly different from present-day Roman Catholicism. As I noted in the seminar paper to which I referred previously, it was the Church of Ireland, with its Ascendancy patronage and (mostly) better educated clergy, which looked to the early Irish church for its church dedications, while the resolutely Ultramontane nature of nineteenth-century Irish Catholicism determined the nature of its export to the diaspora communities in Birmingham, Liverpool and the new world. Similarly, it was learned Protestant clergy, with few exceptions, who edited and translated many of the earliest texts, including the hagiographies and other overtly confessional materials. As Patrick Corish pointed out in 1985,[51] the title of James Ussher's 1622 book, *A Discourse of the religion anciently professed by the Irish and Scottish, showing it to be for substance the same with that which is at this day by public authority established in the Church of England*, clearly set out an agenda which was to be followed for some centuries afterwards.

Although the denominational perspective has largely ceased to matter – whether due to ecumenism or secularism – there is still room for considerable disagreement on the basic issue. An important contribution to the question of ecclesiastical structure was Colmán Etchingham's 1990 work, *Church order in Ireland AD 650-1000*.[52] This rather unwieldy volume is a published version of the author's PhD thesis, but it also draws on a number of the author's earlier articles, most importantly on the key question of *paruchia*, which may be defined as a network of monastic affiliations, or a monastic federation of a non-territorial nature. As with the nativist versus non-nativist argument to which I referred previously, there seems to have been, in more recent times, a return to a more nuanced position, whereby two types of ecclesiastical government, the monastic and the episcopal, are acknowledged to have co-existed for at least a couple of centuries after the Patrician mission. This, of course, was the position taken

---

[51] P Corish, 'The Early Irish Church and the Western Patriarchate' in P Ní Chatháin and M Richter (eds), *Ireland and Europe: the Early Church* (Stuttgart, 1980) 9-15.
[52] Colmán Etchingham, *Church order in Ireland AD 650-1000* (Maynooth, 1999).

by Kathleen Hughes thirty years ago! But some of the more detailed questions examined by Etchingham in this book provide useful insights into the nature of authority in hagiography and the annals, the legal and economic standing of the *manaig* (*manach*, monk or tenant) and patterns of tithe and land inheritance in the early church.

I referred earlier to the amorphous term 'spirituality' which has inspired some of the best and some of the worst modern writing. As I was working on this paper I took a tea break to scan my newly arrived airmail copy of *The Tablet* and landed on an article about Glastonbury by the paper's deputy editor, entitled 'My day in Avalon'.[53] I spent much of my early childhood in villages in North Somerset and recall Glastonbury as a small and sleepy place, with the Tor and the ruined abbey as its best-known monuments. I now learn that its main street is full of shops with names like 'Man Myth and Magick', the 'Goddess and the Green Man' and that behind these shop windows 'there is a bewildering array of merchandise on display, from small fountains featuring Buddhas or fairies surrounded by pebbles to hideous statues of King Arthur and an invariably naked Guinevere'. The parish priest of the local Catholic church tries to maintain an amiable dialogue with some of the many visitors who flock in to enrol in workshops such as 'A seven-week course in witchcraft and Wicca for the twenty-first century'. He does not see his work as being 'in opposition to the New Age culture' and says that occasionally someone will stumble on the connection between Mary and the Goddess, for instance. But ironically, most of the many visitors, while claiming to be deeply interested in the past, do not bother to step inside any Christian monument at all. The eclecticism which characterises the New Age movement often stops at the doors of the institutional churches. Is it merely the familiarity which breeds contempt or something more sinister? Recent Vatican pronouncements on the dangers of the New Age movement seem to suggest the latter. But while some of this New Age material is overtly hostile to Christianity, its influence can also be seen in the work of some writers claiming to be Christian. How is the serious scholar to distinguish between these approaches?

Any serious *historical* study of the 'spirituality' of the early Celtic churches must start with the early texts themselves and with what is known of their specific contexts, among which feature important practices such as pilgrimage, and the cult of relics.[54]

---

[53] Mian Ridge, 'My day in Avalon', *The Tablet* (30 August 2003) 11-12.

[54] A T Lucas, 'The Social Role of Relics and Reliquaries in Ancient Ireland', *Journal of the Royal Society of Antiquaries of Ireland [JRSAI]* 116 (1986) 5-37; H S Crawford, 'A descriptive list of Irish Shrines and Reliquaries', *JRSAI* 53 (1923) 74-93; 151-176.

Peregrinatio, or pilgrimage, appears to have been understood slightly differently in Ireland from the pattern on the continent or even in England.[55] While a *peregrinus* was primarily someone who went overseas, it could also denote someone who went on an internal pilgrimage, within Ireland itself. Thomas Charles-Edwards[56] has shown that this particular use of *peregrinus* is linked very closely, through its vernacular equivalents, to indigenous notions of exile and alien status. As we know, tribal identity and position within kinship group and social hierarchy were defining markers of identity, and the importance of these ties is illustrated by the way in which the originally imported notion of Christian orders was assimilated to the secular grades in the legal working out of compensation, honour-price and the like. Repeatedly throughout the narrative texts, exiles and outcasts are portrayed as dangerous and marginalised. Both the *cú glas* [grey hound or wolf], that is the foreign exile, usually a Briton, and the *ambue*, the Irishman exiled from his own tribe, are regarded with contempt. Similarly, a man who leaves his tribal territory to go after a woman from another territory, is condemned not merely as a fornicator or adulterer but as a fool who has lowered his own standing. The contemptuous term *re tóin mná* [following a woman's backside] does not merely indicate deep seated misogyny, as Muireann Ní Bhrolcháin[57] rightly argues, but serves as a reminder of how much is lost in the foolish pursuit of personal desire. Against this background, like so much else embedded in the old pre-Christian social order, the new Christian dispensation results in a revolutionary subversion of the established values: Patrick himself was a *cú glas*, and the servile status which the seventh-century hagiographers show him patiently enduring was a reminder of the gospel message that Christ came to serve not to be served. So the *peregrinus* becomes, over time, one who is honoured and revered. He is called the 'exile of God' and has a legal status, by the mid-seventh century, equal to that of a king. The notion of the *plebs christiana*, the Christian people, represents an implicit challenge to the notion of the pagan *túath* and, Charles-Edwards argues, by the beginning of the seventh century the two had become conflated, so that excommunication from the *plebs*, or the *ecclesia*, will also entail expulsion from the *túath*. Once again, we see these tensions and conflicts worked out through narrative in some of the sagas, in this instance the story of Diarmait mac Cerbaill and his conflicts with the feisty trio of Ciarán, Rúadán and Columcille. Exiled warriors fleeing from secular justice seek sanctuary

---

[55] P Harbison, *Pilgrimage in Ireland* (London, 1991).
[56] Thomas Charles-Edwards, 'The Social Background to Irish Peregrinatio', *Celtica* XI (1976) 43-59.
[57] Muireann Ní Bhrolcháin, '*Re Tóin Mná*: In Pursuit of Troublesome Women' in *Ulidia: Proceedings of the First International Conference on the Ulster Cycle of Tales* (Belfast and Emain Macha, 1994).

with the Church, while Churchmen denounce and threaten rulers who infringe the sovereignty of sanctuary. It must be assumed that in reality, compromises and stand-offs would have been the result.

So far I have touched on major areas of research and publication which have been studied for almost two centuries. I have not referred to theoretical or critical perspectives, except perhaps in a semi-serious aside. I shall conclude with a brief reference to one area of study which has benefited considerably from the input, not only of established scholars but of a number of gifted younger researchers, who are interested in theoretical issues, such as the role of gender in the creation and transmission of texts. This is the field of hagiography, which has been considerably boosted over the last twenty years or so with the work of scholars outside the Irish area, such as Thomas Head[58] and the many feminist scholars working on women's piety and gendered sanctity in the continental tradition. Most people have now accepted the caveat expressed by Kathleen Hughes[59] and others, that saints' *Lives* tell us more about the context in which they were written than about the factual details of their subjects' lives. But that is just the starting point and, for many scholars, the saints' *Lives* have proved to be a richly rewarding field. For those, too, to whom these ancient lives are part of a living tradition of faith, much is to be gained from serious academic study of the texts. It is only in relatively recent times, after all, that the West has seen faith and reason as opposing categories.

For the scholar, the saints' *Lives* in Latin and Irish – and there are several hundred versions of the lives of a variety of saints, wonder workers and eccentrics as well as historically attested abbots and solitaries – are full of information about the belief systems of the early Irish, the old question of pagan/Christian interface, as well as social institutions and values. University College Cork is probably the best place to study early Irish hagiography at the moment and the volume entitled *Saints and Scholars*, published in 2001 by a triad of leading academics, John Carey, Máire Herbert and Pádraig Ó Riain, provides ample evidence to support this claim. There is much more to be done. There are huge problems still to be solved in connection with the editing of texts, not to mention the question of translating them for the benefit of the growing number of keen interested students without Latin, let alone older Irish. Complex stemmata are constructed and dismantled as the textual critics revise the earlier compilations and editions. Then the philologists such as David Howlett draw our attention to idiosyncratic and perhaps highly significant features

---

[58] Head has published numerous studies of hagiography, including his anthology of hagiographic texts, *Medieval Hagiography* (New York and London, 2000). He also maintains a useful web-site: http://www.artsc.wustl.edu/~tfhead/

[59] Hughes, *Early Christian Ireland*.

of Hiberno-Latin. And finally there are questions of interpretation, and the interplay between hagiography and heroic saga or romance.

I referred earlier to younger scholars, in Ireland and elsewhere. Elva Johnston[60] is one impressive young Irish scholar who has written most significantly on the role of gender in the hagiographies, comparing and contrasting the representation of both male and female saints in the Irish and Continental traditions. Another young scholar, from the Netherlands, Jacqueline Borsje, has examined the role of women in Adomnán's *Life of Columba*,[61] showing that the misogyny often attributed to clerics cannot be so easily assigned to the great Apostle of the North. On the other hand, Johnston's latest article, in *Peritia*, analyses the representation of women in a culture which was processed by male clerics, a culture which in her words 'obscured female experiences beneath the distortions of highly gendered christian attitudes'[62]. Her solution, however, is not to construct some kind of compensatory ideology based on the notion of all-pervading misogyny but to study closely and attentively the texts themselves, looking for what Lisa Bitel[63] calls textual silence and discontinuities, as well as implicit representations of social mores and value systems. Ann Dooley has advocated a similar reading 'against the grain' of secular sagas, and the representation of women in them.[64]

One can look at the treatment of marriage in the lives of women saints and compare this with the views on marriage and sexuality generally in the *Collectio Canonum Hibernensis*,[65] as well as the rather divergent view which emerges from the secular tradition represented in the *Corpus Iuris Hibernici*.[66] For women saints in Ireland, marriage represents an obstacle in their path, whether it is a well-meaning arrangement drawn up by their men folk, or a tyrannical demonstration of paternal authority. Brides-to-be resist, sometimes in a spectacular fashion, by spontaneously combusting on the wedding night, though remaining unhurt by the flames, while the terrified bridegroom runs away. Time prevents me from going into greater

---

[60] Elva Johnston, 'Transforming Women in Irish Hagiography', *Peritia* 9 (1995) 197-220; idem, 'Powerful Women or Patriarchal Weapons? Two Medieval Irish Saints', *Peritia* 15 (2001) 302-10.
[61] Jacqueline Borsje, 'Women in Columba's Life, as seen through his biographer, Adomnán', proof copy kindly lent by the author. The paper has now been published.
[62] Johnston, 'Powerful Women'.
[63] Lisa Bitel, *Land of women: tales of sex and gender from early Ireland* (Ithaca, New York, 1996).
[64] Ann Dooley, 'The invention of women in the *Táin*' in *Ulidia*, 123-133.
[65] See Thomas O'Loughlin, 'Marriage and sexuality in the *Hibernensis*', *Peritia* 11 (1997) 188-206; Akiko Tatsuki, 'The Early Irish Church and Marriage: an Analysis of the *Hibernensis*', *Peritia* 15 (2001) 195-207.
[66] Principally located in the tract known as *Cáin Lánamna*, edited by Thurneysen in D Binchy *et al* (eds), *Studies in Early Irish Law* (Dublin, 1936) 1-80.

detail but I would just say that, in my view, sanctity overrides gender in the Irish hagiographies to a much greater degree than in comparable narratives outside Ireland and this warrants further exploration.

Although sanctity in Irish women saints is to some extent 'somatised', that is located in the body, either by fasting, self-mutilation or denial, this pattern seems much less obsessive than in other traditions. This is an interesting variation: does it derive from the so-called 'benign ecumenism' of the early tradition, and ultimately from a more positive view of the feminine in the pre-Christian belief system? Many would like to think so but this view runs up against some difficulties, particularly the fact that evidence from non-literary sources seems to suggest that pre-Christian Ireland was no feminist paradise and the feminine element in the mythology was essentially metaphorical or symbolic. On the other hand, as Peter O'Dwyer[67] has shown in his book on Marian devotion in Ireland, the earliest Marian prayers do include powerful images such as that of Mary the Sun of Women (*Grian inna mBan*) which suggest pre-Christian associations. (It has been argued that the place of Mary in Irish Catholicism has helped to ensure a strong female role in Irish society and history, from the many generations of indomitable Irish mothers to the last two presidents of the Republic. Contrast this with the daunting machismo of what Ruth Dudley Edwards labelled the 'Faithful Tribe' of present day Ulster.[68])

This paper has only touched on a few important areas in early Irish studies and of course there have been obvious omissions, including the fields of archaeology and art history, where it must be left to the appropriate specialists to share their findings with the historians and linguists. In conclusion, I should like to return to the title of the conference.

In what sense was there a Roman 'intrusion' into Ireland? Why would this be seen as a more important starting point than, say, the putative original incursion of the goidelic Celts either during the Hallstatt period or slightly later, or of the better-attested iron-working La Tène Celts from Gaul or Britain? The early Christian Irish were themselves interested in ancestral incursions, as that difficult mythological text the *Lebor Gabála* demonstrates. Evidence of Roman presence on the east coast of Ireland suggests no prolonged periods of activity and it is generally accepted that Romanisation came about through the Christianising process, which came with cultural and intellectual baggage of a Mediterranean nature. Would St Patrick have considered himself a Roman, as did St Paul some centuries before, in the same way that many Australians in the early twentieth century thought of themselves as British? Today we label him a Romanised British Celt if we want to be scholarly (or a Welshman or a Briton if we want to

---

[67] Peter O'Dwyer, *Mary: A History of Devotion in Ireland* (Dublin, 1988).
[68] Ruth Dudley Edwards, *The Faithful Tribe: an intimate portrait of the loyalist institutions* (London, 1999).

annoy our Irish friends), but these are modern labels which would have made no sense to anyone at the time. And why was the Norman, or rather Anglo-Norman, 'intrusion' seen as so significant? There were other intrusions, of course, before the Normans, and these were much more invasive in nature, in the short term at least: I refer to the Viking raids of the ninth and tenth centuries. Some have suggested that because the Vikings became assimilated, their contribution to the course of Irish history is less significant, and because their numbers were smaller, they were easier to absorb than the Normans. On the other hand, the Anglo-Normans too became assimilated to the extent that later Irish tradition distinguished between the *sean gall* — the 'old' foreigners, who were of the same religion as the Gaelic Irish, and ultimately intermarried with them — and the 'new' foreigners, who maintained a distinct identity based among other things on religion. These are important issues, which the historian must continue to address. Concepts of 'identity' are often defined in oppositional terms, ('we' are 'not-you') and in recent times Ireland, like most European nations, has had to confront these issues anew with the appearance of migrants from outside Europe in what has been a remarkably homogeneous population. The past has lessons to teach us all and the historian has a crucial role in these public debates, in Ireland and Britain no less than in Australia.